24/2/15

17 March

7 Sept

Nipper

The Amazing Story of Boxing's Wonderboy

Alex Daley

Published by

TPD Associates

First published in 2011

© Alex Daley

A catalogue record for this book is available from the British Library

Pictures are reproduced courtesy of the Daley family and from the author's collection

ISBN 978-0-9567494-0-6

Typeset by Get Set Go, www.g-s-g.co.uk

Printed and bound in Great Britain by CPI Antony Rowe

www.nipperpatdaly.co.uk

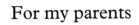

For my parents

'Perhaps the greatest tragedy the sport of boxing has to offer is the story of Nipper Pat Daly... So long as boxing is carried on and men have memories Nipper Pat Daly will not be forgotten.'

– Gerard Walter (*News Chronicle* and *Daily Mirror* sports reporter),
White Ties and Fisticuffs, Hutchinson, 1951

Contents

Foreword

by Nipper Pat Daly's youngest son (the author's father)

I suppose if my father had been a famous footballer or cricketer I would have wanted to be one too. But what he excelled at was boxing, and so it was natural that I should take a keen interest in the noble art. From an infant I was aware that my dad had been a famous boxer, and so, without realising, it was always there, always with me.

From the age of about seven I would accompany him, along with my older brother John, to the different gyms he ran over the years in various parts of London. We would usually travel by the old red London buses and arrive at the gym before 10am. John and I wore black boxing trunks – which in my case always seemed three sizes too large – plain white vests, and black plimsolls. Dad, like Professor Newton before him, always wore cream trousers, a cream sweatshirt and black boxing boots while teaching. Under my dad, the gym regime was always no nonsense and 100 per cent commitment, and so my natural propensity to 'mess about' was kept well in check. Perhaps because of the order imposed by dad – it reminded me too much of school – I was an irregular attendee, but to dad's credit I was never forced or nagged into going.

Dad's method of training his pupils would in modern parlance be called proactive; which means he would spar with each and every one, the severity of the session depending on the size and ability of the pupil – at the end of the round he would point out any faults he had noticed. At the core of his teaching were the tenets of correct footwork and an accurate straight left – from these flowed every other punch and move.

I once saw him spar a round with a pro who visited a gym he ran in Peckham, south London. At the end of the round the pro – who admittedly was of limited ability – was flustered and demoralised because of dad's use of a constant, rapid straight left that found its mark unerringly. Dad, if I remember rightly, was then about 50.

The teaching of boxing as applied in the gymnasium was almost a religion to my father. Although he showed little interest in current boxers and the state of current boxing, it was always his dream to bring one of his

1

pupils to championship level. But he never found the equivalent Newton–Daley partnership in any of the gymnasiums he ran. No matter how good the teacher – and he was a great communicator of the art – the intrinsic ingredients of a champion have to come from the boxer himself: ring intelligence, natural stamina and sheer guts, the last two you could never teach. In all his teaching life, to his regret, he never found a synthesis of all three attributes in one boxer.

My son – whose production of this biography is a testament to his dedication, love of his subject and sheer stamina – has produced what I consider a worthy tribute to an extraordinary boxer and extraordinary man. I hope you like it.

Terry Daley

Acknowledgements

I am grateful to many people for the help and kindness they offered me during the writing of this book: some of them are sadly no longer with us, and some of them I now count as friends.

Firstly, I would like to thank the members of the Daley family – Mary, John, Ken, Terry and Maureen – who shared their memories of Pat and their personal impressions of the man behind the gloves.

Others who kindly shared their recollections of him include John Black, Bill Chevalley, Peter Kent and Terry Goldsmith; the last of whom very patiently spoke over the phone to me at length from the Bahamas, and sent me countless emails about his days at Nipper's gym. Eddie Reeves, who never met Pat but well remembered his name, spoke to me at length about Marylebone in the '20s and '30s and gave me a great insight into what life was like there.

My thanks to Kevin Batchelor, who assisted with the index for this book and provided a great deal of useful feedback. I am indebted to boxing historian Miles Templeton for allowing me access to his comprehensive fight records for Nipper Pat's opponents. Thanks to these I was able to study each of their careers in depth, and write about each of them with some authority. The chapter 'Yesterday's Heroes' owes its depth of insight to Miles's exhaustive statistics on twentieth-century boxing. Boxing historians Derek O'Dell, Richard Ireland and Harold Alderman, MBE, were also very helpful. Derek generously sent me a large batch of his fight records, and Richard and Harold likewise posted me material.

I would also like to thank the following people, who have helped at different stages and to varying degrees, and who all gave readily of their time:

Mary Powell and LEBA, Martin Sax, Rob Snell, Bryan Evans and Colin and Howie Johnson (Nipper's Welsh relatives), Ron Olver, Pat MacManus, Johnathan Oswin, Bryan Yates, Eddie Quill, Brian Ekins, Peggy Newton, Andrea Stanton, David McCleave (Dave McCleave's son), Charlie McCleave (cousin of Charlie and Dave), John McDonald, Sharon Liddon, Larry Braysher, Peter Judge, Ron Morgan, George Happe, Dave Evans, James Duffy, Trevor Jones, Sara Denham, Dereck S. Couzens, Heather Acton, Peter Cuthbert, Jeff Ellis, Bob Lonkhurst, John

Sheppard, Barry Deskins, Mike Hallinan, Peter Street, Tony Mizler, Jamie Parker, Tarka King, Penny Perrick, Tony Connolly, Claude Abrams and the staff at *Boxing News*, the staff at the British Newspaper Library, the staff at the City of Westminster Archives Centre, and the staff at Bancroft Road Library.

I apologise for any omissions, which are purely accidental.

Introduction

'Of course I've heard of Nipper Pat Daly,' exclaimed TV pundit, writer and sports personality Reg Gutteridge with some incredulity. 'Mind you,' he added after a pause, 'I've not heard that name for years.' It was a privilege to speak with Mr Gutteridge for some 20 minutes back in the summer of 2007, and to hear first-hand some of his favourite anecdotes from a lifetime in boxing.

His knowledge stretched back to when his father and uncle – the famous Gutteridge twins, who seconded everyone from Eric Boon to Primo Carnera – introduced him to the sport that became his bread and butter. He told me that Premierland, the legendary East End hall where Nipper Pat built his career, was slightly too early for him; but he well remembered watching boxing elsewhere during the depressed 1930s. He recalled, in particular, seeing contests at the Holborn Stadium (site of Nipper Pat's biggest fight), which was bombed to bits during World War Two.

It was wonderful to speak to a man who had witnessed first-hand the long lost sporting epoch I intended to write about, and all the more so one whose commentary skills and writing I greatly admire. I left Reg hoping we'd speak again (we never did), but also with the sad realisation that he was one of the last men alive who could talk first-hand of the fight game of the inter-war years; and moreover one of the last who recalled the days when Nipper Pat Daly was a household name. Reg passed away in January 2009.

Another splendid writer, the late Gilbert Odd, was the man first tasked with writing this biography. Unfortunately, that book never reached fruition, but during the early 1980s Nipper Pat wrote down his memoirs for Odd, many of which, I suspect, were forwarded on to him with no copies made. Luckily, copies of *some* of them – eloquently penned in old-fashioned handwriting – remain with the Daley family and are reproduced throughout this book. I believe they add a real feel for the era, and, although Pat was a matter-of-fact type of man, at times we get a real insight into his thoughts and feelings; as great an insight, anyway, as a man of his phlegmatic nature would ever offer. Parts of the book written by Pat in the first person are from these notes made originally for Gilbert Odd.

Without realising it, I started researching this book back in 2002, when I decided to learn more about my paternal grandfather, who had died when I was seven, who I was told was in his day a very gifted professional boxer, but of whom I otherwise knew very little. As time passed and I delved deeper into Nipper Pat's career and the age in which he fought, I became increasingly sure that I had unearthed an incredible yet long forgotten human-interest story.

Before I knew it, I was immersed in a bygone world of smoky, ramshackle boxing halls, fly-by-night promoters, unscrupulous managers, and fighting men whose courage went beyond the call of duty. It was a sporting scene unlike any I'd heard of or known, and I could scarcely believe that it happened not so long ago. For the boxers of that era, trading leather was less a sport than a means of survival. Their limitless courage, their single-minded resolve, and their willingness to fight anyone, anywhere at any time sets them apart. It was an era stranger than fiction, crammed with controversy, colour and larger-than-life characters, like a chapter from a Dickens novel.

Nipper Pat Daly was as extraordinary as the era in which he boxed. He was one of the most amazing talents to grace a boxing ring, and his achievements while in his mid-teens – when he not only beat but outclassed a string of champions (all grown men of course) – go unsurpassed. Although he never won a British championship, he could have become the youngest to do so given the chance. Indeed, the chief question concerning fight scribes in those days, was at which weight would the kid win his first *world* title? He never got that far, but all the evidence suggests he should have. To discover what went wrong and to understand why he retired from the sport he loved when only 17, please read on.

Britain's recognised weight classes in the 1920s and '30s

Flyweight	8 stone and under
Bantamweight	8 stone 6 lb and under
Featherweight	9 stone and under
Lightweight	9 stone 9 lb and under
Welterweight	10 stone 7 lb and under
Middleweight	11 stone 6 lb and under
Cruiserweight (now light-heavyweight)	12 stone 7 lb and under
Heavyweight	Any weight

A caricature from *The Sporting Chronicle*, 4 Sep 1929.

1

The Champion and the Child

In May 1928 Giovanni Sili, flyweight champion of Italy, arrived in London to do battle with one of Britain's best eight-stone boxers. It was his first bout on British soil and most likely his first time in the country. He had probably heard of his opponent, who for some months had been setting newspaper columns aglow with vivid reports of his ring exploits, but he had never seen him in action. Nipper Pat Daly – the 'Marylebone wonder' – had arrived seemingly from nowhere and quickly established himself as Britain's most precocious boxing talent. Big things were forecast for this gifted young man – comparisons were being made with the greats of yesteryear, and some had already tipped him as a future world champion – but in no way did this deter or frighten the Italian.

While this young British prospect had chalked up some notable victories, he had never faced a fighter of Giovanni Sili's class. The 23-year-old Italian had captured the national title the previous November, dismantling Enzo Gaggiula in Milan. And five weeks ago, in Paris, he'd fought the top-ranked Frenchman Emile Pladner, who within a year would be world flyweight champion. The man from Roma was proud to be champion of Italy – a distinction he'd earned through years of dedication. He was well known for his punching power – tragically, in his next title defence later that year, Sili's opponent Enzo Cecchi would die following a knockout. If the young Brit was as gifted as they said, then Sili's powerful right hand would surely nullify his boxing talent. Age, experience and weight of punch were all on the Italian's side.

The fight would be staged at the headquarters of British boxing: Covent Garden's illustrious National Sporting Club (NSC), an establishment that fashioned the rules of modern boxing and for decades ruled the fight game with an iron fist. Traditionally this stuffy members-only establishment – in which fights were observed in near silence – was the reserve of the wealthy and well-connected. On a normal NSC night, a hushed, dinner-jacketed assembly looked on as two working-class lads fought hell for leather for their entertainment. The only sounds audible were the gasps and grunts of the fighters and the dull thud of leather against skin or glove. The NSC once held a monopoly over British title fights. It chose the challengers and told both men under what terms and on which date they would fight. No one apart from the Club's elite patrons could watch these contests; the 'great unwashed' could only read about them in newspapers. But by 1928 the status quo had altered; the Club had lost its grip and promoters with deep pockets had moved in. They now staged championship fights at large venues, such as Olympia and the Royal Albert Hall – all paying customers were admitted and the NSC's blessing was no longer needed. Faced with financial ruin, that year, for the first time in its history the Club had opened its doors to the general public for special events. With great reluctance, but the utmost necessity, the cloth-cap and muffler brigade were finally allowed through its sacred gates.

One such occasion was the Anglo-Italian boxing night of Friday 18 May 1928. The bill comprised two 15-rounders and three 10s – each pitting a top Italian against an Englishman. Mr A. Molinari, the promoter, hoped the evening would raise funds for the Italian hospital in London and sold his tickets at a premium: £1 10s for ringside, £1 1s for stalls, from 15s 6d to 5s 9d for reserved seating and 3s 6d unreserved – all sizeable sums for the day. Come fight night, the cheaper seats and standing areas were crowded, but much to the organisers' surprise, the dearer seats were only sparsely filled. Did price hikes alone account for so many notable absentees? Or was the prospect of a working-class invasion simply too much for some Club members to bear?

Nipper Pat Daly, who opposed Giovanni Sili in one of the 10-rounders, arrived at the Club with his trainer and manager, 'Professor' Andrew Newton, at around 8pm. If the bouts all went the distance – which they virtually did – he would not be due on until 12:30am, so could expect a long wait. Sprawled across two of the NSC's floors were a series of dressing rooms for the boxers. Pat and his party settled into one next to Giovanni Sili, and waited to be called out. Among the Daly team was Leo Phillips, another Newton pupil, who in the '30s boxed out of Birmingham and became a top welterweight. At this time he was 14 years old and accompanying his famous stable-mate at Newton's invitation, on the condition he brought his violin. His job that night was not to box but to play songs chosen by the Professor. In a moment of inspiration the Prof picked the famous Neapolitan ballad, *O sole mio*, and did not let Phillips change the tune all night. 'Play it again, Leo,' he growled, 'we'll show 'im we're not afraid of 'im.' His plan, presumably, was to unsettle the Italian and gain a valuable psychological edge.

Meanwhile, in the Club's main hall, two great nations waged war. Salvatore Ruggirello drew first blood for Italy in a contest that ended bizarrely. His opponent, Jack Stanley of Deptford, slipped on a patch of water in the ninth, landed awkwardly and was counted out. Later it transpired that he had dislocated a kneecap. Next, Primo Ubaldo made it two-nil to Italy, forcing Erith's Jim Shaw to retire between the ninth and tenth with a badly cut eye. But Bristol lightweight George Rose salvaged some English pride with a 'no thrills' points win over Milan's Saverio Turiello. England then fell irreversibly behind when Mile End bantamweight Lew Pinkus lost a barnstormer of a fight to Dino Tempesti. Italy had triumphed, but nobody present dared leave their seat just yet. The most intriguing bout on the bill was up next.

With Professor Newton in tow, Pat left his dressing room and strode out into the magnificent Club hall. On one side was a stage, a relic from the building's theatrical days, over which the curtain was permanently raised. On here, their pens eagerly poised, sat pressmen on rows of benches. Overhead, stretching along the other sides of the hall, were ornately crafted balconies, shaded by chandeliers; clusters of men leaned over them for a bird's-eye view. Beneath them was the gallery, which on this night was the busiest part of the hall. In the very middle, gleaming brightly beneath electric chandeliers, was a white, roped squared ring, clearly visible to all in this old amphitheatre. To men accustomed to watching fights in grimy, ramshackle buildings, this magnificent hall, with its splendid décor and prestigious past, was a real treat. As Pat approached the ring, a volley of cheers rang out through a dense fog of tobacco smoke. With an appreciative smile he climbed through the ring ropes, crossed to the farthest corner, and sat down in a relaxed posture. Sili appeared next and he too received a warm welcome, particularly from an Anglo-Italian contingent getting its first glance at a national champion. Ducking beneath the ropes, he shot a cursory glance at his opponent; he then paused and started to laugh.

Whatever the champion had read about England's young prospect, however he had envisaged him, he was not prepared for the undernourished cherubic face gazing up at him from across the ring. In contrast to the Italian's own stocky, bronzed physique and rugged countenance, was this pale, gangly adolescent with a face like a choirboy. In place of muscle mass, around shoulders, thighs and calves was angular bone draped in a milky whiteness of skin. His opponent didn't look like a prizefighter – he looked like he needed a good square meal. Yet if Sili had studied the youth more closely; if he had looked beyond the immediate; he would have spotted an already flattened nose – the product of scores of professional fights – and would have noticed in those eyes an unshakable gaze, devoid of fear, belying the boyish features. The Italian, however, had not.

'I did not come all the way to England to fight a child,' he sneered, and began to remove his gloves. He explained both to his seconds and to the referee that for the champion of Italy to be matched in this way was not just a joke but an insult. In any case, he added, he would like to avoid killing 'this little boy' if he could help it. 'If you don't fight you'll be letting your country down,' they told him. 'Think of all the Italians who've turned out to see you box!' At first he maintained that he would not proceed with the contest; the mere thought of him fighting this skinny youth was absurd. But after further cajoling, finally he relented, and the fight was back on.

The two boxers were then called to centre ring for final instructions, and for the first time stood face-to-face. Pat was a few inches taller but also a shade lighter than Sili (they met at catchweights with separate weigh-ins). Unfazed by the furore of a few moments before, Pat met his rival with a confident stare. In response, the Italian narrowed his eyes and curled his lips in utter disdain. Back in his corner, he muttered churlishly to his seconds, then shot Pat another scornful glare, as if to say, 'This will not take me long.' To this the Londoner grinned and shrugged his shoulders.

At the clang of the first bell Sili shot from his corner in a crouching stance, bobbing and weaving as he moved. He seemed determined to finish the fight quickly and teach the matchmaker and this impertinent infant a lesson. *Boxing* (the sport's trade paper) surveyed the action as follows:

> 'This Sili knows a thing or two and he tried them all out. Crouching almost to a sitting posture and swerving his head and body from side to side, he presented a constantly moving target and would then leap into furious action, swinging, hooking and lashing out in desperate attempts to send a winner over. Pat kept cool and boxed brilliantly, refused to be tempted into experiments, made use of his excellent left at every available opportunity, used the uppercut judiciously, but wisely refrained from taking risks. The boy had sensed at once that his opponent was laying traps and he wouldn't be caught.'

The Italian pulled out every trick in his repertoire, but to his astonishment he found his opponent wise to them all. In a bid to confuse the youngster he tried alternating his stance between orthodox and southpaw. Each time he did this, however, he was caught by a stinging straight left or well-timed right. Round after round the British lad bombarded his man with piston-like lefts. Time and again poor Sili was forced to retreat behind raised gloves, astonished by the pace and precision of these blows and left shaking his head in disbelief.

In the later rounds – his face now a bloodied mess – Sili charged at Pat in a desperate series of punch-slinging rushes. But he was swiftly stopped in his tracks by a hard left or well-placed uppercut, or made to look clumsy by a neat sidestep and counter.

At the close of 10 action-packed three-minute rounds, ringsiders, among them some of the leading figures in Anglo-Italian society, rose to their feet amid rapturous applause. They had just seen the finest fight of the evening and a show of boxing worthy of the best. The lad from London was the undoubted winner, as Signor Sili sportingly acknowledged. Sidling up alongside him, through cracked and swollen lips, Sili smiled to his conqueror and remarked in broken English, 'You-a look like such a baby, but you are a great, great fighter!'

Boxing's correspondent was thrilled by what he had seen, declaring, 'Pat gave one of the best performances of his already brilliant career, and won well... Nipper Pat put up one of the best displays of scientific boxing seen anywhere for quite a while.'

Giovanni Sili, flyweight Champion of Italy, had to be led from the ring by his seconds. The blazing ring lights had faded, the audience were now shadows, and both of his eyes were swollen shut. His 'unworthy' opponent was unmarked. Pat was 15 years old.

2

West London to Wayne

'Boxers, like poets, have to be born and cannot be made.'

John Murray (Editor of *Boxing*), 25 October 1927

Patrick Daley, the father of this book's protagonist, was a man who enjoyed a fight. He lacked the discipline and self-control needed for boxing but was well known for his tear-ups on the cobbles. Although he spoke with a broad cockney accent and had been born and bred in London, he nevertheless maintained that he was Irish.

Born in Marylebone, west London on 29 March 1884 to Irish immigrants Denis and Honorah, Patrick was one of nine brothers and sisters – only three of whom reached adulthood. He grew up in one of Marylebone's poorer, largely Irish quarters, amid a maze of crowded backstreets and courts nestled behind the Edgware Road. The men of this quarter were mostly labourers, and with little else to do besides the occasional trip to a music hall, a culture of hard work and heavy drinking prevailed. As a teenager Patrick worked as a road sweeper, then at 20 enlisted in the Army's Dorsetshire regiment. After three years' service he transferred to the reserves. He had quickly grown tired of Army life, and he was also growing tired of the murky air and crowded conditions of inner London. A total change of scenery was what he needed.

Accompanied by elder brother Denis (known as Dinny), Patrick packed his few possessions and headed for south Wales, in the hope of finding steady work in more agreeable surroundings. The brothers lodged with coalminer Will Evans in the picturesque southwest Powys town of Ystradgynlais. They found jobs at the local colliery and soon became acquainted with Mr Evans's two strikingly beautiful daughters. On 25 September 1909 – just over a year after arriving – Patrick Daley and Mary Ann Evans (known as May to friends and family) were married. (Her sister, Margaret Hannah Evans, married Denis Daley shortly thereafter.)

Newlyweds Patrick and May moved to 6 Brookland Terrace in the nearby village of Abercrave. On 17 February 1913, their first child – a boy, named after his father – was born. Patrick Clifford Daley was a robust, intelligent and good-natured child who had his mother's brown hair, brown eyes and good looks. To save confusion with his father, his immediate family called him Clifford; but later, to his friends and to thousands of boxing fans, he would be known as Pat or simply 'Nipper'. For the majority of his boxing career Pat's last name was spelt without the 'e', so in the interests of consistency, hereafter it shall be spelt 'Daly'.

Abercrave had its own colliery in which Patrick and nearly 200 others laboured for long shifts, digging coal with picks and shovels. It was dangerous, backbreaking work, but there was every incentive for the men to graft hard, as they were paid according to the tonnage they produced. Patrick's time down the pits, however, was about to be cut short.

Britain entered the First World War on the 4 August 1914, and as an Army reservist Patrick was among the first called up to serve. Like countless other wives, daughters, sisters and mothers, May, then aged 22, was left alone to fend for herself and her infant son. Most of Britain expected a quick victory and the civilian population volunteered in their droves. Indeed, for some, the greatest fear of all was that the war would end before they reached the front line. No one could have foreseen the four years of horror and carnage that were to come.

As fate would have it, Patrick's time in the trenches would be relatively short lived. In 1915, just months after enlisting, a German bullet tore through his left shoulder. It left the arm an inch or so shorter than his right and made him unfit for war service. He was discharged and returned to Abercrave. Luckily, the injury had not truly handicapped him, so he resumed his job at the colliery.

In 1918, Patrick, May and Pat relocated to 100 Princess Street in Marylebone. On 29 September that year a second child, Cornelius Henry Daley (known as Con), was born. By then Patrick was working as a labourer at an aircraft works, which may well have been the Palmer Tyre Company in nearby Hatton Street – a road the family would later live in.

The following year tragedy struck. After falling seriously ill, Con was rushed to Paddington Green Children's hospital where, despite the efforts of staff, he died on 8 November at only 13 months old. The cause of death was listed as diarrhoea, which was probably the result of a viral infection. Today, in the western world, such conditions are easily managed, but in

1919, without the aid of an intravenous drip, the resultant dehydration was a common cause of infant mortality. At the time of his baby brother's death Pat was six years old.

Perhaps seeking to distance themselves from the site of so much sorrow, a few months later the family emigrated to Canada. One of May's sisters, Liz, had already moved there with her husband and, word had it, work was plentiful in Alberta's coalmines. On 11 May 1920, Pat and his parents left London aboard the SS *Tunisian* and docked at Montreal, Quebec 13 days later.

Upon arrival they headed for the small Alberta mining town of Wayne, nestled in a vast prairie landscape known as the Badlands. To reach it they crossed a winding moon-like valley, and 11 one-way plank-bedded bridges. Today Wayne is a ghost town, strewn with disused houses and mining relics, and only 40 diehard souls still live there. But in 1920 it had a thriving coal industry and was home to up to 1,500 people. The town had all the family necessities – a goods store, a school, a church and a 15-bed hospital. There was also a police officer stationed at the town, although his main objective was to apprehend moonshiners (Alberta's prohibition laws were then in effect and bootleggers were doing a roaring trade). Wayne's houses were very basic and very small wooden shacks, but the town had a close-knit, predominantly Welsh community, which suited Pat and his parents.

The work at the Alberta mines was just as gruelling as back in south Wales, but community events were held to help lift spirits. Pat would recall that on their annual sports day a mysterious Red Indian rode into the village and enrolled in each of the running events. The crowds of locals were abuzz with speculation as the stranger lined up beside their own runners. The mystery man won every event, collected a tidy sum in wagers, then rode out of the town, never to be seen again. His sudden appearance and disappearance provided reams of material for schoolyard chatter in the months to come.

To keep busy, Pat served as an altar boy at the town's Catholic church. And what began as a hobby quickly blossomed into an out and out obsession. So enthralled with religion was Pat that he persuaded his mother, herself a Welsh Baptist, to convert to Catholicism. Of course she did this more to humour the boy than through genuine religious conviction; and like most childhood fixations, Pat's devoutly religious phase soon passed. It was replaced, however, by a new obsession, itself almost a religion. He would later recall:

> 'My dad used to help run bunkhouse scraps out there and believe me these contests would have put to shame some of the so-called fights today. I used to go off to morning service, serve at the alter, make responses in Latin, then at midday I was one of the cheering bunkhouse crowd, yelling my little head off as a couple of miners went at it.'

These bunkhouse battles captured the imagination of this seven-year-old who could no doubt picture himself as one of the combatants, gliding across the ring and swapping blows to the delight of a cheering crowd. Little did he know that in a few years he would be doing just that – not to scores of miners in tiny bunkhouses, but to thousands of paying fans at esteemed venues such as the Royal Albert Hall and the National Sporting Club.

On 25 March 1921, Patrick and May's third child, Robert – known as Bob or Bobby – was born (another boy, Kenneth, followed in 1926). With an extra mouth to feed Patrick's wages were stretched further than ever. Pat and his mother were happy in Wayne and reluctant to leave the shelter of its close-knit community. But Patrick had grown bored with Canada, and with funds wearing thin, he decided to try his luck in Australasia. Naturally, the rest of the family travelled with him. But three days in New Zealand and half a day in Australia were enough to convince him that jobs 'down under' were scarcer still. May had her heart set on returning to Canada, but her husband surprised her by producing three long-haul tickets, destination… England. Patrick had already booked a passage for her and the boys to return to London. They would sail via passenger liner, while he travelled separately, earning extra cash as a freight ship's stoker.

On arrival they stayed with Patrick's sister, then moved into a house of their own on Hatton Street, Marylebone. Unwittingly, the seal had been set on a gifted young man's future.

3

The Professor's Prodigy

'All around me as I grew up were boxers and would-be boxers. And the youngsters like myself dreamed of the days we would be champions. Champions like Danny Frush, Pedlar Palmer, the Johnny Brown brothers, Jack Hyams, Joe Bloomfield, Harry Mason, Kid Lewis, Nipper Pat... not all champions in status but all of them East End champions.'

R. L. Finn, *Grief Forgotten*

Just behind the Edgware Road lies Hatton Street. It is short and narrow and runs parallel with its famous bigger brother. Unlike most of the surrounding roads, its name to this day is unchanged. But in the 1930s a 'slum clearance' operation altered its appearance forever. The little rows of terraced houses were ripped down and replaced by a characterless council block. Although the street was far from a slum, it was thought more practical to demolish than to modernise.

When the Daley family lived there – first at number 19 then, as the family grew, at number 24 – the street was as it had been for a hundred or so years. Its houses were lit by gas, had no bathrooms and no hot water. The lavatories were outside and householders washed in an old tin bath, hauled into the kitchen or backyard and heated with kettle water. Those who could spare the money would wash in a cubicle at the public baths instead. But despite the absence of creature comforts and the scarcity of money, it was a pleasant place to live. 'It was a bit like Coronation Street,' recalled Pat's youngest brother Ken, 'the kind of place where everyone knew everyone and we were very, very happy there.'

Flanked by Oxford Street and Regent Street in the south, the exclusive squares of Bayswater to the east, and the broad, well-to-do avenues surrounding Regent's Park in the northwest of St. John's Wood, Marylebone was an area split by class and money. Poor and squalid streets were found in close proximity to the wealthiest of London addresses. Eddie Reeves, who grew up on Fisherton Street (a couple of roads from Pat) in the 1920s and '30s, remembers what life was like:

'As kids we could roam far and wide. You'd wander into these [wealthy] areas and there were many ways that you could earn a crust here and there. By dashing across and opening a taxi door and saying, 'Here you are, sir,' and hoping he'd put a copper or two in your pocket. Or you progressed further up to Piccadilly and you got hold of something some way or another... Quite a lot of the men folk liked to drink and unfortunately quite a lot of them spent all the money in the pub, which left some of the women in dire circumstances. So we had Uncle Horace, the chap with a hump and the three brass balls hanging above his shop. He would lend mum a few bob on your father's suit for a week. It never got her out of debt because she had to find it on the Saturday to get it out again...

You did a paper round, not because you wanted to, you did one to put a few bob in the house. You gave it all over. I think the wage was something like three shillings a week, of which your mum would probably give you sixpence – if you were lucky. And in those days, if you had your newspaper delivered, you was worth a few bob. We used to deliver papers to these big blocks of luxury flats, like Abbey Lodge, which backed on to Regent's Park. But you couldn't go in through the front door – you used the tradesmen's entrance. You went round the back and went up in a tradesman's lift and the maid would answer a door that opened onto the kitchen. That was the difference in the people that lived there – the class division.'

Other ways Eddie and the local children earned money included selling jam jars to the rag shop, salvaging old boxes to chop up and sell as firewood, and helping spectators at the annual Harrow versus Eton cricket match, at nearby Lord's, find parking spaces for their cars. 'You learned to have your little schemes to get a copper or two here and there. It's just the way that kids were then,' he recalls.

A couple of minutes' walk from Pat's house was Church Street and its famous market. Packed with barrows and stalls, it supplied most of the Daley family's groceries and, as Eddie Reeves remembers, it served as a focal point for the local community:

'It was an all-day street market open every day apart from Thursdays. Barrows from Edgware Road up to Grove Road. It had every sort of barrow you wanted. On a Saturday it was all bustling. The men got paid on a Saturday; the wives got their money, the men'd go down for a pint and the wives'd do the late shopping on a Saturday night. In the winter they'd have the old oxyacetylene lights burning, with the barrows underneath them.

We all lived fairly adjacent and walking through that market you'd always knock into somebody you knew… It was a real community. But you go there now – which I have been – and you've got these big, tall high-rise blocks, and then this dirty old lonely market; an absolute ghost town, with not half the love or feeling for the place. I might sound like a poet saying this, but there's a lot of warmth missing today that *they* had yesterday.'

Equally close by, on the corner of Richmond Street and Fisherton Street, was Richmond Street RC School, where classes were taught by nuns, renowned locally for their iron discipline and liberal use of the cane. Pat attended lessons there until he reached the age of 14. By coincidence, in the year below him at the school was another future pro boxer, Charlie Thomas, who later became his stable-mate and described Pat as his idol. Often taught in classes of more than 60, working-class children received a rudimentary education. School, for most, was merely a stopgap between infancy and decades of poorly paid work. If you were poor in '20s Britain, it was unlikely schooling would elevate you financially; but a successful career in the prize ring just might.

Professional boxers were the heroes of working-class schoolboys in '20s and '30s Britain – football and all other sports then played second fiddle. Every national newspaper had its own boxing expert who covered fights across Britain, while the weekly trade paper, *Boxing*, had a circulation of hundreds of thousands (its modern counterpart, *Boxing News*, today sells just 10,000 copies per week). 'To witness the return of one of the local stars of boxing,' wrote author Thomas Burke in 1932, 'would make a film star really ill.' Practically every town and every part of every city in Britain had its local ring heroes. With the utmost partisanship, schoolboys and grown men alike would fervently follow their local men and support them in their bid to reach the top. Most, of course, never reached it; but as long as they gave their best between the ropes, they could usually count on the loyalty of the fans.

Fights were staged in practically every corner of every province and in every district within every city. Sometimes a single venue would open its doors two or three times a week, and the boxers customarily fought several times a month, some even several times a week. Countless halls, warehouses, public baths and ice rinks were commandeered and adapted to stage boxing. In the 1920s top-class London shows could be seen everywhere from Whitechapel and Hackney, to Kingston, Blackfriars, Fulham and Edmonton.

The East End was a hotspot for London boxing, but west London had its share of fighters and venues too. During the Great War an arena called the West London Stadium operated at 60 Church Street and brought some of the sport's biggest names to Marylebone. Jimmy Wilde, Digger Stanley, Pedlar Palmer, Tommy Noble, Alec Lambert, Joe Conn, Danny Frush, Bill Beynon and Mike Honeyman all boxed beneath its roof. The venue had since closed, but other west London arenas – such as the Vale Hall in Kilburn, Lime Grove Baths and Paddington Baths – quickly replaced it.

Boxing had long been popular in Britain – big British names such as Jimmy Wilde, Jim Driscoll, Freddie Welsh, Owen Moran and Ted Kid Lewis had pulled in the crowds before and during the Great War. But in the gloomy post-war years a new wave of ring-glamour – sourced from across the Atlantic – would envelop Britain's working classes like never before. The world champions at the time were truly legendary figures. They included the iconic, giant-killing heavyweight Jack Dempsey, the 'Human Windmill' Harry Greb at middleweight, the hard-hitting 'Toy Bulldog' Mickey Walker at welterweight and the 'Ghetto Wizard' Benny Leonard down at lightweight. Unlike today, there was then – aside from disputes over vacated titles – just one titleholder at each weight, and only eight universal weight classes. Ironically, despite this newfound fight fever, Britain had lost its once high place in world boxing. America now held all but one of the world titles; the UK's last world champion, the legendary but now past-his-prime Jimmy Wilde, was about to lose his crown to a hungry Filipino called Pancho Villa in New York.

The search for Britain's next boxing star was on, and the country's gyms and fight halls were abuzz with activity. Today Britain has only a few hundred active pro boxers. But during the 1920s and '30s there were invariably over 6,000 active professionals at any given time – around 10 times the number there are now. Unlike today, the majority of these boxers fought in the lighter (fly, bantam, feather and lightweight) weight classes. Competition was hot; the prospect of glory slim; but that did not deter countless working-class lads endeavouring to punch themselves clear of poverty.

Pat's first acquaintance with fighting arrived shortly after he returned to Marylebone. According to Ken, he was a quiet, fairly subdued child and, with his Welsh accent (of early years) and his lack of street-wiseness, he probably stood out from other west London kids. But if any of them harboured ideas of bullying the little lad, they were in for a rude shock. Pat's father had taught the boy to look after himself, and so, even as a nine-year-old, he took insults from nobody:

'My fighting life started on a back street in Marylebone. My cousin Harry Sivers and I were booting around a sixpenny rubber ball (a joint week's pocket money) when the local bully kicked it over a roof. "I'll get it, Cliff," said Harry. (Like the rest of my family, he called me by my middle name.) Harry, like the other kids in our neighbourhood, was afraid of this boy. I was not. To give him a chance I asked the bully to retrieve our ball. "Not so likely," he replied and a fight started but was quickly over. He lunged at me with both fists flying. I landed one punch and he was in the gutter, crying. His mother came out and, though her boy was twice my size, called me every name under the sun. She ended with, "If you want to fight, there's a place in Marylebone Road where they'll put you in your place." I knew the place she meant. It was run by "Professor" Andrew Newton.' *Topical Times*, 27 May 1939

'Professor' Newton was a larger-than-life character with a thick, sprouting moustache and a shock of unmanageable hair. He carried a gnarled, gold-topped cane and smelt strongly of oil of wintergreen (an embrocation he rubbed in to stave off rheumatism), the scent of which permeated his gym. He was not a real Professor – in fact, he could scarcely read or write – but the moniker he adopted fitted him just the same: he had devoted his life to the study and perfection of scientific boxing.* Some reckoned him the greatest boxing instructor of the day; the sporting press dubbed him 'the One and Only' – and, being a man of no small ego, he wholeheartedly agreed.

---

*   The 'Professor' appellation was adopted by numerous other boxing instructors, and was particularly popular during the nineteenth century. Ned Donnelly and Bat Mullins were two other notable fistic professors. Newton's obituary in *Boxing* (3 April 1940) describes him as 'the last of the old boxing professors'.

Youngest of eight, Andrew J. Newton was born in Watford, Hertfordshire on 22 July 1864. According to Eugene Corri's *Gloves & The Man*, he started boxing rather belatedly at the age of 22. He relocated to St. Pancras in London and within two years had won the 1888 ABA lightweight title. He captured the title again in 1890, twice flooring H.A. Fawcett (Cestus BC) in the third round of the final. (Amateur fights then consisted of two three-minute rounds and a final four-minute round – with plenty of knockouts scored in that extra last minute.) He was by then fighting under the banner of Isledon BC.

Despite his obvious talent, Newton only had two or three pro fights. He worked during his 20s as a stone polisher for a stonemason, and in his spare time taught boxing for extra cash. In about 1900 he opened his first gymnasium, 'Newton's School of Arms and Physical Culture', at 55 Barnsbury Road, Islington. The philosophy of his coaching, from first till last, was to hit without being hit. His lessons were open to boys and men of all ages and classes, both amateurs and professionals. His clientele were as diverse as the populace of London itself, and ranged from local working-class schoolboys through to grown men of wealth and position. He produced champions of Oxford, Cambridge and Sandhurst; champions of the Navy and Army, and he served as long-standing boxing instructor to Dulwich College.* ABA champions Hugh Brown, Arthur Beavis, Lieutenant-Colonel Dudley S. Lister and Dave McCleave; British heavyweight champion Gunner Moir, British middleweight champion Roland Todd, plus a host of other top-line pros, were all trained by the Professor.

In 1907, when the Barnsbury Road lease expired, he relocated his gym to 241 Marylebone Road, a building with its own rich history. In Victorian times it had been one of several homes for 'Red Coat Boys', as shoeblacks were called. These poor boys, mostly orphans or foundlings, were employed and housed there by a boot-blacking manufacturer called Day and Martin. As a 10-year-old Charles Dickens was sent to work in the Day and Martin factory at Old Hungerford Stairs, sticking labels on bottles and boxes for two years as his father languished in debtors' prison. (There are references

---

* Newton pupils Sir Iain Colquhoun and Major-General G. Le Q. Martel were both Army and Navy champions. T.B. Hardy (1842-1897), a well-known marine painter, and Edwin John (son of the famous painter Augustus John), who briefly boxed as a pro in the 1930s, were two other notable Newton students.

to Day and Martin's boot polish in both *Oliver Twist* and *The Pickwick Papers*.) Thanks to social advancement, Red Coat Boys' homes eventually became extinct. In 1900, William Ecclestone, a gargantuan-sized boxing enthusiast, said to weigh somewhere between 22 and 40 stone, purchased the premises. 'Jolly Jumbo', as he was nicknamed, set up a gymnasium with a full-sized ring on the first floor, while the ground floor – formerly the shoeblacks' dining area and recreation room – was used to stage professional billiards matches. (At some point the building also served as a cinema, Mansell's Picture Palace, which held London's first 'penny picture shows'.)

Jolly Jumbo's gym – known as the Cosmopolitan Club, then later as the National Athletic Club – staged private boxing shows for the next seven years, including, on 8 September 1902, a bout between former world champions Pedlar Palmer of Canning Town and George Dixon of America. The Prince of Wales – the future King Edward VII – watched the fight with interest from the Club's reporters' box. Upon the King's death in 1910, Professor Newton renamed his gymnasium the 'Empire School of Arms' as a tribute.

The Empire School of Arms stood three doors from Edgware Road, on the left-hand side of Marylebone Road as one approached Paddington. The building, which had a deceptively narrow front, stretched back an entire block. Situated in a large Victorian house, the gym was reached via a long passageway. Across its walls hung photos of various boxing personalities; pictures of military officers (all former Newton pupils) in full dress and, in pride of place, one of the Professor – dressed in bowler hat, black overcoat with astrakhan collar, white duck trousers, umpteen pairs of gloves strung around his shoulders, sporting his trademark walrus moustache. On the other side of the gym another long passage led to a back exit on the adjacent street, Crawford Place.

Nina Hamnett – a prominent pre-war artist and notorious bohemian, who had a romance with a Marylebone boxer called Vernon Campbell – visited the gym in the late 1920s and recalled it in her autobiography:

'I went down one Sunday to see the boys training and to meet the great Professor. Sunday morning is the best time, as most of them have to work during the week as navvies. Nipper Pat Daly was then in his prime. He was a funny little boy of fifteen and a half, and a very fine boxer. If ever there should have been a champion it ought to have been Nipper. But that is another story.

The Professor was most charming and gave me demonstrations of right hooks, upper cuts, etc... I met his niece, who played the piano for the boys to do their exercises. Her harmony was not very good, but there was a lot of pep and energy in her performance. No wonder, for I heard afterwards that she was a very fine boxer herself and used to spar with many of the boys. Professor Newton sang out: "Left, right, left! Now agine!" "Old up that left 'and unless you want to stop a right 'ander!"

The gymnasium was very large and very dirty. On one side were wooden steps on which were old mattresses, plaster casts of Greek statues and on one side of the ring, against the wall, a seat was spread with a Union Jack. This was for the guests of honour. Many of the boys were seven or eight years of age and the Professor was really charming when he got into the ring with them. If they looked well he would say: "'It me 'and 'ard," and would fall down flat on his back, to the joy of the little boys...

When we came out in the Marylebone Road, half a dozen workmen laid down their pickaxes and shouted: "'Allo, 'ow are yer?" and we both solemnly shook them by the hand. They were boxers who had to work that morning and could not train. They apparently were not losing any strength or weight digging up the road.'

The artist was evidently struck by the gymnasium and also by Pat himself. She produced a drawing of the gym (later sold to an American), and included a signed photo of Pat in his boxing stance among her book's illustrations.*

★★★

Since learning of its existence, Pat had pleaded with his father to take him to Newton's gym for a tryout. Initially his father refused as, by his own admission, Pat was a child of babyish appearance. 'They'll laugh at you, son. Wait till you're a little older,' instructed his dad. But after a prolonged

---

* After meeting Vernon Campbell at the Fitzroy Tavern, Fitzrovia in the late 1920s, Hamnett's interest in boxing had burgeoned. She watched a show at the Comrades' Hall in Camden Town, and when the promoter, Johnny Hughes, offered her a free pass, became a regular attendee. She took large parties of friends, which often included the poet Roy Campbell, to the Comrades' Hall, and later to the Chalton Ring in Somers Town. She often drew pictures at the matches, and also persuaded some of the boxers to pose for her at home. She also watched fights at Premierland, The Ring (Blackfriars), Olympia and the Royal Albert Hall.

period of nagging, he finally relented, and one day in 1922 took the boy to 241 Marylebone Road – just a few minutes' walk from their home.

The Professor didn't know it yet but a once in a lifetime opportunity had literally knocked at his door. As Pat crossed the threshold his heart began to race. He paused as he reached the gym doorway and above it, in imposing letters, saw the following sign:

EMPIRE SCHOOL OF ARMS

Home of Boxing.

Full-sized Ring,

and

Every requisite

to

Develop Champions.

As he wandered through the gym the nine-year-old was mesmerised. Around him were punch bags and punch balls of every description – some fixed to the ceiling, some to the wall and some, rather peculiarly, fixed knee-high to the floor.* There were shelves filled with boxing gloves and rows of neatly stacked medicine balls and Indian clubs. The walls were adorned with pictures of bygone greats and famous contemporary fighters. Among them he saw Georges Carpentier, Jack Dempsey, Sam Langford, Jack Johnson, Tommy Burns, Kid Lewis and Roland Todd – the last of whom had been trained by the Professor. There was the squeak of swinging punch bags, the dull thud of leather, and in every direction were groups of fighters sparring, hitting punch bags, throwing medicine balls or doing floor work; each one working feverishly, oblivious to his presence.

---

* The 'Ground Punching Ball', as this device was called, was patented by the Professor. It comprised a heavy round board with a heavy 'Army' punch ball attached to its centre. The ball was punched around alternately with both hands, then with one hand only, and then with the left hand and right foot. The position was then changed, right leg foremost with the right hand and left foot used. Other exercises included striking with the feet only, right hand and left elbow, and *vice versa*. Its purpose was to perfect timing, balance, hitting with the knuckles, and to strengthen various muscles. A lighter ball was used to develop speed and anticipation and was punched across instead of around. A moment's hesitation saw the ball drop to the board.

Towards one end, near a window, flanked by rows of long steps, stood a magnificent ring with a special felt base. It was the ring in which George Dixon and Pedlar Palmer had spilled their blood 20 years before; a roped space in which countless leading fighters had learnt their trade, and where the legendary world heavyweight champion Jack Johnson had once sparred with Newton while in exile in Europe.

Spotting the two visitors, the daunting, upright figure of the Professor loomed up to Pat and his father. The latter explained that he had brought his son down for a trial and would like him to have some lessons. The wily old trainer looked the boy over sceptically then glanced around the gym. These types of try-outs were trivialities to Newton, who'd seen thousands of hopefuls pass in and out of his door. But, to Pat, it was thus far the greatest moment of his young life:

> 'The Professor looked around and called to a young ginger boy, bigger than myself. I must have looked nervy as my father shouted out, "Are you feeling alright Pat? Calm down, son." But our spar was a wash-out, Ginger was no match for me. The Prof looked surprised, stopped the scrap after a minute and called to an older, well-made boy. "Jimmy, come over here and put 'em on for a minute with this kid." Jimmy Lindsay, a boy the critics later said was faster than Teddy Baldock, stepped over. We fought a fast three minutes and I loved every second of it. Afterwards, lads from around the gym came over, one or two slapped me on the back and my father said "well done". The Prof seemed impressed.' *Topical Times*, 27 May 1939

Pat's father paid the standard 30 shillings for a quarter year's tuition. It was the only fee of its kind he would be asked to pay, as it soon became clear that for a lad of Pat's ability no fees were needed.

Pat was taught that measured, straight hitting was far more effective than wild, energy-sapping, conspicuous swings. He was paired up with a sparring partner and told to practice the left lead and guard continually until it was perfected. The left lead – now universally called the 'left jab' – was known in Britain in the '20s and '30s and for some time afterwards as the 'straight left'. It was a fast, hard, jolting punch, delivered from the shoulder like an arrow from a bow. Pat was taught to shoot out his straight left whenever an opportunity arose. He would use it to mount an attack and also to defend against one. 'As your opponent advances,' he was told, 'the weight of his oncoming rush increases the force of your blows. It is his face hitting your fist, as much as your fist hitting him.'

Next he learnt the other blows in a boxer's repertoire – right cross, left hook, uppercuts and body punches – and was taught how to throw them in combinations. He was shown how to block blows with his glove, forearms and shoulders, how to avoid them with a slip, duck or sidestep, and how to counter whenever a chance arose. He learnt how to box at range and then how to fight in close. He was taught how to open and close distances with nimble footwork and eventually the art of feinting and drawing a lead. These skills were mastered methodically and one at a time. Above all, the importance of self-control was drummed into him: the boxer who loses his head, he was told, will ultimately lose the fight.

Dudley S. Lister came under the Professor's tutelage as a schoolboy at Dulwich College. He won the ABA heavyweight title in 1925, had a distinguished Army career – reaching the rank of Lieutenant-Colonel – then turned to journalism. In his textbook on boxing, *How to Box*, he recalled a Newtonian training exercise that called for clear thought and rapid reactions. Referred to as 'controlled loose play', the instructor sets a scenario, presenting openings or initiating attacks, to which the pupil acts accordingly:

"'Time!' would shout the "One and Only", and off we went together. No action was allowed without his orders apart from the sparring stance, propelled by purposeful footwork, as we followed each other's moves about the ring. Then, interspersed with constructive criticism as to posture, would come sharp commands as to phases of action to be undertaken.

"Lead!" would snap the Professor, and such an order always meant a left lead to the head. As your punch came in it was "block guarded" and a light counter flashed to any uncovered portion of your target. "Double lead!" "Lead and Right to the body – lead!" And this latter instruction resulted in your straight left being blocked and a counter left swing from the Professor being "gone into" with your right to his body.

And the executive word was always "Lead!" at the end of any string of instructions, which meant that the brain had to keep working fast whilst the body was moving, ever ready to snap into the openings presented, or sway away from, or block and then counter, the advertised attack. "Deflect this straight left and counter with left to the body – lead!" And in his left would come, and you would do your stuff – or not, as the case might be.

And all such sessions of "controlled loose play" would end by the Professor, who was not strong on aitches, saying, "Has you please!" and there would be a spell of glorious free boxing until some uncontrolled wildness caused the great old boy to put you back on the leading rein again.'

One of Pat's earliest sparring partners was the Professor's niece Annie Newton, a war-widow with a young daughter. Born at Highgate, north London in March 1893, she was mostly raised by the Professor and at an early age taught to box. Before the Great War she had been part of the 'Newton Midgets': a troupe comprising herself, her brother David, the Professor's son Andy and the Prof himself. They toured some of the best-known music halls in London – Collins's, the Islington Empire, the Euston Theatre and the Canterbury Music Hall – where they performed a unique club-swinging, ball-punching and boxing act choreographed by the Professor.

Annie held the distinction of being the only female ever to enter the ring at the auspicious National Sporting Club where, along with the other 'Newton Midgets', she gave her usual exhibition on one of the Club's co-founder Arthur Bettinson's benefit nights. As a sideshow on professional bills, before crowds at venues such as the Alcazar in Edmonton, Hackney's Manor Hall and Peckham's Winter Gardens, during the 1920s she boxed three-round exhibitions with male opponents. Pat appeared a number of times in exhibitions with Annie, which featured sparring, ball punching and demonstrations of the Professor's unique system of training. So successful were the displays between the woman and the boy that they often outshone the contests themselves. Pat would recall:

'For a woman, Annie Newton was in a class of her own as a fighter. She claimed the Women's Boxing Championship of the World and undoubtedly she was. When I first went to the gym she was commissioned by the Prof to look after me and she did a good job and taught me some of the art of boxing, ball punching and club swinging. From 1922 to 1925 I was her chief sparring partner and she kept me very busy sparring with her, ball punching, club swinging and also various exercises.'

In the daytime, within the confines of a crowded classroom, Pat gazed listlessly at textbooks and listened impassively to teachers as his mind wandered off to his theatre of dreams. School and family life, it occurred to Pat, were hours of wasted boredom. Four nights a week – though he would have preferred seven – he rushed off down the street, boxing togs in a little case, and arrived at the only school that he felt mattered – Newton's Empire School of Arms.

On his few spare nights Pat often visited the 'pictures'. The films then were all silent, but with no television sets at home, the experience of seeing Charlie Chaplin or Buster Keaton on the big screen felt very special. Cinematic technology was then in its infancy and mid-film projection breakdowns often occurred. Invariably, during a breakdown the audience would stamp, yell and whistle until the beleaguered projection-operator got the film back underway. The cinemas were affectionately called 'flea pits' and many locals stayed loyal to their favourite venue irrespective of the featured film. Two of Pat's local picture houses were the Connaught in Edgware Road and Tussaud's on Marylebone Road. 'Best six-pen'orth I ever had,' he recalled, 'was when I sat the programme out twice to watch the film of the Roland Todd v. Kid Lewis fight, when Todd's wonderful defence baffled and beat the Kid.' (The record shows that this bout took place two days before his tenth birthday.)

The tiny lad imbibed boxing lessons with ardent enthusiasm and mastered every punch and move with extraordinary deftness. He soon outshone older, much more experienced Newton pupils as his natural talent began to blossom.

Professor Newton quickly saw in Pat a pupil of unprecedented potential. He became convinced that he had finally unearthed a prospective world-beater and, moreover, a means of cementing his own boxing legacy. Training the youngster became an obsession. 'Daly received more attention from my father than I did in all my career,' wrote the Professor's son Andy, a veteran of hundreds of pro fights. 'He put him through the finer points; for breakfast, dinner, tea and before he left the gym at night he would suddenly aim a punch at Pat to check he was on the alert. If he failed in any particular point he would have to continue until he mastered it.'

The proof of the pudding is in the eating, however. Not everyone can put into practice the moves and strategies learnt painstakingly in the gym. With his speed, strength and reflexes, Pat excelled during sparring. But could he replicate this success in an actual fight? The Professor was keen to find out.

From *Boxing*, 30 May 1928.

4

Jack the Giant-Killer

'Well within my memory, there were a host of tiny gamecocks who asked nothing more than the chance to duck beneath the uncovered hempen strands of some obscure ring and box their hearts out in an effort to shed the shackles of dire poverty and fight their way to the top.'

O. F. Snelling, *Boxing News*, 20 September 1985

Social advancement and the inception of tough new laws killed the shameful British custom of forcing children to toil down mines and up chimneys as cheap labour. In the sphere of professional boxing, however, the country's rules and regulations remained woefully out of date. The only institution that resembled a governing body was the autocratic National Sporting Club, but its policies made few provisions for the well-being of boxers. As a consequence, teenage boys, and some not even in their teens, were entered into professional boxing contests, often conceding age, weight and experience to their opponents. They were often billed as 'midget' matches and appeared as preliminary bouts on the same bills as their older counterparts. There were usually no weigh-ins; if the boys looked roughly the same weight – this being a subjective matter – they would be paired up. Sometimes they fought for a small purse – typically a few shillings – but others boxed merely for their share of the 'nobbings': coins (mostly coppers) thrown into the ring by spectators at the end of a bout. This now extinct custom saw the two boxers collect their winnings from the canvas and divvy them up. Usually a boxer would have to share his end of the nobbings with the 'house' cornermen, and possibly his manager. As a result, what he was left with after fighting his heart out did not amount to much.*

---

* The term 'nobbings', or 'nobbin's' as it is sometimes written, dates from the Victorian era or earlier. In his groundbreaking social critique *London Labour and the London Poor*, 1851, Henry Mayhew makes several references to performers receiving 'nobbings'.

Like today, in the 1920s many young fighters cut their teeth in the amateur ranks before turning professional. But unlike today, a lad of sufficient robustness and talent could circumvent the amateurs and box for money straight away. Pat Daly, the Professor decided, would be one such lad; he would punch for pay from his very first fight. Until he reached 14, it was agreed that Pat's ring earnings would all go to the Professor. At the time this looked likely to only amount to shillings and pence and, as the Prof made no charge for his training, it seemed a fair arrangement.

Since taking over the premises, the Professor had held occasional boxing shows at the Empire School of Arms. With inbuilt stepped seating, and plenty of standing room and chair space, the gym could accommodate a few hundred paying spectators. On 1 October 1924, a contest took place in the gym between Sir John Milbanke, 11th baronet, and Raymond de Trafford (son of Sir Humphrey de Trafford, 3rd baronet), both members of Buck's Club, an exclusive gentleman's club off Bond Street, which created the Buck's Fizz cocktail and served as a model for the fictional 'Drones Club' in the author P. G. Wodehouse's stories.* Mr de Trafford had bet a sizeable sum that he could last five two-minute rounds with Sir John, who was appreciably the harder puncher. Johnny Summers, former British champion at three weights, trained and seconded Milbanke, while Professor Newton handled de Trafford. The gym was crowded with the aristocratic friends of both men and champagne flowed by the bottleful. With Newton in his corner, de Trafford stayed the distance and won the bet. Both loser and victor

---

* Raymond de Trafford (1900–1971) made worldwide headlines in 1927 when he was shot on a Paris train by his lover, rich American heiress Alice de Janzé (who also shot herself), after he reneged on a promise to marry her. Alice de Janzé's wound was superficial but de Trafford suffered a punctured lung and was critically ill for several days. de Janzé confessed to the shootings, but received only a six-month suspended sentence for what the court considered a crime of passion. Despite the public scandal and being almost killed, de Trafford resumed his affair with de Janzé and married her in 1932. She divorced him in 1937, on the grounds of adultery. In early 1941, she was a suspect in the murder in Kenya of Josslyn Hay, the Earl of Erroll. She committed suicide in September that year, using the gun she had once used to shoot de Trafford. She was played by the actress Sarah Miles in the 1988 film *White Mischief*, and Raymond de Trafford was played by Tim Myers.

received a special reception at Buck's the next night, and *The Star* newspaper got an interesting scoop.

Besides giving highly privileged young men the chance to settle a score, the Empire School of Arms staged its own professional shows. Leading men such as Roland Todd, Johnny Broker, Sonny Bird and the Professor's son Andy Newton all started out on Newtonian bills. It made perfect sense, the Professor reasoned, to hold Pat's first fight in the ring he learnt his trade. He made his debut there, at the age of nine, out-pointing George Brown over four rounds before a small crowd. As with many of Pat's early ring encounters there is no known newspaper coverage to provide a date or details of the action. Many small professional shows were not deemed worthy of newspaper coverage, so many professional fights from the period go unrecorded.

Further fights were arranged for Pat on small boxing shows in and around London. The purses vied for were negligible, but these three, four and six-round contests gave him valuable ring experience. In the few newspaper reports that covered these shows Pat received only the briefest of mentions. But much can be gleaned from these snippets, in which he is described as 'cool and confident', 'very stylish', possessed of 'a beautiful stance', a 'brilliantly clever boy' and a lad who 'could not fail to be noticed'. It is unknown how many early fights are missing from Pat's record, but newspaper references, plus his own recollections, suggest he remained unbeaten. Recalling this early period many years later, Pat would write:

'In 1924 boxing was booming, there were boxing shows in almost every district, anywhere where there was room to put a boxing ring 10' square and have room for about 50 or so spectators was a potential boxing stadium, and with the lack of capital the purses were very small. Five shillings was the purse my managers used to receive for a six-round fight. In one such hall in Pimlico I had several fights, also a hall at Camden Town and one at Euston.

The Euston hall was run by Johnny Hughes, ex-flyweight champion of Great Britain. Before I went on Mr Hughes asked me to take it easy with John Brent, my opponent, to let the bout go the full distance (six rounds), as there had been several KO's and as it was only 8:45pm – the show started at 8pm – he did not have enough bouts to last until 10pm, the advertised finishing time. Mr Hughes said, "You've got an easy job so you can take your time". I said, "All right Mr Hughes, it'll go the full six rounds." I do not remember the first round as the "mug" had hit me on the chin and put me down, I was quite groggy for the whole of that round. As the gong went for the second round I was unsteady, but I pulled myself together and outpointed him for the remaining five rounds to win on points. I had promised Mr Hughes to let it go the distance, so I kept my promise, despite the fact that I wanted to kill my opponent. I was 10 years old.'

On 8 February 1924, nine days before his eleventh birthday, Pat boxed an exhibition with George Brown in a theatre at the Hertfordshire town of Letchworth. Former world bantamweight champion Joe Bowker was headlining in a boxing comedy routine he performed with another top pro called Wally Pickard. The pair had made their act famous, appearing throughout the '20s on charity shows at high-profile venues such as the NSC and the Royal Albert Hall. The Letchworth show was promoted by Major James Arnold Wilson, a well-known figure who had just been granted the freedom of the City of London. (His fortunes, however, were about to change. Six months later he was bankrupted when an attempt to pack out Wembley Stadium for a match between Londoner Jack Bloomfield and the American Tommy Gibbons spectacularly backfired.)

At the time, many promoters were in the habit of asking John Murray, the Editor of *Boxing*, to appoint a reporter to referee their fights. Various staff members – including a young Gilbert Odd – were farmed out to officiate the smaller-paid jobs. But, for this one, Murray nominated himself.* With Murray refereeing each of the fights, the famous boxers' manager Ted Broadribb acting as ring manager, and former world champion Bowker topping the bill, the Letchworth show was a prestigious occasion. Pat felt honoured to be sharing a bill with Bowker and was

---

* The practice of appointing newspapermen as referees, along with famous fighters serving as ringside judges, ended with the introduction of British Boxing Board of Control licences in 1929.

determined to put on a good show. As he approached the ring, from amidst the din of the crowd, a wag yelled, 'Blimey, 'ere's Jack the Giant-Killer!' and the theatre erupted with laughter. The little lad reddened with embarrassment, but when he entered the ring his awkwardness vanished. Pat quickly silenced his detractors with a splendid display of fast, clean boxing. The laughs had turned to cheers. The crowd enjoyed the action so much that the bout was extended from three to five rounds. 'Jack the Giant-Killer' had had the last laugh.

The next newspaper coverage of Pat arrives six months later, at the annual August bank holiday horticultural show at Prestwood, Bucks, where he took on 14-year-old former Public Schools Championship competitor Ernest Morris of Manor Farm, Saunderton Lee, Princes Risborough. Morris, three years the elder, 'had the advantage of weight and reach, and went off at a rare rate, finding Daly naturally a wary customer, cool and confident. Both fought a really good three rounds to a draw,' wrote *The Bucks Examiner*. After the fight Pat boxed a three-round exhibition with another Newton 'midget' called Young Baker. At the time he weighed less than 5 stone 6lb.

The highlight of boxing shows for some fans – apart from, of course, the actual action – was betting on the outcome. Bookmakers would crowd round the ringside and yell out odds before and during a contest. There would be new odds, and a fresh rush to place bets, as the fight swung one way or the other. With relatively large sums at stake, feelings often ran high between gamblers and bookmakers. As a consequence, arguments at ringside, and even fistfights, were not unheard of. At one of Pat's early fights an observant bookie called out odds of 'five-ta-two on the nipp-a' referring to the smaller, younger-looking boxer that was Pat. The Professor thought this had a wonderful ring to it and decided in future to bill the boy as 'Nipper Pat Daly'. One of Britain's most memorable ring names was born. By the time of his next recorded bout this new nom de guerre was in place.

The north of England had its own 11-year-old boxing prodigy, 'Nipper' Johnny Summers, who was causing a stir round the fight halls of Leeds, much as Pat was round the small halls of London. Like Pat, he had the benefit of expert tutelage. Another self-appointed fistic professor, 'Professor' Louie Marks, managed and taught Summers. The boys were the same age, around the same weight, and both had splendid reputations. A match at the Manor Hall on Kenmure Road, Hackney was arranged between the two professors.

The Manor Hall had started Sunday boxing in about 1920. Its promoter, Harry Abrahams (a former fighter), was among the first to offer Sunday shows on a 'pay at the door' basis. Until then, Sunday boxing admission was by programme only. Many big names, such as Al Foreman (who boxed there as Bert Harris), Dick and Harry Corbett, Harry Mason, Archie Sexton, Jim Blake and Ernie Izzard started out at Manor Hall. It had a small – less than 14 foot – ring which left little room for back-peddling and compelled both boxers to come forward and fight.

Pat and Summers met there over six rounds in the early afternoon of Sunday 5 October 1924. With admission priced at 1s 3d and 2s 4d, the intimately sized Manor Hall was filled to capacity. As Summers got under the ring lights in flashy new boxing togs and a smart dressing gown Pat, who had only his school football shorts, looked on in envy. Noticing this, the Professor promptly lent him son Andy's gown, which of course was far too big. As he half-tripped, half-shuffled his way to the ring like a kid in a sack race, the crowd gave Pat a big hand. It struck him at that moment that the applause came out of sympathy. He didn't want that. He'd show them he was master at the game he loved.

To the consternation of Summers's backers, Pat comfortably beat his rival in what *Boxing* called 'one of the prettiest contests ever seen at this hall'. Promoter Harry Abrahams was delighted, but Summers's father was not. Convinced that his son could turn the tables, he demanded an immediate rematch. And so, with the bruises still tender, they had another six rounds at the Winter Gardens, Peckham later that day. Pat repeated his earlier feat and boxed beautifully to earn the decision. Grudgingly, Summers senior had to admit that his son had met his match.

The next evening, Andy Newton took Summers and Pat to watch him fight Joe Shears of Drury Lane in a 10-rounder at the King's Hall, Sidcup, Kent. Sir William Larke, K.B.E. (Director of the National Federation of Iron and Steel Manufacturers), was among the show's sponsors and watched eagerly from ringside. But when Newton stopped his opponent in six rounds and the headline 15-round fight also ended early, the promoter was left with a gap in his programme. To fill it and to save the man some embarrassment, Andy suggested that Pat and Summers have another six-round fight and assured him the lads would put on a fine display. Both promoter and fans were delighted as, for the third time in 48 hours, the pair put on a dazzling display of skill, with Pat again boxing his way to victory. He would later recall:

'After the fight we went round with a hat each and collected £5 between us – a large sum of money for 1924. The next day, when I arrived home at lunch time, Newton senior was waiting for me outside the house and said that he had come to give me a rub-down as I may be a bit stiff. I told him that I was not overly stiff, only a little in the joints of my arms. But he still gave me a massage, and when I turned my back to put my trousers on I heard the sound of money and thought to myself, "He is going to give me money for boxing and I enjoyed it so much!" He did, he gave me 13 shillings. I learned some time later what he had received for the three fights, plus three nobbings – our end came to £9-16-0. [The equivalent of three weeks' wages in industry.]'

In those days, if a pair of boxers put on a good display, they were often re-matched repeatedly. Thus, despite Pat winning on every occasion, during the next four years he and Summers fought four more times. The career paths of these two young hopefuls diverged considerably. By the late 1930s the lad from Leeds was boxing at the 12 stone 7 lb light-heavyweight class, having met such men as Harry Mason, Jack Casey and Archie Sexton along the way.* He also served as a sparring partner to British champions Jack Petersen and Jock McAvoy. Although he had

---

* In the early twentieth century, the 12 stone 7 lb division was known as 'cruiserweight' in Britain. The weight class had been introduced in America in 1903, where it was called 'light-heavyweight', but the National Sporting Club instead used the name 'cruiserweight' when it issued its first 12 stone 7 lb belt to Dick Smith in 1914. The trend continued until after the Second World War, whereupon the British Boxing Board of Control changed the division's title to 'light-heavyweight' to bring it in line with America. Britain's original 12 stone 7 lb cruiserweight class should not be confused with the modern cruiserweight division, which sits between heavyweight and light-heavyweight, and was introduced by the WBC in 1979. To avoid confusion, the 12 stone 7 lb class is referred to as light-heavyweight throughout this book.

reached greater heights than Summers, by that time Pat's career had long ended.

Buoyed by the three wins over Summers, the Professor issued a challenge through *Boxing* 'to match Nipper Pat Daly against any boy under 6 stone and under 12 years of age for a small side-stake and the best purse offered'. He accepted a purse offer from Harry Abrahams, and on Sunday 30 November Pat was back at the Manor Hall to outpoint Young Brooks of West Ham in a six-round 'money match'. In a money match the manager or backers of each fighter deposited a (usually equal) monetary stake with a neutral party – often a promoter, referee or newspaperman – and afterwards the stakeholder released the cash to the winning side. In this case the stakes were £5 a side, but later Pat would be backed for much larger sums.

In January 1925 the Professor again appealed for an opponent for Pat, declaring, 'As Daly is under 12 years of age, he does not mind boxing any boy in England up to 13 years of age, anywhere about 6 stone.' But with no opponent forthcoming, two weeks later he relaxed the criteria. 'Not being able to fix any business for Nipper Pat Daly, Professor Newton does not mind giving a few pounds away, providing that they are under 6 stone 7lb and not over 12 years of age, with or without side-stake.' Whether any challengers were found is unknown. We next hear of Pat in the newspapers five months later.

On 11 July the Newton camp visited Becontree, a new development near Dagenham, where Pat boxed six three-rounders in one night. He began with an actual fight, knocking out the Boys' Brigade champion inside a round, leaving the poor lad in tears. He then boxed an exhibition with Annie Newton, another with Andy Newton, and followed these by boxing three rounds each with brothers Charlie and Dave McCleave (the latter a future British welterweight champion). He finished his night's work by sparring with a local heavyweight. The organisers were amazed by this keenly gifted 6-stone lad, and to show their appreciation they awarded him a little cup. Proudly, Pat hurried home to his mother, shielding his precious trophy as if it were a championship belt.

With each win he notched up, with each new showing of science and skill, the reputation of this pocket-sized pugilist grew and grew. Two weeks after the Becontree display Pat was offered an assignment that signified a step-up in class. Although still only 12 years old, he had graduated from London's small halls. He was now boxing at Premierland.

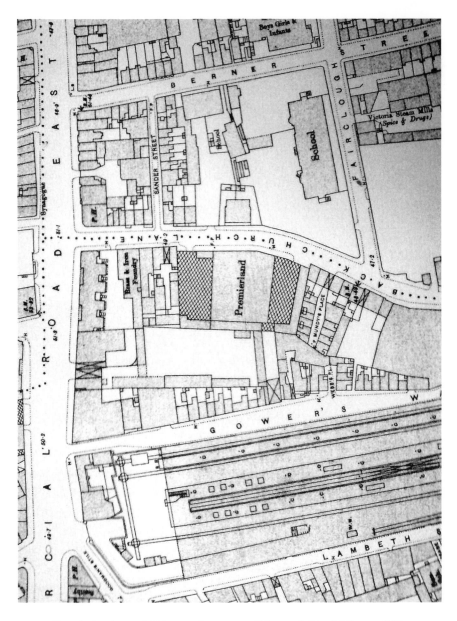

Premierland on a 1913 map (courtesy of Bancroft Road Library, E1).

5

Premierland

On 13 August 1911, at around 4pm, a small fire began at Wonderland, the famous boxing arena on Whitechapel Road. The blaze spread rapidly in the baking August heat, and by the time the local fire brigade arrived it looked to be out of control. An urgent 'district call' brought reinforcements from further afield, but by the time they arrived at 4:30pm the boxing stage, auditorium and dressing rooms were all ablaze, and the flames had shot through the roof and engulfed the first floor of the nearby East London Palace of Varieties. A team of 140 firemen with 12 streamers and three motor pumps fought frantically to save both buildings. They rescued the East London Palace, although the fire damage was estimated at £15,000. But Wonderland, the beloved home of East London boxing, was burnt to a cinder. The fire was attributed to a defective electrical circuit in some cinematograph apparatus being tested for a screening that night. Few locals, however, accepted the official line. Rumours of 'foul play' were rife.

Some claimed the blaze was started by a group of disgruntled boxers who had been short-changed by Wonderland's owner, Jack Woolf; but there was no evidence to support this. More still believed the culprit to be Harry Jacobs, Woolf's former business partner who had been forced out of Wonderland after a spate of public rows between the pair. Circumstantial evidence at least lends weight to this last theory. After falling out with Woolf, Jacobs had staged rival boxing shows at the Paragon Music Hall, but these failed miserably. Shortly afterwards, Wonderland mysteriously burnt to the ground, conveniently clearing the way for Jacobs to open a new arena, without the threat of serious competition. He rented and renovated an empty warehouse (formerly a fish market) on Back Church Lane in Whitechapel, only a few streets from where Wonderland had stood. The new venue, Premierland (pronounced 'Pree-mier-land'), opened its doors on 16 December 1911. An up-and-coming Jewish fighter called Kid Lewis boxed an eight-rounder on the opening bill. Little did anybody know, the 'Kid' was destined for big things.

Jacobs ran shows at 'The Land' (as fight fans christened the new venue) until July 1913, when he was bankrupted by huge gambling debts. The reins then passed to Harry Morris, who in May 1914 staged a 20-round fight there between the legendary American Joe Jeanette and Australian heavyweight champion Colin Bell – Jeanette winning on points. In the autumn of 1914, Premierland closed its doors on the game and during the war years served as a cinema. Jack Callaghan reopened it for boxing when the war ended, then in the early '20s the lease passed to a boxers' manager called Joe Morris, backed by a certain Gershon Mendeloff. The latter was by then known to all as Ted Kid Lewis. The lad who had boxed on Premierland's first show had since won and lost the world welterweight crown and had become a worldwide star.

From the outset, however, Morris (who managed an impressive stable of fighters, most of whom boxed at Premierland) was plagued by complaints from other managers rightly alleging a conflict of interest. With mounting pressure, and the hall's profits in decline, Morris stepped down, leaving Lewis to run it himself. But Ted Kid was a fighter first and last; he knew little about the promoting game, and so signed the lease over to his brother-in-law Manny Lyttlestone who, having worked at the hall's box office, had a sound understanding of the business. He and business partner Victor Berliner took over in late 1924 and gave Premierland a new lease of life.

***

Back Church Lane, in the heart of the East End, juts off of Commercial Road and winds down to Cable Street and the docks. On the right, about 100 yards down, flanked by rows of Jewish shops, stood Premierland, its name boldly emblazoned within an arch above its doors, on either side of which were brick pillars plastered with posters for forthcoming fights. Its roof was pointed in a mock-Greek fashion and steel-girdered underneath like a railway station's. Every Monday and Thursday evening, and every Sunday afternoon, deep queues of fight fans snaked back along the street, hoping to beat the 'house full' sign before the hall's 3,000 capacity was reached. With the '20s boxing boom, Berliner and Lyttlestone became the first to put on three bills a week. Sometimes there were four, with separate Sunday matinee and evening shows, both of which were usually filled.

With the cheapest entrance fees, Thursday nights saw the locals out in force. They were a mix of Jewish and cockney, with a smattering of Irish. Barrow boys, dockers, and street traders from nearby Petticoat Lane, some were current or ex professional boxers, and generally those who weren't had at least boxed for boys' clubs. They knew the game intrinsically and scrutinised the action closely, always quick to voice their displeasure with a dry comment or ironic witticism. They were strongly partisan but nonetheless intolerant of 'foul play' from either fighter. Attending a show there in the late 1920s, German writer Rudolph Kircher found:

> 'In a fight between a young Jewish champion and an English youth who was not a Londoner, the young Jew, in the heat of the contest, hit his opponent an ugly blow below the belt, unnoticed by the referee who was on the wrong side of the ring to see it. The public uproar persisted until the referee became aware of what had happened, and the Jewish fraternity were greatly incensed that the young Jew was not disqualified. From this moment the tide turned in favour of the young Britton and remained with him for the rest of the fight.'

Ringside seats cost 2s 4d, but poorer patrons paid sixpence to stand on steps at the back. For most this meant a cramped, uncomfortable evening spent jostling for a view of events. The more daring, however, clambered atop a large sloping structure above the door, gaining an unobstructed bird's-eye view of the action. After visiting Premierland one Thursday night, author Stephen Graham noted:

> 'It is a great scene. Seldom can you see so many men together in a bright light, unobstructed, in the East End. Cloth caps to bowlers are fifty to one. Almost all wear scarves instead of collar and tie, red scarves, white scarves, green, grey. All are either chewing or munching or smoking. You buy your peanuts at the door, or potato-crisps, or fine big apples or chocolate from the hawkers within... The Jewish and coster elements in the crowd are about equally mixed. The Jewish is rhapsodical in its enthusiasm; the coster, humorous, sporting, smiling, given to sudden shouts and guffaws.'

The crowds at Sunday matinees were more socially mixed. It was the most expensive day to watch boxing at Premierland, but the calibre of fighter tended to be higher. Stars of stage, film and variety were often at ringside. Among them, whenever they played the London Palladium, were the American music stars Layton and Johnstone, along with the gargantuan xylophonist Teddy Brown. After moving from America to London in 1926, Brown became a regular. To accommodate his 25-stone bulk, the hall owners knocked two ringside seats into one.

With Kid Lewis, Kid Berg, Teddy Baldock, Kid Pattenden, Harry Reeve, Harry Mason and Dick and Harry Corbett all graduating from Premierland, the venue earned a reputation as a nursery of champions. Many a young fighter dreamt of appearing there and becoming a regular performer. Excellent money could be made at the top of the bill, and repeated success at Premierland could mean an invitation to box at the more prestigious National Sporting Club or Royal Albert Hall; and eventually, perhaps, a British title shot could be in the offing.

The 'house' referee in the 1920s was former fighter Jack Hart, whose ring career had ended because of an eye injury. His time as a referee would span five decades, and he was to become one of Britain's leading third men. Like most referees in the '20s, Hart surveyed the action from a raised ringside chair. 'We rarely worked inside the ring in those days,' he recalled for *Boxing News* in 1970. 'But, if a pair continually ignored instructions, mostly when told to break, we got in there with them.' This convention ran until 1932, when the British Boxing Board of Control made it compulsory for the referee to work inside the ring. Asked by *Boxing World* in 1972 if he remembered Nipper Pat Daly, Hart answered succinctly, 'That kid with the baby face knew what it was all about. He knew the game from left to right and backwards.'

Pat's Premierland debut was on the evening of Thursday 30 July 1925. His opponent, over six rounds, was Billy Boulger of Canning Town. Former Premierland proprietor Joe Morris took Boulger under his wing after the lad won the district schools' championship. Training regularly with Morris's main prospect Teddy Baldock, Boulger had developed quickly and was already tipped for high honours. Although Morris had relinquished the hall's ownership, he still acted as Premierland matchmaker and no doubt still held some sway. The match between Pat and Boulger received only a brief write-up in *Boxing*, but for the first time in his career, Pat was announced the loser. We are told that 'Boulger had a big pull in weight' and was 'more than a trifle fortunate to secure the verdict'. Had Morris's Premierland connection influenced the outcome, or had Pat just been unlucky?

He would avenge the defeat with a clear-cut 15-round win over Boulger four years later, but for now the Marylebone lad was heartbroken. He had given his all, seemingly outboxed his opponent, yet somehow still lost. It was one of only three verdicts that would go against him throughout his career. But, irrespective of the referee's ruling, the Premierland fans were thrilled by what they had witnessed. They wanted to see Pat again and would get their chance a month later.

Four days after tackling Boulger, Pat took on 16-year-old Charlie McCleave of Bermondsey; again conceding weight and this time four years in age. They met over six rounds at Prestwood's August bank holiday horticultural show, where Pat had boxed the previous year. The *Bucks Examiner* reported that Pat 'not up to the height of his opponent, was no wise daunted, and advanced to the attack with the left again and again and landed on the dial three for nothing before McCleave could get to work... Daly, a pretty little boxer, could not fail to be noticed and well won at call of time.'

Initially, Pat's opponent was wrongly reported as Charlie's younger brother Dave McCleave, but their father was quick to correct the error, writing through *Boxing*, 'I wish to call Prof. Newton's attention to the fact that it was my son Charles who boxed Daly, as Dave is only 13 and weighs 5 stone 4lb, is an amateur schoolboy, and I have no intention of starting him as a professional. I should be pleased if you will make this quite clear, so that Dave's school will have no misunderstanding.' Charlie and Dave McCleave would both soon join Newton's gym. Charlie would continue as a pro, but Dave would stay amateur until he reached his 20s. Regrettably, Pat's parents did not share the sentiments of Dave's father in relation to their son's welfare.

Pat's next fight took place over six rounds at Premierland a month later. *Boxing*'s reporter wrote:

'That brilliantly clever boy, Nipper Pat Daly (Marylebone), gave a truly sparkling display against a taller and older opponent in Jim Hocking (Canning Town). Hocking was no slouch, but Daly knew just too much for him, and was rewarded with the verdict, as also with volumes of applause from "the house". Daly, by the way, who is only twelve years old and goes to scale at 6 st 6 lb, is open to meet any boy in the world at not more than seven stone.'

Advantages gained by weight are relative to the weight class of a pair of boxers. For a heavyweight, conceding a few pounds will make little difference to the outcome of a fight. But further down the scale extra pounds matter more. To a lad of 6 stone 6 lb, allowing an opponent a few pounds could mean conceding a good deal of punching power and strength. Nevertheless, in a bid to find worthy opponents, Pat's trainer was now willing to disregard such disparities:

'Professor Newton wishes to keep Pat Daly busy, and is not particular in giving age and weight away, as Daly is a courageous boy, and wants to bring out what he knows. Any promoter wishing to try out any ex-schoolboy champion can be accommodated for a side-stake or a reasonable purse.' *Boxing*, 14 October 1925

Throughout the second half of the year Pat had a steady stream of matches, with no fewer than 10 fights in six months. His brilliant form and the ease with which he beat opponents continued to arouse interest:

'Daly, being a boy in his early teens [he was, in fact, 12] has not yet developed any of the hugging, holding, and mauling tactics which are tending to kill public interest in the game. His bout with Nipper Johnny Summers at the Manor Hall, Hackney, last Sunday was an object-lesson in the art.' *Boxing*, 7 October 1925

'Most attractive of all the bouts on the programme was the "tenner" between Nipper Pat Daly and Charlie McCleave. McCleave looked to be a trifle heavier and more than a year or two older. The pair put up a model contest, with the verdict going to Daly – a wonderful boxer and a real credit to his coach, Professor Newton.' *Boxing*, 4 November 1925

'Undoubtedly the tit-bit of the evening was the brilliant display of Nipper Pat Daly, "Professor Newton's Boxing Marvel", who gave away weight and some years to Teddy Tompkins, of Clapham, and won a splendid bout of clean boxing on points.' *Boxing*, 23 December 1925

Among these contests were an eight and a 10-rounder, although at this early stage the 10-rounder most probably comprised two-minute rounds. He also had three further fights with Charlie McCleave – two staged only a day apart. By this time it seems Charlie and his brother Dave had joined Newton's gym. In his memoirs, Pat would recall:

'Charlie was my stable-mate and we were *nearly* the same size. Charlie was four years older and, at the time, seven pounds heavier and three inches taller – but that was good enough for the Prof (they can't hurt us). He first sent us to fight each other at Fulham Baths over six rounds, and I gained the verdict on points. In the dressing room after the fight Sam Minto spoke to me about meeting heavier opponents and said that it put too much strain on my youthful body. Eventually, he said, I would "have to pay the price for overworking myself." I was 12 years old at the time and I did not appreciate the truth in his sermon – as I regarded it. And Sam being a negro fighter, one of the first I had ever heard of, I dismissed the subject, but found eventually he was right.'

Although Pat, in his youthful naivety, hadn't realised it, Minto was well placed to impart such advice. Samuel Augustus Minto had arrived in Europe from Jamaica in the early 1900s and boxed professionally since 1909. In a career spanning 28 years he had well over 300 recorded pro fights, plus countless unrecorded booth bouts, making him one of the most active boxers in history. Sadly, he died alone in his flat in the 1960s, the only person at his funeral being the policeman who found his body. But nonetheless, Minto's legacy will live on. He is immortalised in the H. E. Bates short story *The Black Boxer* whose central character, Zeke Pinto, is based on him.

Minto's advice was sensible, yet sadly such suggestions fell on deaf ears where Pat's parents were concerned. Between 1923 and 1928 his father worked as a ship's coal trimmer and was often away at sea for long periods. Whether he would have played an active role in Pat's affairs, had he been home more often, we cannot know. Pat's mother, we might guess, did not consider the risks to her son's health, and doubtless was reluctant to challenge the expertise of the Professor, particularly in light of the much-needed cash Pat would soon be bringing home. It was an aspect of her son's life she probably cared to know little about, apart from the fact that he was happy in what he did and very successful.

Money was sparse in the Daley household at that time. Pat's mother, reliant mostly on his father's income sent home at regular intervals, washed dishes in a restaurant to supplement the wage. When Pat wasn't busy boxing, he helped out at the restaurant and when needed looked after his younger brother Bobby. Apart from some financial worries, family life ran harmoniously for Pat and his mother the whole time his father was away at sea. When Patrick senior returned home, however, things changed.

Unable to match the verbal dexterity of his formidable spouse, when family quarrels erupted Pat's father responded with violence. The frequency of the beatings is unknown but they had a profound effect on Pat's early years. When his father hit his mother, Pat would leap to her defence, bravely shielding her from the blows, doing his best to fight back. Inevitably, Pat then suffered a beating himself.

In the 1920s domestic violence didn't carry the strict legal penalties nor the widespread social condemnation it does today. As can be found in Marylebone's local newspapers, domestic abuse cases that reached court were seldom treated with the seriousness they deserved. A case reported in the *Marylebone Chronicle* on 4 January 1930, for instance, saw a woman take her husband to court after being struck to the ground and seized by the throat for attending a Christmas party. The magistrate bound the accused over, casually remarking, 'he must not take the law into his own hands'.

For Pat, the domestic violence continued until he was fully grown, whereupon, coming to his mother's aid one day, he gave his father what he later termed 'the hiding of his life'. Thereafter, Patrick senior never dared to lay a finger on his wife again. As a man with a strong sense of family loyalty, Pat did not speak openly of this but many years later confided privately to his wife. Ironically, perhaps the controlled violence of the boxing ring offered an escape from the unbridled violence at home.

★★★

Among the last of Pat's 1925 bouts was a fight at a venue fit for Lords and Noblemen. Having heard all about the boy prodigy, National Sporting Club owner Arthur 'Peggy' Bettinson was keen for the lad to show his wares at the NSC. When an invitation arrived to box there, neither Pat nor Newton needed to be asked twice.

6

A Night at the National

The National Sporting Club (NSC) opened the doors to its luxurious 43 King Street, Covent Garden premises on 5 March 1891. Its founders were Arthur Frederick Bettinson, a former parliamentary reporter and 1882 ABA lightweight champion (known to friends as 'Peggy'), and John Fleming, who had managed the NSC's less respectable forebear, the infamously bohemian Pelican Club. Uncompromisingly dictatorial in its rule, the NSC would serve as the headquarters of British boxing for the next three decades.

Before its formation, boxing was often perceived as an unseemly, back-alley activity, staged in secret before crowds of crooks and ruffians. As late as 1885 the championship of England, held at a secret East Grinstead location and contested by Jem Smith and Jack Davis, had been halted by cries of "Police!" shortly after Smith was declared the winner. Those not fast enough on their toes were arrested and hauled before a magistrate. In the eyes of the law there was little distinction between an organised prizefight and a common brawl.

But in 1890 a test case occurred that ushered boxing towards legitimacy. The American Jack McAuliffe was due to fight Frank Slavin at the Ormonde Club in Walworth for a purse of £1,000. A few days before the fight, however, both men were arrested 'to prevent an attempted breach of the peace'. They were bailed at £1,000 each and, when they proceeded with the contest, both were rearrested and committed to Surrey Sessions. Public opinion strongly supported the boxers, and in the event both men were discharged. Although no judge or magistrate had officially declared boxing legal, it was a step towards respectability and social acceptance.

The NSC's foundation saw boxing rapidly transformed into a *bona fide* sport, with boxers seen as heroes rather than villains. Key to this transition was the Club's introduction of a properly constituted set of rules, adapted from the Queensbury Rules of 1866. NSC contests were no more than 20 rounds in length, and rounds now lasted no longer than three minutes, with a minute's gap in between. Gloves were worn for all fights (bare knuckle contests still took place elsewhere until about 1895), and in the interests of safety the referee could stop a bout if he felt one of the men unfit to continue. A scoring system was also introduced to allow the referee to decide the winner, with each man awarded up to five points per round (the 10-point system used today was not introduced in Britain until 1973).

The Club was reserved for members only and catered exclusively to an elite breed of spectator. Some of London's most successful citizens became NSC patrons. Stockbrokers, high-class shop owners, merchants and manufacturers, as well as members of the landed gentry, were on the membership list. What attracted them more than the boxing itself was the chance to gamble large sums with like-minded, similarly well-heeled men in a refined setting (women, incidentally, were barred from the premises). A dining room, grill room and various social rooms and bars made it a popular meeting place for the middle-classes, with a good deal of food and drink consumed before members watched any boxing.

To ensure spectators could concentrate on the action and to maintain an air of stateliness, complete silence was observed during actual boxing. The referee, who sat outside the ring, would halt the contest and call a man over if he had reason to caution him. If he felt that the boxers had failed in their duty to entertain, even as late as the last round, they could be ordered out of the ring and their purses withheld.

In 1897, John Fleming died, leaving 'Peggy' Bettinson to run the Club alone. In a short space of time the role had transformed him from a relatively humble transcriber of speeches into a well-connected London face, on nodding terms with most of the titled men in the land, and a virtual dictator over British professional boxing.

In 1909 the Club introduced a championship belt at eight self-nominated weight classes. The 'Lonsdale' belt – named for its President, Lord Lonsdale – was awarded to each of Britain's champions, and for some years gave the Club a monopoly over British title fights. The NSC chose the challengers, terms and dates for all championship contests, and they could only be seen by Club members and their guests at 43 King Street, Covent Garden. This state of affairs prevailed until the Great War; but afterwards things changed.

With the war over and the 1920s boxing boom in full swing, ambitious promoters such as Charles B. Cochran, Major Arnold Wilson and Harry

Jacobs staged rival championship-level shows at large venues such as Olympia, the Albert Hall and the Crystal Palace, where big money could be made. With its meagre 1,300 (800 sitting, 500 standing) capacity, the NSC could not hope to generate enough revenue to match the purses offered at these vast venues. There was now little incentive for the big-name fighters to box at the Club.

The NSC could no longer pick the British champions with any authority. The Club, for instance, insisted that Bombardier Billy Wells was the British heavyweight champion, but every fight fan knew that Joe Beckett had beaten him twice. British title fights were being staged independently of the NSC and a belt was no longer a requisite for winning a title. For a time the Lonsdale belt system threatened to fall into disuse. But, unlike the institution that spawned it, the system survived and is still in use today.

While preserving its Covent Garden HQ for its members, in an effort to compete, the NSC hired the sizeable Holland Park Skating Rink in west London, where it staged shows for the public between 1921 and 1925. But 'Peggy' Bettinson seemed stuck stubbornly and sentimentally in the past. He flatly refused to barter alongside other promoters for the right to stage fights, and so unsurprisingly the Holland Park venture, and with it the Club's hopes of survival, failed.

In truth, by the 1920s the NSC had served its purpose and was surviving on borrowed time. It had brought British boxing from its dark age into the more civilised modern era; but stripped of its assumed powers, it was now effectively just another commercial promoter, financially dependent on the success of its shows and competing (unsuccessfully) on the open market.

But, spent force or not, 43 King Street, Covent Garden was still the fistic equivalent of Lord's Cricket Ground. To box at the Club's famous headquarters and follow in the footsteps of such legends as Peter Jackson, Pedlar Palmer, Tommy Burns, Sam Langford, Georges Carpentier and Jimmy Wilde, was an honour for any young fighter.

On 4 November 1925 Pat made his NSC debut as part of the annual Lion Hospital Aid Society charity show organised by referee Moss Deyong. His opponent was Jim Hocking of Canning Town, whom he'd comprehensively beaten at Premierland two months before. *Boxing*'s report reveals nothing about the action, simply stating it was a good bout that ended in a draw. Whether Pat had had an 'off night' or been subject to a bad decision is therefore unclear; but it seems he made a good impression all the same.

Following a long illness 'Peggy' Bettinson died on Christmas Eve morning in 1926, but not before passing judgement on the Professor's newest prospect. Andy Newton recalled for *Boxing News* in 1941 that, 'The late Mr A. F. (Peggy) Bettinson, and the late Harry Jacobs, stated that Daly was the best youngster they had ever seen, and both wanted an interest in his contract.'

After his Wednesday night NSC bout we can guess that Pat was both the talk and the envy of the school playground next day. Peculiarly for a '20s working-class child, if only in professional boxing circles, he had achieved a measure of fame. Fight fans, ranging from the ring-wise, rough-and-ready patrons of Premierland to the Corona-smoking dignitaries of the NSC, were all now aware of this talented kid, and scribes and promoters were taking note.

7

Strikes, Setbacks and Lady Boxers

Premierland was the setting for Pat's first fight of 1926. After just two contests at the East End's fistic Mecca he had moved up the bill and was boxing a 10-rounder. His opponent, Johnny Quill, was tall, rangy, clever, and two years Pat's senior. He lived just round the corner from Premierland on Brook Street, now part of Cable Street – site of the famous 'Battle' in which local residents clashed with Oswald Mosley's 'Blackshirts' in 1936. Pat cleverly outpointed Quill then, some months later, they became sparring partners and pals when Quill started training at Newton's gym.

Quill later became a leading lightweight and welterweight, defeating top men such as Billy Bird, Stoker Reynolds and Fred Webster. In 1934 he stopped Pat Butler just seven months before Butler became British welterweight champion. Quill was himself climbing the ladder towards title contention when out of the blue tragedy struck. He was training in Brighton for a British-title eliminator against Birmingham's Charlie Baxter when he fell ill with a cold. His condition rapidly worsened, and eventually became so severe that he was admitted to St. George's hospital in London. After five weeks' hospitalisation, he died there suddenly on 29 June 1935, following an operation for pleurisy. He was an astute young man and left behind a small library of books, including a dictionary filled with pen marks and folded pages. He was educating himself for a career in journalism, which he hoped to break into when his boxing days ended. Although by the time of his death he had moved to Manchester Road on the Isle of Dogs, the people of Cable Street had not forgotten their local hero. As his funeral procession passed along the famous mile-long street, mourners crowded the pavement from end to end to pay their respects. There were over 100 wreaths, and so large was the turnout, that mounted police had to clear a path for the hearse. It was a send-off truly befitting Johnny's talent. He was just 24.

Still a month shy of his thirteenth birthday, 11 days after the Quill fight a picture of Pat appeared on the cover of *Boxing*. It was captioned, 'Nipper

BOXING, January 20, 1926.
VOL. XXXII, No. 855.

3d. **JACK HOOD WINS WITH ONE HAND.** **3d.**

BOXING

Vol. XXXII No. 855   JAN. 20th, 1926.   Registered at the G.P.O. as a Newspaper and for Canadian Magazine Post.

The Only Paper in the World solely devoted to Boxing.

"NIPPER" PAT DALY
Professor Newton's wonderfully clever midget who has been winning all along the line of late.

Pat Daly, Professor Newton's wonderfully clever midget who has been winning all along the line of late.' It was an honour for any boxer to see his image adorn the trade paper's front page, but for a 12-year-old the acclaim was incredible. As special as the boy pugilist was, however, the Newton stable had another unique fighter, who at the time threatened to put even Pat in the shade as a novelty; namely the Professor's niece, Annie Newton. In his memoirs, Pat would recall:

> 'A match was made between Annie and Miss Madge Baker billed for the World's Ladies' Championship. It was similar to a war being declared as they claimed all the attention of the newspaper headlines, placards, adverts on buses, trams, lorries, cars and anything else that could carry an advert. Reporters were telephoning and visiting Newton's gym all day and every day, and as Miss Newton's chief sparring partner, and being in charge of the gym during the daytime, I was kept very busy. People were very excited about the match, which was unique.'

In a society where women had yet to earn the right to vote, where a woman's role was still widely seen as housewife and nest-builder, the mere thought of women boxing was enough to provoke widespread derision, if not outrage, from certain quarters. "Women's participation in all masculine sports should be banned by law,' actor Robert Hale told the *Daily Express*. 'Why these mad women must emulate men I cannot conceive. One can only assume that they are chiefly those who normally command no attention and who seek notoriety at all costs.' Even British boxing's chief ambassador, Jimmy Wilde, publically aired his disapproval, telling the same newspaper, 'The idea of women in the boxing ring is repulsive, and will receive no support from real lovers of the art. Girl boxers will ruin their matrimonial chances. No man could fancy a professional bruiser for a bride!'

Annie was originally billed to oppose Madge Baker, a pupil of the late British and European bantamweight champion Digger Stanley, over six rounds at Hoxton Baths on 1 February, for a side-stake of £25. But after an emergency committee meeting, Shoreditch Borough Council told promoter Harry Abrahams that unless the fight was removed from his programme he would not be allowed to hire the baths. Seemingly unfazed,

Abrahams rescheduled the match for Sunday 14 February and changed the venue to the Hackney Manor Hall.

The postponed contest may well have taken place, were it not for the intervention of a 78-year-old Baptist minister. Reverend Frederick Brotherton Meyer, a moral crusader and pastor of Christ Church in Westminster Bridge Road, had played a key role in the abandonment of another prizefight back in 1911. Meyer had rallied leading members of Britain's churches to speak out against a planned fight between world heavyweight champion Jack Johnson (a black man) and Englishman Bombardier Billy Wells. The Archbishop of Canterbury wrote to Home Secretary Winston Churchill, urging him to stop the fight for fear a Johnson victory could spark dissent in Britain's colonies. And when the Bishops of London, Oxford, Ripon, Durham and Truro, plus the headmasters of Rugby, Dulwich, Mill Hill and Taunton schools, and Boy Scout founder Sir Robert Baden-Powell, joined the chorus of discontent, Churchill did as they asked. The fight was outlawed and Johnson, Wells and the organisers were marched into court charged with planning a 'breach of the peace'. Hoping to repeat his success of 15 years earlier, Reverend Meyer wrote to Home Secretary Sir William Joynson-Hicks, complaining about the women's match.

Sir Joynson-Hicks, well known as a reactionary and for his efforts to curb nightclubs and other risqué 'roaring '20s' businesses, replied immediately, offering Meyer his support. His letter appeared in several national newspapers:

'Dear Rev. Meyer – I have received your letter relating to the proposed boxing match between two women which it is suggested is to take place on Monday next. I have considered with great care whether there is any law which I can put into force to prevent it taking place, but if the proposal is to arrange a sparring match in which the object is not to win by reason of the severity of the injuries such an exhibition would not be illegal, and I should have no power to interfere – mainly, I think, because the Legislature never imagined that such a disgraceful exhibition would be staged in this country. I can only express my entire sympathy with your views and say that I hope and trust that the influence of decent public opinion will prevent such an outrage taking place.' As printed in *The Times*, 30 January 1926

Joynson-Hicks was evidently unaware that the proposed match was a real fight with side-stakes, rather than an exhibition, and he also got the date wrong. He had ruled that the match was not illegal, but his comments, it seems, were enough to give Harry Abrahams cold feet. Defying the government and bucking public opinion would hardly have enhanced his reputation as a promoter, so with mounting pressure he abandoned the fight and announced through the press that it was 'off'.

Annie Newton was introduced from the ring at the Manor Hall the following Sunday. She told the assembly that she was very disappointed; she had trained extremely hard for the fight and could not 'understand why people should object to a purely scientific match between two women'. She added that she was now keener than ever to establish the right for women to box.

According to Andy Newton, the Madge Baker–Annie Newton fight took place in private at a later date. In a 1969 *Boxing News* article, entitled 'Annie (KO) Newton', he states that she participated in 50 six-round contests, five of which were held in South Africa. He adds that in 1907 she knocked out a decent flyweight, Kid Logan of Islington, during a sparring session at the Professor's Barnsbury Road gym. Pat would recall:

'The Prof always gave his star Annie as much publicity as he possibly could. She was a big attraction. As Annie grew older she did not lose any of her skills – either ball punching or boxing. I always had a soft spot for Annie, and when she died she left a space that has never been filled.'

Annie, who died in 1955, was perhaps born a century too soon. Had she boxed in modern, more liberal times, she would probably have been a rich woman.

With the excitement of the Annie Newton-Madge Baker affair at an end, Pat turned his attention back to his own career. Two weeks after the Quill fight, he and Deptford's Teddy Tompkins topped the bill on an Andy Newton promotion at the Pimlico British Legion. Tompkins would scale 7 stone 8 lb for a fight at the Albert Hall two weeks later, which suggests that he outweighed Pat by over a stone. Even so, Pat had outclassed him at the same venue the previous month, inflicting the Deptford lad's only recorded defeat. 'House full notices were up outside,' noted *Boxing* and 'the spectators as they filed out stopped to secure tickets for the next show.' Reviewing the action, the newspaper wrote:

> 'Daly was at a disadvantage in both height and reach, yet took up the attack from the start, and scoring fast, took the honours of the opening five stanzas. Weight then began to tell and Tompkins, the bigger lad, had a shade on the next two rounds, but Daly nearly had Tompkins going in the eighth with a hurricane attack. Tompkins survived this, however, and making every use of his weight may have had a shade in the closing two rounds. The referee called it a draw, but personally we thought that Daly had done enough to win.'

'Draws are at times arranged to suit the promoter in order to ensure a return match,' admitted Andy Newton in a *Boxing News* article in 1941. With far greater scrutiny and big money often at stake, this obviously was less likely on larger-scale shows; but it was not uncommon practice among small-time promoters, and it may account for the decision in the Tompkins–Daly match.

In his next fight, 20 days later, Pat outpointed George Brown over six rounds at Peckham's Winter Gardens, then the next day opposed Canning Town's Boy Deary in a Premierland 10-rounder. Pat, according to *Boxing*, 'looked to be well ahead on points', but in the eighth he was disqualified 'for a low punch which was obviously accidental'. Today boxers are seldom disqualified for a single blow below the belt. But in the '20s, when the rules allowed the injured fighter no recovery time and protective cups were not widely worn, the offender could be disqualified the first time he landed low, even if the blow was accidental. Inevitably, this led to many needless disqualifications, and also plenty of angry post-fight exchanges. It says much for the cleanness of Pat's boxing that this was the only disqualification of his career.

Precisely two months after the Deary fight Pat was back at Premierland, this time tasked with a tough assignment. He was facing former amateur schoolboy and Federation champion Moe Mizler of St. George's. Son of Jewish-Polish immigrants, 16-year-old Moe had turned professional to support his parents' struggling fish business on Watney Street market. Moe was an elder brother of that brilliant stylist Harry Mizler, who held the British lightweight title in the '30s. Together Moe and another brother, Judah, coached Harry and moulded him into a champion. Moe was himself a splendid boxer but he did not possess his younger brother's patience. Unlike Harry, who was a consummate boxer, Moe also relished a tear-up. He was three years older than Pat and accordingly taller and heavier. The fight – scheduled for 10 rounds – promised to be an explosive affair.

'As can be imagined, the exchanges were brilliant,' reported *Boxing*, 'and were a real treat to watch.' But during the fifth a clash of heads caused a nasty cut over Pat's eyes; and despite his protests, the referee rightly refused to let him continue. 'It was most unlucky,' concluded the sports paper, 'as Daly was shaping like a master at the time.'

Pat no doubt was disheartened. Twice in a row, he had seemingly mastered his opponent, then been thwarted by circumstances beyond his control. But he was not the type to dwell on such things, and he was no doubt aware that occasional disappointments were part and parcel of boxing.

The following month the famous 1926 General Strike halted boxing promotions across the country. Mine owners had imposed widespread wage cuts in response to Chancellor of the Exchequer Winston Churchill's reintroduction of the Gold Standard. For nine days Britain's key industries were crippled as nearly 1.5 million workers struck in support of the miners. It was a key event in Trade Union history, as shortly afterwards a law was passed that made all future sympathy strikes illegal. With so few fight shows taking place, *Boxing* was not published for two weeks.

There was a seven-month gap between the Mizler bout and Pat's next recorded fight. The Professor made numerous appeals for opponents through *Boxing*'s challenges column, but none came forward. Despite being happy to concede age and weight, it seems that there were few lads capable of extending Pat. With no other likely opponents on the horizon, the Professor appealed for an old adversary to have another crack at his colt:

'Prof. Newton is ready to match Pat Daly and Nipper Johnny Summers for a return engagement over ten two or three-minute rounds, for £10 to £20. As these lads are both growing schoolboys he favours a catch-weight match and promises promoters one of the most scientific bouts seen in London. Replies to Prof. Newton, Empire School of Arms, 241, Marylebone Road, N.W.1. (Padd. 3836.)' *Boxing*, 29 September 1926

Although Pat had already beaten Summers four times, the NSC promptly snapped up the match. True to form, Pat outboxed the Leeds lad, treating the NSC's members 'to a truly classic display' (*Boxing*), at one stage flooring Summers with a thundering right to the body. Andy Newton topped the bill in a 15-rounder against Alec Atkins of Lincoln, stopping his man with a solar plexus punch in the seventh. 'Had he but used a little more restraint and calculation,' wrote *Boxing*, 'he might well have finished the affair in double-quick time... The one and only Professor would doubtless prefer that he should travel on the classic lines exhibited by his pet pupil, Nipper Pat Daly.'

It was the busiest and most successful year of 26-year-old Andy's career. He had 30 fights that year, with only four losses; two of which were disqualifications. Born 28 July 1900 at his father's Barnsbury Road gym, it could be said that Andy – real name Isaac Andrew Newton – was truly born into boxing. In 1913 he partnered world heavyweight champion Jack Johnson in a ball-punching, club-swinging music hall act that they performed at the Euston Theatre of Varieties on Euston Road. Johnson paid a visit to 241 Marylebone Road, where he sparred two rounds with the Professor and another with Newton pupil Julian Bernard Hall.*

In 1918 Andy joined the Army, whereupon he won the Service boxing championships and earned the nickname 'the mad Englishman' from Marshal Foch, supreme commander of the Allied armies. It was an epithet that fitted perfectly, for though he had learnt the art of boxing from his father, Andy preferred to throw caution aside and blaze away with both fists. He loved the thrill of combat and was highly adept both at inflicting and taking punishment. His raw, non-stop aggression at times did not sit well with the boxing connoisseurs, nor indeed with his father, but it made him a hit with most fight fans, who admired his strength and courage. In spite of his bravery, however, Andy was not averse to pulling a showman's trick when the chance arose.

---

* On 13 April 1913, 26-year-old Julian Bernard Hall ('Jack' Hall to acquaintances), a well-known airman, golfer and amateur boxer living on independent means, was shot dead at his flat in Denman Street, Shaftesbury Avenue by his lover, Jeannie Baxter, who stood to benefit from his will. Baxter was acquitted of murder but convicted of manslaughter and sentenced to three years in prison. Hall's estate was valued for probate at £19,607 – a small fortune in 1913.

On a damp May evening in the penultimate fight of his career, he faced the French (and future world) middleweight champion Marcel Thil over 20 rounds. The fight took place in Edmonton, where Andy was a local hero, but after being hopelessly outgunned and dropped several times, coming into the tenth he was in dire straits. Things grew worse when, suddenly, Andy yelled with pain and clutched his right shoulder, as the arm fell limply to his side, apparently rendered useless by injury. But as his army of fans sighed with dismay, thinking the fight over, Andy charged at the Frenchman using his 'good' arm to fence him off. He survived to the end of the round but was prevented from coming out for the eleventh by the referee. 'What a game boy!' cried the appreciative crowd, and they cheered him all the way to his dressing room. Having watched the encounter, Pat and the Professor joined him there but were both amazed to see the 'dead' arm return to life. Effortlessly, Andy slipped on his shirt, buttoned it and moved the arm around with no hint of discomfort. It was a miraculous recovery for a man who, according to the newspapers, had torn a ligament. Thinking on his feet, it seems Andy had snatched glory from defeat and also saved himself a further 10-round drubbing from the Frenchman.

Outside the ring Andy was as shrewd and colourful as he was within it. Two of his favourite pursuits were women and gambling, and despite being married with a young son, he readily indulged in both. He was a confident, outspoken young man, abundantly endowed with the 'gift of the gab', which he put to very good use. By the mid-'20s he had taken over his father's business affairs and was promoting his own small-hall shows. Failing eyesight would force him to retire from the ring in 1928, whereupon he took a hand in Pat's matchmaking and took half Newton senior's share of each purse. The Professor, however, remained Pat's official manager.

Pat's final engagement of 1926 was on an Andy Newton bill at the newly opened Pembroke Garage Club, which stood on Halkin Street, off Belgrave Square. Little is known of the venue but, given its opulent locality, it is likely to have been a private club for the wealthy. With Andy topping the bill against leading middleweight Lauri Raiteri, and Pat featuring on the undercard, the show sold out a full hour before opening. There was a double success for the Newton stable with Andy stopping Raiteri in eight, and Pat once more smartly outboxing George Brown – this time over eight rounds.

Pat returned to the Garage Club on 2 February for his first contest of 1927. *Boxing* reported that he proved 'far too clever for a heavier opponent in Taff Sharpe (Tottenham), and forced the latter to retire in the third round.'

It was his final contest as a part-time fighter. He was about to turn 14, and a fulltime ring career beckoned.

8

Fulltime Fighter

'There is a young boy out Marylebone way, one, Pat Daly by name, who may well prove to be the best of all hopes who have been turned out for many a year. That experienced old warrior, Professor Newton, became fully convinced long since that in Daly he had lighted upon the "find" of his lifetime... the one and only professor has entered into the only legal managerial contract of his career, and will have young Daly continuously under the eye.'

Boxing, 23 August 1927

As a rule '20s children finished school at 14 and then had to work to augment the family income. Among Richmond Street RC's 1927 school leavers were boys heading off in all directions. Some found apprenticeships; others jobs on the railways; and more still had family ties to London's meat, veg or fish markets. But the less fortunate found work sporadic and uncertain, and were obliged to take whatever was offered. Pat's career, however, had long been mapped out by the Professor. With the encumbrance of school now at an end, the boy would box fulltime.

The Professor signed Pat to a contract that gave him 50 per cent of the first £200 Pat earned in a year, and one third of his annual earnings thereafter. According to *Boxing* Pat was the only fighter ever contracted to the Professor, but Andy Newton recalled three others: British heavyweight champion Gunner Moir, South African lightweight champion Fred Buckland, and an unnamed amateur who ultimately decided not to turn pro.

Pat was paid a weekly wage of 10 shillings for his attendance at Newton's gym, where his day comprised a mixture of work, sparring and training. His duties included floor-sweeping, window-cleaning and, when needed, cleaning the mess left by Newton's dogs. The Professor was an avid dog-breeder; Red Setters and Bull Terriers being his speciality. He sold Jack Johnson a Black Pomeranian when the world heavyweight champion was in exile in Europe. Having been born into modest means in the 1860s, the Professor had had little education and, as a result, was largely illiterate.* So Pat was also tasked with reading and answering much of Newton's mail. Despite leaving school at 14, Pat had an excellent grasp of written English. 'He could write a letter as well as any solicitor,' remembers his widow Mary; and during his time at the gym he got plenty of practice.

The arrangement gave the Professor a tight rein over his pupil and also kept the boy's feet planted firmly to the ground. 'Window cleaning may not be classy,' he told the *Topical Times* in 1939, 'but my fourteen-hour day, work and sparring mixed, would have been the salvation of many a champion who has come a cropper through not being able to win his fight outside the roped square.'

When he wasn't at the gym or involved in a contest, Pat was sometimes called upon to second other boxers. He mentions this twice within his memoirs; the first occasion in the year he left school:

'In 1927 the Prof sent me to Peterborough to second two of his boys, namely Dick Pretlove, who was to fight "Butcher" Arthur Adkins from Nottingham, and Billy Pinn (Walworth) who was to fight George Watkins, a local boy from just outside Peterborough. Before the Adkins fight was due to start I went to Adkins's dressing room to inspect the tape on his hands. Adkins and his manager at first humoured me and allowed me to inspect Adkins's hands or rather the way they were taped, but when I said that there was too much plaster on his hands – and there was – and that some of it would have to come off, the air turned blue as the language became choice. So I said that if it was not taken off in my presence, there would not be any fight. I was quite adamant about it, so with the prospect of going home without any wages they took some off. The fight went the full 12 rounds and Adkins won on points. Billy Pinn beat George Watkins on points. Two years later, [when] I had grown a little, I fought and beat Adkins on points at Nottingham Baths over 15 rounds. Imagine a fight manager of those days being ordered about by a 14-year-old.'

---

* A handbook on boxing technique and training released by the Professor (Newton, A.J., *Boxing with a section on single-stick*, Pearson, 1904) was evidently ghost-written. Bloomsbury republished the book in 2005 with the year of the first edition wrongly given as 1910.

It today may seem astounding that a boy of 14 could be entrusted with the care and safety of professional boxers. If one of the men looked to be taking too much punishment – and '20s referees were not apt to stop fights easily – it was down to Pat to decide when to throw in towel. If he intervened prematurely he would scupper his man's chances, yet if he waited too long, he would see his stable-mate take a needless beating, and perhaps endanger the man's health. It was a heavy burden for shoulders so young, and Pat's recollections of another seconding job show just how grim a task it could be:

> 'I was in Dick Pretlove's corner (chief second), the Prof had some other business on. Dick was fighting Kid Rich of Aldgate, 12 rounds. Dick's left ear began to swell and Rich being a killer played on the ear, punching it at every opportunity and the ear was swelling rapidly. Suddenly it burst with a sickening plop and blood ran down Dick's side and ran to the canvas and splashed over ringside spectators. The referee stopped the contest and I was left the job of treating Dick's ear.'

The Pretlove-Rich fight took place at Premierland on 1 March 1928, 12 days after Pat's fifteenth birthday. *Boxing*'s report reveals that Pat's recollections (over half a century later) are remarkably accurate. He remembers the correct scheduled distance and also the side of the injured ear. He neglects to mention, however, that Pretlove took the fight at short notice and had a damaged ear before he went on. This underscores the hazards of regular fights without sufficient rest in between.

Pat's first contest after leaving school was also his debut at north London's leading fight arena. Whitewashed and alcoved to look like a Moorish palace, the Alcazar cinema was built in the year of Pat's birth, 1913. It stood on the west side of Fore Street in Edmonton, almost opposite Fairfield Road, just a few yards north of Angel Road. Fight shows were staged there every Monday evening from February 1925. Behind and adjoining the cinema was a large ballroom, perfect for indoor boxing; but what made the venue exceptional were its picturesque gardens at the rear. When the weather was warm contests were held outside in what *Boxing* called 'the prettiest open-air boxing arena in the world'. The ring stood amid sloping grass banks, surrounded by flowerbeds, a stream and fruit trees in full bloom. The ground was a sort of amphitheatre, bound by the stately trees in the gardens of the adjacent well-to-do houses that stretched to the railway line, which ran from Liverpool Street to Enfield Town. On a balmy summer's evening, thousands sat on deckchairs around the ring in this idyllic setting; their sporadic yells rivalling the roar heard up the road at White Hart Lane whenever 'Spurs scored a goal. As the daylight began to fade, the gardens were lit up by countless coloured fairy lamps, which gave the shows a special ambience. Outdoor fights were usually advertised with the proviso 'In Hall if Wet' but in colder months all fights were held indoors. Harry Abrahams (of Manor Hall fame) was promoter, referee and matchmaker at the Alcazar, and his brother Jack was the MC.

In the mid-1920s Andy Newton was the Alcazar's most popular and regular performer – his two-fisted tornado tactics had earned him a huge local following. In 1925 he boxed a draw at the 'Alc' with that classy stylist Jack Hood (later British welterweight champion), and it was also the site of his two battles with the aforementioned future world middleweight king, Marcel Thil. On 2 May 1927 Newton opposed Thil in their first fight, and Pat was on the undercard, re-matched with Taff Sharpe of Tottenham. Under a fusillade of heavy hitting, Newton was pulled out by his father in the ninth with two badly damaged eyes. Pat again beat Sharpe, this time by fourth-round knockout. Afterwards, in the boxers' dressing room, Thil gave Pat some French sweets and offered him words of encouragement. Pat, who was seldom impressed by any boxer, spoke very highly of Thil's abilities, and placed him among the great middleweights.

Three weeks later another great middleweight from foreign climes arrived in Britain for the first time. On 24 May, a little tank of a man with a pug nose and dark, slicked-back hair stepped off the transatlantic ship the *Berengaria* at Southampton. Beside this 24-year-old was a slim man, two decades older, with a stern, calculative face and piercing blue eyes. They spoke with American accents and were instantly recognisable as Mickey Walker, the reigning world middleweight champion, and his manager Jack 'Doc' Kearns.

'Kearns was a man who could go a dozen ways at once, and did,' wrote Oscar Fraley, his biographer. 'For there was a combination of the swashbuckling D'Artagnan, the rollicking Robin Hood, the daring Jimmy Valentine, the wily Richelieu and withal, one possessing the charm, wit, impishness, and savoir faire of a larcenous leprechaun.'

A few years earlier Kearns had managed the iconic world heavyweight champion Jack Dempsey. In 1921 Kearns and promoter Tex Rickard brought boxing its first million-dollar gate when a crowd of 91,000 watched Dempsey destroy the legendary Frenchman Georges Carpentier in four rounds at Jersey City. Since then Kearns and Dempsey had parted company, and the famous manager had a new star in Mickey Walker.

Walker began as world welterweight champion, but in December 1926 stepped up to middleweight to wrest the 11 stone 6 lb world crown from the head of his countryman Tiger Flowers. Outside the ring Walker enjoyed a life of free-spending, hard-drinking and womanising (he was married seven times to four different wives), helped run whisky into New Jersey during prohibition, and counted Al Capone among his acquaintances. A more colourful duo than he and Kearns would be difficult to find.

Walker was set to defend his world title against Britain's middleweight champion, Tommy Milligan of Scotland, in a Charles B. Cochran promotion at London's Olympia. It promised to be the biggest sporting event held in Britain that decade, and gossip and news from both camps filled the sports pages of every paper in the run-up to the fight.

Much like his lifestyle, Walker's training camp was flash and expensive. He had hired Tagg's Island, an island pleasure resort for the rich and well-connected, sited near Hampton Court on the River Thames. 'Doc paid fifty dollars a day to each of the seven sparring partners,' remembered Walker in his autobiography, 'in addition to my two trainers, two rubbers and a masseur. And there were plenty of other expenses. I never did learn exactly how much it cost us. I didn't care.'

Pat arrived at the gym one morning in June and was greeted by a big grin from the Professor. 'I've got you a fight with Mickey Walker,' he told Pat. 'We better get you ready.' Thinking that he was being kidded, Pat simply smiled, but then Newton, looking serious, promised he'd be in the ring with Walker before the week was out. Eventually Pat tumbled that he was to spar with the champion at his Hampton Court training camp. He recalled the encounter vividly in his memoirs:

'Kearns was very businesslike and arranged what order we would spar with his present champ. As he looked at me I could see the disappointment in his eyes, and he said, "You're far too light for this job." I weighed 7st-12lb (110lb). My manager explained to him that I was engaged for my speed, not my strength. Mickey, who was talking to another of his partners, noticed that we were talking, rather excitedly came to us and on hearing the cause of the argument said, "Okay I'll just spar with him last to speed me up, and he better be fast."

I sat at the ringside and watched Mickey spar two rounds each with a Malcolm Campbell, middleweight champion of Scotland and Tom Fowler, a heavyweight who had served his time as a sparring partner to most of our leading heavies. Walker, not a brilliantly clever boxer but clever just the same, with a KO punch in either hand, and I was his sparring partner. One of his punches could kill me. Still, I had a job to do and I intended to do it as well as I could. While watching Mickey spar I had noticed that he would make his partner miss with their initial punch by swaying backward, and then counter [the hopelessly reaching boxer] with his right. At the first opportunity I had, I feinted with my left lead, Mickey drew back from his hips and was temporarily defenceless as I moved forward and connected with a perfect right hand punch on his jaw. Mickey stopped boxing, shook hands, patted me on the back and said, "That was a great punch kid."

After I had finished my training I was told that we had been booked to appear at Jimmy Butler's boxing booth at the Welsh Harp, Hendon in the evening and that I was to stand on the front of the booth and take on all comers. I did two houses, which means I had two fights, three rounds each. Still, it brought my manager in a few shillings and saved me wasting time. I only fought two fights as there was not time for any more, as it was 10pm and the fair was closing down.

I'd had an easy day, only having sparred with the world middleweight champion and fought two opponents at a booth. I was very proud at having sparred with the world's middleweight champion, and also pleased that Mickey had pulled his punches.'

'No sooner had time to start been called than Daly hit Walker five times with his left on the nose,' remembered Andy Newton for *Boxing* in February 1940. 'They finished the two rounds and were given the best reception of the day. I was having dinner with Walker and his manager, Jack Kearns, at night, when Walker remarked: "Gee, that kid hit me more times in two rounds than I have been hit in a 15-round contest. He surely did me good. Bring him down every day." The same remark was passed by Al Foreman [a British lightweight champion], who boxed several times with Daly.'

'[Kearns] wanted guys who'd test me,' remembered Walker in his autobiography. 'He felt that if one of them could hurt me, I'd work out a way to defend myself against him and therefore have a sounder defense when I met Milligan.' Pat had inadvertently taught Walker to watch for the feint when he employed his signature sway back and right-hand counter, and so Milligan never got the opening Pat had. Kearns was evidently impressed. On 28 June 1927, two days before the big fight, *Boxing* reported:

'Among those who have paid visits to 241, Marylebone Road, within the last week was a prominent American manager, who not alone paid a high tribute to the management of the school but expressed in no unmeasured terms his high opinion of the Professor's clever pupil, Pat Daly, who was having a work out at the time.'

Kearns appealed to the Professor to allow him to take Pat to America. In the States, he told Newton, the law would prevent the boy from boxing more than six rounds, yet the financial rewards would be palpably higher. The combination of youth and precocious talent would quickly make Pat a star. But the Professor, knowing all about Kearns's reputation for sharp practice, flatly refused. The boy, he said, was under contract and would remain in London under his charge.

In a fierce battle at Olympia, Walker floored Milligan several times before knocking the Scot out in the tenth to retain his world crown. Nine days before the big match, Pat boxed a 10-rounder at Premierland (his first fight there for 14 months) against local lad Kid Silver of St. George's. Judging by *Boxing*'s report of the fight, Pat's fulltime training regime was paying dividends:

'This was a lively, brilliant little bout. Daly bids fair to fulfil all the prophecies of his mentor, Professor Andrew Newton, and being pitched against a classy opponent, was able to exhibit some of his real quality. The exchanges in this affair provided an object lesson for other

The Long and the Short of It at Premierland. Phil Scott made the big noise, but Pat Daley set the stars travelling.

From *Boxing*, 21 June 1927.

older and more prominent fistic performers present, and one felt, as one watched, that if Nipper Pat goes on as he has been of late, we shall not have to look elsewhere when we are seeking for world champions some four or five years hence. Daly, who is only 15 years of age [he was, in fact, 14], already knows more about the game and can put in more punishing work than several of our present champions.'

'If we have ever seen an assured future world-beater we saw him in Pat Daly,' wrote *Boxing*'s Editor, John Murray, in his regular column. The newspaper's cartoonist drew a caricature of Pat punching, firstly, an exaggerated illustration of his opponent's nose, then a punch bag specially shaped like the nose. British heavyweight champion Phil Scott, in a showman-like feat, fought and knocked out two opponents on the same bill; but even this achievement, the cartoonist says, was upstaged by the 14-year-old. 'Phil Scott made the big noise,' reads the caption, 'but Pat Daly set the stars travelling.'

A fortnight later Pat returned to Premierland on a bill that pitted three Midlanders against three Londoners. Bethnal Green boxers Harry Burman and Billy Mack lost to their 'Brummy' counterparts and, according to *Boxing*, Pat's opponent, Charlie Rowbotham, 'opened up a good favourite to complete the hat trick for the Midlanders'. However, he 'had a bit of a shock when he faced Nipper Pat Daly of Marylebone... he could not stand against the pace and science of the Marylebone "Nipper".' Pat gave the Midlander a one-sided drubbing until the referee stopped the bout in the fifth. Although outclassed that afternoon, Rowbotham, who was a year older than Pat, went on to beat some of the best bantam and featherweights in the country. (He died on 5 February 1938 from tuberculosis, aged just 25.)

Another 'Brum', 'Tank' Fowler (brother of leading bantamweight Len Fowler), was Pat's next opponent at Premierland precisely a week later. Pat conceded three years and several pounds but all the same, according to *Boxing*, he 'hammered the life out of Fowler, and the "Brum" was absolutely out on his feet, but was persuaded to carry on.' Pat had Fowler down in the fourth and seventh, but gamely the older lad battled on. At one stage Harry Mason (British light and welterweight champion several times) rushed to the ringside and pleaded with Fowler to 'chuck it in'. But he refused and hung on to last the full 10 rounds.

Pat's next opponent, three weeks later, was 19-year-old Alf Gudge of St. George's, an ex-amateur for Columbia B.C. Conceding height, reach and half a stone in weight, Pat was far too quick and resourceful for Gudge, and won well over 10 speedy rounds. But collisions during the contest caused cuts above and below the Nipper's right eye. He was set to box a series of fights at Premierland but first the eye-damage needed to heal. Two months elapsed before his next fight.

9

Top of the Bill

'He is unquestionably the best and most promising piece of fighting stuff this country has produced for many years, and it will be both a crime and a national disaster if he is allowed to be cut to pieces before he has even approached his prime.'

Boxing, 8 November 1927

Premierland promoters Victor Berliner and Manny Lyttlestone were in a fix. The start of their new Monday-night boxing season was fast approaching, yet no headline match had been found. The famous Kids – Berg and Lewis – were topping that week's Thursday and Sunday bills respectively; but the combined purses of these two stars left little spare cash for the Monday-nighter. They needed a popular yet affordable top-liner; someone who would draw the crowds without breaking the bank. This, of course, was a combination not easily found. But suddenly they had a brainwave – why not use Newton's Nipper? The boy was already upstaging established top-liners whenever he boxed on the undercard; and the fans were already clamouring to see him. Why not, then, give him pride of place? There was of course the question of whether a 14-year-old physique could stand the strain of a 15-round fight. Had anyone so young ever boxed such a distance before? And would attempting to stage such a fight be foolhardy? They telephoned the Professor, who assured them his boy already had the stamina and strength to go 15 rounds. No doubt some uncertainty remained but, with Newton's assurances, they pencilled in Pat to headline their 3 October show.

His opponent, Jack Ellis of St. George's, was relatively new to pro rings, but had already travelled the 15-round distance three times. He'd had a glittering amateur career, boxing as 'W. H. Ellis' for the Limehouse, Poplar and District Boxing Club, and had reached the flyweight final of that year's ABAs. Since turning pro he'd beaten Johnny Quill and Kid Rich, and was stopped only by a cut eye when he faced Moe Mizler. Up till now Pat had received just £3 each for his Premierland matches, but this time the advertised purse was £50 – split 60 per cent winner; 40 per cent loser. Ellis was heavier and older but Pat possessed superior reach.

In the early rounds, Pat piled up the points and kept his opponent at bay with fast flurries of lefts. But midway through, the St. George's man forced his way inside and landed some punishing body-shots causing the Marylebone lad to hold. The referee cautioned Pat for holding, but he quickly recovered and regained control of the fight. Pat 'continued to keep the fighting at long range, despite Ellis's constant efforts to get close,' said the *Sporting Life*, 'and the latter was shaken in the closing stages by hard left and right hooks to the jaw.' The referee called it a draw but the *Sporting Life* disagreed. 'The verdict created a little surprise, and Daly seemed unfortunate in only sharing honours.' *Boxing* similarly felt that, 'Daly was brilliant all the way, while Ellis did just enough to earn a draw.'

Given Pat's age, the rounds were probably two minutes long as opposed to the modern standard of three minutes. But this was still equivalent to the maximum 10 three-minute rounds boxed in non-title fights today. Pat had stood up well to his severest test to date. Thoroughly delighted, Berliner and Lyttlestone promptly booked him for a string of 15-rounders.

A fortnight later he met Barnsley's Jack Glover (who used the alias Glover's Nipper) for a 15-round Premierland purse of £75. Boxing mainly in the north, Glover had amassed a fine record, beating some top lads, including Sheffield's Dick Inkles. In his last fight – his London debut – he'd boxed a draw with Moe Mizler over 15 rounds. The Daly–Glover match was made at 7 stone 12 lb.

Pat set the pace from the start with a stream of lighting straight lefts to the Barnsley lad's face. Glover proved very tough but, try as he did, could not get into the fight. 'Pat used both left and right in wonderful style and was always the master of the situation,' wrote *Boxing*. 'The manner in which he side-stepped the Barnsley youth's rushes had the crowd gaping at times.' Pat won the fight by a country mile, leading *Boxing* to call it, 'A model contest from which many champions could have picked up instruction.' Unperturbed by this one-sided defeat, Glover's Nipper lost just two of his next 20 fights, which included a points win over future world flyweight champion Jackie Brown of Manchester.

The following week *Boxing*'s Editor, John Murray, wrote a scathing criticism of the mismanagement of young fighters, heading the piece, 'The waste of first-class material'. 'What will become of Nipper Pat Daly?' he ponders. We are told that Pat is both:

'a really great long-range fighter [and] that rare product at such a youthful age, a quite expert in-fighter. We have seen him produce uppercuts, most unexpectedly, in situations where one would have imagined that there could be no opening for an uppercut. His accuracy of delivery is almost uncanny, while he packs an unusually heavy punch for a boy of his years and poundage. He has everything... We venture the assertion that there is not a better, a more scientific boxer, to be seen any where else in the world today... Yet there are, it would seem, quite serious risks that Nipper Pat may find himself used up, or drained dry, before he can ever come into the kingdom he is so plainly destined to rule... We have to own to a genuine feeling of surprise when we consider the Professor's management of his most brilliant pupil... He should not be sent in for contests of 15 rounds.'

But Murray's protests, it seems, fell on deaf ears. Two weeks after the Glover fight, Pat had another 15-rounder. He was supposed to fight Moe Mizler at 7 stone 10 lb, but when Mizler withdrew he was instead re-matched with Jack Ellis and again forced to concede weight. It was a chance for Pat to make amends for their previous drawn fight, which most felt he had won. In the audience that evening was sports journalist Dave Caldwell, who recalled for *Boxing World* in 1972:

'I was working ringside at Premierland, the original East End Hall of Splosh, when I noticed the small boy in knickerbockers sitting behind me with Professor Newton. "Enjoying the boxing son?" I asked. "Yes Sir" was the polite reply. Less than an hour later I was watching goggle eyed, the lad, who had been introduced by [the MC] Buster Cohen as Nipper Pat Daly, box the ears off one Jack Ellis of St. George's. Earlier that year, Ellis had been runner-up in the ABA flyweight final. After the bout I learned that Daly, now approaching his 15th birthday, was something of a veteran.'

'It is seldom that such clever boxing is witnessed as took place at Premierland last night,' wrote *The Evening Standard*, but even so it was not an easy fight. Ellis used his weight and the strength of his years to force Pat, uncharacteristically, to box on the retreat. But he sidestepped many of Ellis's charges, and damaged the ex-amateurs eyes early on with what *The Evening Standard* called 'a delightful exhibition of left-hand boxing'. During the fifth Pat was caught by some heavy body blows and looked as if he might go down; but his footwork and speed got him out of trouble. 'A terrific fight took place in the closing rounds, and both lads came in for punishment, but Daly was always a good winner, and was loudly applauded on his victory,' concluded the newspaper.

As the winner, Pat received £60 of the £100 purse. Half, of course, went to the Professor, and no doubt a slice of Pat's share went into the family pot; but nonetheless it was very good money for 1927. John Murray, whilst applauding Pat's performance in his 'Editor's ideas' column, also deplored the nature of the match:

'... we shall still hope that a certain contract having now been wound up, there will be no more 15 round tests for Daly for quite a few years to come. We adhere as firmly as ever to our first opinion that 6 rounds, or at the most 10 (2 minute) rounds, are ample for even a boy of Daly's exceptional stamina, at his age. He is unquestionably the best and most promising piece of fighting stuff this country has produced for many years, and it will be both a crime and a national disaster if he is allowed to be cut to pieces before he has even approached his prime.'

10 days after the return fight with Ellis, Pat faced one of the best lads in the north. Dick Inkles of Sheffield could easily have passed for an office clerk; but his slender, almost fragile appearance greatly belied his fighting abilities. He was a relentless little whirlwind of a pressure-fighter, with a crouching, bobbing and weaving style. The advertised purse was again £100, and the weight 7 stone 10 lb. Pat and Inkles shared top billing with former British and European bantamweight champion Harry 'Bugler' Lake, who faced Stepney's Johnny Mann, also for a purse of £100. Johnny Cuthbert, the reigning British featherweight champion and a man Pat was destined to meet in the ring, was in Inkles's corner giving advice.

Each of the 15 rounds was fought at a blistering pace. Inkles relentlessly bustled in, determined to impose his strength and make it a close-range battle. This forced Pat out of his usual stride, and he had to go at full speed to stay in front. 'He boxed very well to beat the pride of the north, Dick Inkles,' wrote *Boxing*, 'but he had to fight hard indeed.' Pat deservedly got the decision but *Boxing*'s 'man on the spot' had some choice words for the Professor:

> 'It is pleasing indeed to learn that Nipper Pat Daly, the clever youngster from Marylebone, has finished with 15 round contests. It may have cost the proud Professor so-and-so to keep young Pat, but there is no doubt that it would have cost him more for doctors' bills had he continued signing this boy of 14½ years for 15-round contests against much older and stronger lads. Pat's distance is six rounds, and only against boys.'

It is unclear why the writer thinks that Pat has finished with 15-round fights, but presumably his contracted series of matches at Premierland was at an end. Far from lightening Pat's workload, however, the Professor already had plans to increase it. Having read so much of the exploits of London's 'wonder boy' in *Boxing*, fight fans from other cities and towns were eager to watch him box. The Professor had little trouble negotiating a string of matches for Pat at arenas across the country. In addition to his usual London fights, over the coming months he would tour the provinces.

The first of his provincial fights took place at Nottingham's Victoria Baths 11 days after the Inkles bout. Public baths and ice-skating rinks were often hired and adapted for boxing promotions. A temporary wooden floor was placed across the pool or rink, a ring was rigged-up on top, and the baths' or skating rink's in-built seats were supplemented by benches or chairs placed around the ring. Pat and his opponent, Tom Fitzsimmonds of Leicester (formerly of America), weighed in that afternoon at 7 stone 10 lb, give or take 2 lb under forfeit – Pat coming in at 7 stone 10½ lb.

'We expected to see something out of the ordinary in Daly,' wrote *Boxing*, 'and were certainly not disappointed.' Pat bossed the fight from start to finish, outboxing his man at range and outpunching him in close. He was far too quick and clever for the Leicester lad, and a verdict for Pat was the only one possible. 'There was something reminiscent of the famous Jimmy Wilde about Nipper Pat Daly of London,' observed a reporter from *The Nottingham Guardian*.

A week later Pat returned to Premierland, tasked with another 15-rounder, this time at 7 stone 12 lb. But Pat's original opponent, Freddie Collins of Leeds, withdrew and was replaced by fellow Leeds lad Alf

Thornhill, which *Boxing* said meant that Pat, 'had to concede a few years and a few pounds, and did it with the most astonishing ease. Nipper Pat was the master from the first gong till the last, and we do not think that his opponent Thornhill was entitled to a single half-round.' This time the reporter was less reproachful of the Professor, concluding:

'It is a moot point whether the wonderful Nipper is more highly favoured by a long than by a short contest. Anyway, the old Professor believes that the kid can travel more comfortably over 15 rounds than over 6 or 10… Moreover, his name at the head of a bill is sufficient to pack the East End N.S.C. [a sobriquet for Premierland], and this must be a record for any lad who has still several months to travel before he can nod to his 15th birthday greetings.'

Even in the face of hard common sense it seems success is hard to criticise.

***

'You must see this boy' enthused an advert for Pat's next fight, in which he opposed Ginger Johnson of Edlington. They met at 7 stone 12 lb over 10 rounds at the Peterborough Corn Exchange on 19 December. 'Nipper Pat is a real wonder and his display was superb,' wrote *The Peterborough Advertiser*. 'He was ever on the offensive, and the use he made of a lightning left was really wonderful, while his right was no less rapid and effective. His opponent was game and smart, but in resource and hitting capacity he was no match for the Nipper, whose win on points was beyond dispute.'

Christmas dinner for Pat must have been strictly rationed that year, for on 29 December he was again booked to meet Freddie Collins of Leeds in a 7 stone 12 lb 'money match'. But once more the Leeds lad failed to show, and was replaced this time by Jimmy Thornton, a good-class flyweight from Bethnal Green.*

'Daly was all too clever for the local lad,' said *Boxing*, 'and there was nothing sensational in the bout, for young Pat was easily the master, and

---

* Thornton boxed from 1927 until December 1933, when spinal tuberculosis forced him to quit boxing. Despite receiving treatment at numerous hospitals, he died in November 1935, aged just 24. He had amassed a respectable pro record of 115 traceable contests: 61 wins, 28 losses and 26 draws.

Thornton, realising this, could do nothing but hold, for which offence he was ruled out in the 6th round.'

Pat was more critical of the performance. Recalling it for the *Topical Times* in 1939, he said:

> 'That's a fight I like to forget. After six rounds of holding, waltzing and general spoiling the referee disqualified Thornton. About the only bright feature was the work of a Premierland "wag" up aloft. Halfway through the wag's voice rich with artificial horror rang out, "Stop this bloodshed!" That gave the house a laugh and they wanted it with that sort of "top-line" fight.'

An edition of *Boxing* on sale that day featured the Professor, Pat, and his stable-mates Arthur Norton and Leo Phillips on the cover. In the centre is a group of trophies, which incidentally were just for show. The Professor, Norton and Phillips, as no doubt posed by the photographer, gaze reverently towards Pat. It was a fitting image to end a year that had seen him rise from relative obscurity to claim his place as Britain's best young hope.

10

Bring on the Flyweights

Boy Sharpe of Nottingham had an unusually hard punch for a lad of 16, and a string of knockout wins in the local rings had earned him a reputation. Four days after tackling Jimmy Thornton, Pat travelled to Nottingham to face this lad in a 7 stone 10 lb match at the Victoria Baths. Weeks earlier, Pat had caused quite a stir when he outpointed Tom Fitzsimmonds in fine style, but this time many locals believed their boy would have his number. Sharpe's backers were so confident that they wagered a £25 side-stake with the Professor. If their lad got past the Londoner's defence – which, inevitably, at some point he would – his heavy hands would put paid to any points deficit. Or so they believed.

Having heard of Sharpe's punching prowess, Pat allowed him no openings to land his favourite shots. 'Daly's defence was almost perfect,' wrote *Boxing*, 'and he kept rattling the local with stinging shots to the face and had him beaten from the first round.' Sharpe fought back fiercely but Pat proved far too clever, and the Nottingham lad only just survived the fourth thanks to the bell. Pat floored him for two long counts in the fifth but again the end of round bell intervened. Early in the sixth he was down again for eight, but indignantly leapt to his feet and charged at Pat in furious fashion. This, however, would prove his undoing, as another right to the jaw flashed over and downed him once more for eight. He was up and down repeatedly after that until, finally, the referee stepped in, picked him up and carried him to his corner, declaring Pat the winner.

The ruthless efficiency of the victory had left onlookers astounded. 'Daly a coming Champion' declared a headline in *The Nottingham Journal*, its reporter heralding him, 'the successor to Jimmy Wilde – if I am not mistaken.'

The Marathon Stadium in the Lancashire town of Preston was the site of Pat's next fight. The venue, which stood on Frank Street in the heart of the town, had opened for boxing in September 1926. Its promoter, Frank Conway, staged weekly shows which drew close to 3,000 fans. Four days after blasting away Boy Sharpe, Pat met Johnny Summers of Leeds there in the pair's sixth encounter. As before, Pat won cleverly over 12 thrilling rounds; he then returned to London to prepare for a fight at Premierland 10 days later. His opponent should have been Jimmy Rowbotham of Birmingham – whose younger brother, Charlie, he had stopped there six months earlier – but when Rowbotham withdrew, he instead faced Kid Rich of St. George's.

Rich was a Jewish lad whose Ukrainian parents had fled persecution to start a new life in England. However, like many Jewish immigrants, they escaped the pogroms only to live poor in London's East End. Boxing, for young men like Rich, was less a sport than a means of survival. He took fights whenever and wherever he could and, win or lose, always put on a gallant display. Meeting some of the country's best flyweights, he'd already had well over 50 pro bouts; and eight months earlier, had faced future world flyweight champion Emile Pladner in Paris. Rich was built along the lines of a pocket Hercules, and his squat, bulging physique looked incongruous next to Pat's skinny, elongated frame. The disparity may well have caused concern among onlookers, but when the action commenced, their fears were soon allayed.

'Nipper Pat, who is coolness personified, took general command of the exchanges from the start,' wrote *Boxing*. Hopelessly outboxed at long range, Rich strove his hardest to get inside and set up two-handed attacks. But Pat halted most of his advances and, when the St. George's lad did get inside, drove him back to long range with fierce uppercuts, before continuing to pepper him with straight lefts. 'Rich took all that was coming in the gamest fashion and although his left ear was badly damaged in the sixth he still preserved till the close,' said *Boxing*. 'But Daly was all too clever for him and won almost as he liked.'

Less than a fortnight later, on 29 January Pat returned to Premierland on the more prestigious Sunday matinee show. He was billed to box Young Jim Driscoll of Cardiff at 7 stone 12 lb for a £100 purse and £25 a side, but yet again his opponent withdrew, so he instead fought Sheffield's Fred Bromley (also known as Jack Bromley), who had lost only six of 32 recorded fights. Bromley had former British and European middleweight champion Gus Platts in his corner, but this did not affect the outcome. 'Daly's speedy left hand and footwork were too much for Bromley to contend against,' said *Boxing*, 'and despite Gus Platts's efforts, the Sheffielder had to be content with the loser's end.'

That week, *Boxing* stated that the Professor was 'ready to lift the age limit' in order to find Pat competitive matches. 'He keeps on winning and this without worrying whether he has to concede 3 or 4 years in age. Daly can go to scale at 7 st 12 lb and is open to meet any boy or man in the country at this poundage for the 7st 12 lb championship.' The championship referred to was, of course, unofficial. Boxers below flyweight were often called 'paperweights', and Pat was frequently billed as the 'Paperweight Champion of England' – a claim that few could dispute.

Evidently dissatisfied with his previous showing, Kid Rich challenged Pat to a rematch via *Boxing*, which was promptly arranged and staged a week after the Bromley fight. They met at 7 stone 12 lb and, once more, Pat's left 'played havoc with Rich at long range'. In close, however, using what *Boxing* called 'some doubtful tactics', the St. George's man gave Pat plenty of problems. But all the same, Pat again finished the fight a clear points winner. To mark the win, *Boxing*'s cartoonist drew caricatures of both boxers.

A match with a fighter called Kid Hughes, billed for the following Monday, appears to have fallen through, leaving Pat a rare respite of 14 days. His next fight took place on 19 February, two days after his fifteenth birthday, at the Leeds National Sporting Club, which stood at 88 Templar Street on the junction with New York Road. It was owned by local businessman Albert Heslop and had no affiliation with the famous London NSC, which no doubt resented the corruption of its name by this working-class Yorkshire hall. A handbill for Pat's fight flamboyantly exhorts, 'Come and see the 15 yr. Old Champion of the World, Nipper Pat Daly, London. The Boy Wonder.'

His opponent, Harry Yates of Ashton, was six years Pat's senior, and when the pair weighed in that afternoon, the Ashton lad came in 2½ lb over the agreed 7 stone 12 lb limit. The Professor was denied the usual forfeit but still agreed to let Pat box. According to *Boxing*, Pat gave 'a wonderful display of boxing and finished up a good winner by a comfortable margin of points.'

Years later, Harry Yates would enthral his young nephew, Bryan Yates, with stories of his boxing days. 'I asked Harry who he considered his best opponent,' remembers Bryan, 'and without hesitation he said "Nipper Pat Daly". He was pleased to have gone 10 rounds with Nipper, more so than [future world flyweight champion] Jackie Brown. Harry had Brown down for a count of eight but let him off the hook, whereas he found it hard to land a punch on Nipper. Harry fought some cracking flyweights, and to consider Nipper over them all is a real tribute. He couldn't believe a 15-year-old lad had such talent.'*

★★★

On 1 March Premierland held a special fifteenth birthday testimonial for Pat, organised by a group of admirers. For some weeks *Boxing* had appealed for donations to pay for a birthday gift. 'Buck up, you who are anxious to encourage the best "hope" we have had for many years,' it told readers, 'make this lad remember his 15th birthday by the size and value of his presentation.' A week before the event, £10 19s 6d had been raised, including £5 from Victor Berliner and Manny Lyttlestone, £2 2s from a Mr H. Cristall of Ontario, Canada, 10 shillings from Syd Carter, and 5 shillings from Tom Quill. Come the big day, in what *Boxing* described as the 'tit-bit of the evening', Pat was presented with his birthday gift: a gold watch and chain for Sundays, and a silver replica to wear on weekdays.

The following Monday, in the company of the Professor and Andy Newton, he travelled to Stockport for an afternoon weigh-in at 7 stone 12 lb (under £5 forfeit). That evening, at the Stockport Armoury, he faced Johnny Summers of Leeds for the last time. Despite all previous decisions going to Pat, Summers's camp believed an upset was possible. Side stakes of £25 from both sets of backers were deposited with *The Sporting Life* newspaper. Unsurprisingly, however, Pat dominated the 15-round fight and won by a wide points margin.

It was his final match at 7 stone 12 lb, as he could no longer shed the required weight. It is interesting to note that the average male grows fastest between the ages of 14 and 15, yet despite growing taller, through training and dieting Pat had remained the same weight for six months.

---

*   There is a sad postscript to Harry Yates's ring career. In 1950 he was knocked down by a lorry on Stockport Road. He was left with a fractured skull and never fully recovered. After the accident he suffered memory loss, recurrent headaches and depression, and could no longer hold down a regular job. Tragically, in late 1955 he took his own life.

He was now, however, a full-fledged flyweight and about to enter a weight class brimming with talent.

His first fight at flyweight was against Mark Lesnick of Stepney, a rough, tough, muscular little fighter who was not averse to rule-breaking. Lesnick had around 80 amateur fights and won the London Federation Championships at 6 stone 7 lb and 7 stone (junior and senior) in 1922 and 1923, then turned pro in 1924. Born to a poor Jewish family on 10 December 1906, he was obliged to box pro to pay the bills. Almost all of his fights had been at Premierland where he was considered the 'house' fighter, and over half his wins so far were by KO or stoppage. He had beaten top-class men such as Young Bill Lewis of Bethnal Green, Harry Hill of Birmingham and Dod Oldfield of Leeds, drawn with former European flyweight champion Michel Montreuil, and been in with British flyweight champion Johnny Hill.

'If Mark had applied for a pro licence today,' wrote Ron Olver in a 1987 *Boxing News* article, 'given the same circumstances it would definitely not have been granted. Reason – Mark had bad eyesight from birth. And I do mean "bad". But in those days, with no Board of Control, it was a case of "anything goes". Mark's bad eyesight was probably one reason for his all-action style. He liked to get in close as often as possible, so that if he couldn't see 'em, he could feel 'em.'

Lesnick's tearaway tactics had got him disqualified four times, while on three other occasions things had got so messy that the fight had been stopped and ruled a 'no contest'. 'Lesnick has soon become acquainted with all he should not do in the ring,' wrote *Boxing* after his first 'no contest' fight. Shorter, slower and at a disadvantage in reach, Lesnick was also stronger and, at 21, six years older than Pat. Rough tactics were on the agenda before the fight even began.

As the first bell chimed, Lesnick charged from his corner, slinging shots wildly and showing scant concern for where or how they landed. 'Lesnick is too keen to get to close quarters,' noted *Boxing*, 'and the sooner he learns where to place his punches the better. It isn't that he loses his head, but he is a very bad judge of distance, and doesn't know where the border line is... Daly wanted a straight fight, but was continuously "claimed" by a tough, strong fighter.' Eventually Pat grew tired of being fouled, and since the referee was taking no action, he decided to foul back. 'Young Pat knows a trick or two himself,' wrote *Boxing*, 'and he followed suit when Lesnick started, with the result that one of the poorest bouts imaginable was seen.' By the tenth round referee Jack Hart had seen enough. He halted the bout and declared it a 'no contest', leaving *Boxing* to muse, 'Had Jack Hart allowed the contest to go on, as he allowed Lesnick's low punches to pass, Daly might have put paid to Mark's account. Lesnick was getting demoralised towards the close.'

A representative from the soon to be reformed British Boxing Board of Control was in attendance and insisted that both boxers' purses be withheld. Victor Berliner, not wishing to upset his big ticket-seller, paid Pat out of his own pocket. 'Daly was a victim of the "no contest" decision,' declared *Boxing*, 'because he lacks the strength at his age to cope with the roughing and wrestling tactics of such men as Lesnick. At the boxing game he could lose Mark any day.' Despite, as *Boxing* put it, being 'badly punched in the groin', Pat was back in the ring four days later.

The venue for his next fight was among the finest in the north of England. The Liverpool Stadium, which stood on Pudsey Street, opened on 13 July 1911 and could accommodate 4,000 spectators, each of whom was guaranteed a tip-up chair and a decent view – scarce commodities among Britain's pre-war fight arenas. In addition, the Stadium had a sliding roof, which gave fighters and fans extra ventilation throughout the stuffy summer months. The venue staged regular shows and drew capacity crowds until its closure and demolition in 1931.*

Pat's opponent was a local 19-year-old called Lud Abella. Born Ludwill Pablo Abella to Spanish-Filipino parents on 8 October 1908, he first boxed as an amateur for the Hercules Athletic Club, then later moved to the well-known Liverpool ABC, run by Ted Denvir and Jack Dare. In all, Lud had around 50 amateur bouts – reportedly losing just two – and in 1926 won the Northern Counties flyweight title. Also that year, he reached the ABA flyweight quarterfinal but was beaten by Eddie Warwick, who'd been champion three years running. Abella turned pro in 1927 and built a fine reputation round the northern rings. He was more of a fighter than a boxer but was never found wanting for tenacity or grit.

---

* In 1932 it was replaced by a larger, 6,000-seater venue of the same name, which purpose-built on nearby St. Paul's Square.

After an 8-stone afternoon weigh-in, the pair entered the Stadium ring at 7:45pm for their 15-round fight. Pat opened proceedings in speedy style, raining perfectly timed punches on Abella from all angles. Naturally, the shorter Liverpudlian favoured infighting, but when he got inside he was surprised to find the Londoner more adept than he was. 'Daly was repeatedly cheered for his super cleverness,' observed *Boxing*, 'and although Abella fought fiercely, he was outpointed every round. The crowd appreciated the Londoner's boxing, and he received an ovation... As we anticipated, Nipper Pat Daly made a great hit with the Liverpool fans, and is likely to reappear at the Stadium shortly.'

There was only a four-day gap before Pat reappeared in a northern ring. On 19 March, the people of Blackburn got to see him take on 18-year-old Tommy Brown of Salford at the King Street Drill Hall over 12 rounds. Brown, a graduate of Salford's famous Adelphi Lads' Club, had lost only two of his 32 recorded pro fights, and one of these defeats had been due to a cut ear. Among his many victories was a points win over future world flyweight champion Jackie Brown of Manchester. (Incidentally, Tommy went on to defeat such stars as British bantamweight champion Johnny King and world flyweight title claimant Valentin Angelmann.) But '20s boxers weren't privy to such statistics, as no official records were kept. Probably Pat knew little or nothing about his opponent, and had little idea that he was in for a hard night.

In a brief appraisal, *Boxing* noted that, 'Spells of boxing, which were a delight to watch, were followed by occasional spasms of real hard fighting. Both took hard punches nonchalantly, and the house showed its appreciation by roars of applause.' Perhaps because of the class of his opponent, or possibly the strain of fighting three times in eight days, Pat had a far tougher time than usual. 'Tommy Brown gave the Professor's colt the hardest fight of his career,' concluded *Boxing*, 'but Daly fully justified his title of the "Wonder Boy".' 'In announcing Daly as the winner,' noted *The Blackburn Times*, 'Mr Ben Green, the referee, described the fight as wonderful. Brown, he said, was not disgraced and he considered him the best fighting flyweight in the North of England. Daly, he remarked, was the wonder boy of Great Britain.'

Perhaps pre-empting criticism for the frequency of the boy's fights, Professor Newton announced through *Boxing* that he'd be giving Pat a rest. However, no rest was forthcoming, for 11 days after the Tommy Brown battle, he took on former stable-mate Jimmy Lindsay of Fulham over 15 rounds at Fulham Baths. Despite Lindsay's class as a boxer (he outpointed top men such as Benny Caplan, George Garrard, Douglas Kestrell and Billy Boulger) Pat put on a straight left master-class and 'hit Lindsay much as he pleased'. Switching his attack to the body and throwing right crosses to the head with splendid judgement, he gave the Fulham lad a torrid time, 'driving him round the ring and flogging him at every turn,' as *Boxing* put it. 'It was an easy win for Daly, who did not lose a single round.'

In a rematch with Lud Abella four days later at Premierland, 'Nipper Pat scored all the points there were, while Abella hung on and wrestled. The referee, for some reason best known to himself, called it "a draw",' reported *Boxing*. It was Pat's second 15-rounder that week, but even so, it seems that he had fully deserved to win.

Two years later, during a campaign in America, Abella was involved in another contentious decision when he drew with Joe Glick, a Brooklyn fighter who had recently challenged for the world junior-welterweight crown.* The gangster backers of Glick were so upset by the decision that Lud had to flee the arena and spend several days in hiding. After a three-year Stateside stay – during which he was recklessly overmatched against world-class operators such as Barney Ross, Steve Haiko and Lew Feldman – Abella returned home and moved to the Midlands, where he boxed until the late 1930s. He lost an eye while on active service during World War Two and was discharged. In later years he took out a manager's licence and ran his own Birmingham gym.

★★★

Pat's next fight was planned for the Easter Bank Holiday weekend a fortnight later, but when it fell through, the industrious Professor found another way to keep him busy while earning some extra cash. 'As I had missed a 15-round contest at Premierland on Sunday,' remembered Pat,

---

* Now also known as 'light-welterweight', this 10-stone division was introduced in America in 1923, but wasn't recognised in Britain, which had only eight weight classes. When Jack Kid Berg won the junior-welterweight title from Mushy Callahan at the Royal Albert Hall in 1930, Lord Lonsdale rose from his ringside seat, waving his stick, and told the announcer that there was no such weight. The division was abandoned in 1946, but revived in 1959.

'my opponent, Young Siki, had not turned up, the Prof sent me the next day (Bank Holiday Monday) to work at a boxing booth at the [Lea] Bridge Road.'

Travelling booths were a veritable breeding ground for boxing talent before the Second World War. Usually attached to a fairground, booths toured the length and breadth of Great Britain, moving from town to town or district to district. Each possessed its own set of fighters, who were held on a retainer of food, lodgings and a small weekly wage – the latter augmented by nobbings from the crowd. With several short bouts a day, the booth life offered many young boxers an unmatched chance to sharpen their skills and gain experience by meeting a diverse range of opponents. Challengers were sometimes simply unskilled young men, wanting to show off to their friends or girlfriends. But invariably, when they got word that a booth was in town, the local boxing men turned out to test their skills against the booth fighters. Thereby the booths brought out a great deal of latent talent and gave many young boxers a start in the game. In addition to the novices, it was common to see well-established pros on a booth, for although the remuneration was small, it kept them at peak fitness, saved them the cost of gym fees and the trouble of finding sparring partners, and often they picked up fights at the halls of the towns and cities they visited. Besides boxing, it was a booth fighter's job to erect the booth, assemble the ring, second the other boxers and time-keep when needed. After a few days, they dismantled the whole structure and loaded it onto lorries to be driven to the next town or district. Champions such as Freddie Mills, Benny Lynch, Tommy Farr, Joe Beckett, Jim Driscoll and Jimmy Wilde were products of boxing booths.

Essentially, a booth was a large marquee with an ornately decorated, platformed facade. The booth fighters – usually five or six – lined up along the platform and the blare of a trumpet or the banging of a drum summoned the expectant crowd. A man called the 'barker' then introduced each of the fighters and, dangling a pair of well-worn boxing gloves in one hand, called for a challenger from the crowd, to whom the gloves would be thrown. 'Roll up and try ya luck – see if you can knock our boy's block off.' If the challenger lasted three rounds, he would win a small monetary prize.

The booth fighters were obliged to take on 'all comers', which often meant conceding age and weight. If no genuine challengers were found, there was usually a 'plant' hidden amid the crowd who'd yell out, 'I'll take him on' and step in if needed. This type of staged bout was called a 'gee' fight, and was put on to encourage the locals to have a try. Once the challengers had been found, the crowds filed inside the marquee (which usually had standing room for several hundred), paid an admittance as they passed, and then that set of contests – known as a 'house' – got underway.

'When I started work I created something of a sensation,' recalled Pat, 'as it seemed that most of the young men in the crowd wanted to take me on, as I was 15 years old, skinny and did not look like a fighter.' Any misapprehensions over his fighting abilities, however, were quickly dispelled when Pat got to work. It seems the Marylebone lad had a busy day. The event made the columns of that week's issue of *Boxing* and its commentary was tinged with irony:

> 'Nipper Pat Daly has started on a rest cure. This commenced in a boxing booth at Lea Bridge on Easter Monday, when Nipper Pat boxed 36 rounds during the day. As Professor Newton states, there is nothing to equal "a change of occupation" to provide a complete rest.'

Just as long as Pat kept on winning and the money rolled in, no 'change of occupation' was likely. The Professor was eager for his boy to fight as often as he could, and Pat for his part did not object. 'I could no more have hung up my boxing gloves than stopped breathing,' he would recall. 'Fights were the fun of my life.'

He was riding the crest of a wave. With his God-given talent and the Professor's expert instruction, he seemed invincible. A surprise, however, lay in wait.

11

The Kleiner Bube

'The Nipper is developing physically and mentally at an astonishing rate, and if he doesn't annex a World title one of these days, we are double Dutchmen.'

Boxing, 13 June 1928

Young Siki (whose real name was Andy Devine) was a 20-year-old Liverpudlian of either black or mixed-race heritage, which made him quite an anomaly on the '20s British fight scene. Some contemporary newspapers state that he arrived in England from America, but all these years later the facts are hard to determine. At any rate, we can be sure he took his moniker from the French-Senegalese light-heavyweight world champion, Battling Siki, a flamboyant character whose end came tragically when he was gunned down on the streets of Hell's Kitchen, New York in 1925.

The Liverpudlian Siki learnt his trade on the boxing booths and had fought professionally since 1924. He was not the most skilful of boxers but held a powerful punch in each hand. After Pat's original match with him fell through, a swift rearrangement meant that they met at Premierland on 29 April in an 8 stone 2 lb Sunday matinee 15-rounder.

The fight began on familiar lines with Pat bombarding his shorter opponent with jolting, piston-like lefts. Siki repeatedly charged at Pat but could not get past his tormentor's educated punches. 'Siki to all appearances,' wrote *Boxing*, 'had become resigned to the position of receiver general.' At this point, the fight appeared an easy task for Pat. The one-sidedness of the exchanges, however, had lulled him into a false sense of security. A moment's carelessness in the fourth saw a right cross from Siki crash through his defence and onto his chin. A crescendo of gasps shot around the hall as the boy fell flat on his back. According to *Boxing*, this was the first time Pat had been floored.* Probably through injured pride, he rashly leapt to his feet before the referee's count reached two. But with his senses scattered, he was an open target for another right hand smash, and down he went again. This time Pat looked incapable of rising and the Professor shrewdly threw in the towel, meaning the defeat goes down as a corner retirement and not a knockout. It was some time before Pat regained his senses, but the fight had taught him a valuable lesson – never again, without first clearing his head, would he bounce straight up from a knockdown.

A boxing defeat in the 1920s was not the career-blight it might be today. The long unbeaten records enjoyed by today's carefully matched young prospects were almost unheard of in pre-war rings. With boxers performing so regularly and with so little care taken over matchmaking, the occasional loss was inevitable, even for the very best. Pat's defeat to Siki, therefore, was not a major setback. But even by the harsh standards of the day, allowing a 15-year-old boy to be knocked out by a grown man – to some at least – was grossly irresponsible. The defeat had not won Pat's mentor any fans among the sport's more conscientious followers. But bizarrely, in an apparent turnaround of opinion, *Boxing*'s John Murray now fully backed the Professor:

> 'The only and wonderful Professor has been criticised for his handling of young Daly and has been told that he is asking an immature boy to do too much. Well, we have made it our business to study the boy and have satisfied ourselves that he has in no way suffered either in stamina or vitality. We have to confess that we were among the first to criticise the Professor's strategy, and not only anticipated but forecast inevitable disaster. Hence we hasten to tender our apologies, both to Daly and to the Professor. There can be little doubt that the achievement must be attributed to the Professor's system of physical training.' *Boxing,* 16 May 1928

Also that week, Murray previewed Pat's imminent clash with the Italian flyweight champion, Giovanni Sili, calling it 'the severest test to which a

---

* His memoirs indicate that he was also knocked down in a fight with John Brent in early 1924, when aged 10 – see page 36.

lad of 15 years of age has ever been exposed.' 'One thing is certain,' he adds, 'Nipper Pat will make even prominent boxers sit up and take notice whether he wins or loses. Young Daly is a boxer, a boy who is definitely booked for a World's title, provided he remains under his present careful and expert management.'

According to Andy Newton, Sili was a four to one bookies' favourite and 'many hundreds of pounds changed hands that night. One bet of £400 to £100 was accepted by one of my father's pupils, who backed Daly in all his contests,' he wrote in *Boxing News* in 1940. As described in the book's opening chapter, Pat systematically dismantled the champion with a wonderful display of boxing. To put the win into perspective, the legendary Georges Carpentier, himself considered a 'boy wonder' in his teens, stunned the fight world when he annexed the French title at 17; Pat, however, had beaten a national champion a whole two years sooner. Writing of the Sili fight in his memoirs, he recalled:

'The next day a messenger brought a box containing an Easter-egg, the top of which was slanting and in the middle, inside the egg, was an effigy of a boxer, and the name *Nipper Pat Daly* on the outside of the egg. It looked quite handsome, especially as it was sent for me, and was the first time I had seen anything so nice. [Ten months later] The same person came into my dressing room at the Albert Hall, where I was to fight Petit Biquet over 10 rounds, to explain that he would act as a second in Biquet's corner as he had always done when Biquet fought in England. I gave him my blessing, and he wished me "Good luck".'

Pat's long list of victories and his defeat of the Italian champion now made him a credible challenger for the British flyweight title, then held by Johnny Hill of Leith, Scotland. The boxing public was keen to see the match take place, but the British Boxing Board of Control had some qualms about allowing a 15-year-old to box for a national title. 'At the Board of Control offices they may entertain a notion that Nipper Pat is too young to compete for any high honours,' wrote *Boxing* on 20 May. 'Still, it should not matter so very much. Nipper Pat is due to make history, and will assuredly make it, irrespective of any hindrance the Board of Control or any other more or less official organisation may attempt to devise.'

Regardless of the Board's position, Pat believed that a British title shot was now within his reach; and he would willingly box any eight-stone man to realise it. Another flyweight prospect on the fringes of title contention was 21-year-old Dod Oldfield of Leeds. He had beaten leading men such as Lew Sullivan, Mark Lesnick, Jim Hanna, Minty Rose and Harry Hill, and also held the flyweight championship of the north (an unofficial '20s equivalent of the Northern Area title). A 15-round Oldfield–Daly match was fixed for 21 June and immediately sparked excitement among the fight fraternity. In its preview *Boxing* noted:

'Nipper Pat is credited with possessing the best left hand of any boxer in England. He is only 15 years of age and is therefore liable to be short on physical strength; but he has the skill and the method. Oldfield has also the wider experience as well as the stronger seasoning and sounder maturity; but he will have to place his best foot foremost, and to keep it there, if he wants to win over Professor Newton's pet pupil.

Both are clean, open fighters, and of the classic style. They box, both scientifically and correctly, and the spectators will witness a contest as contests should be waged. Both are aspirants to the flyweight title, though one assumes that before Nipper Pat can get near to this distinction he will have outgrown the class. This will be the stiffest test of his career, and if he can win over Oldfield it will be practically impossible to check his upward advance. One has to admire the confidence of both the Nipper and of his mentor, for Oldfield is some mouthful to be chewed.' *Boxing*, 20 June 1928

Meanwhile, on 7 June, Pat had a warm-up bout at Premierland. His intended opponent, Jack Ellis of St. George's, withdrew, leaving fellow East Ender Kid Rich to take his place and face Pat for the third time. It was another rough and tumble affair with Rich inflicting some savage close-quarter punishment but, as *Boxing* noted, 'Pat's clever boxing all through the bout rightly earned him Jack Hart's verdict.'

The clash with Oldfield took place at the Ilford Skating Rink on Ilford High Road precisely two weeks later. With wooden boards placed across the skating rink, and chairs positioned all around the makeshift ring, the 6,000-capacity arena was packed from floor to ceiling. The night began with the former world bantamweight champion, Teddy Baldock, refereeing a six-round preliminary. Another six-rounder and a 12-rounder formed the rest of the undercard. The American Maxie Rosenbloom (a future world light-heavyweight champion) was billed to appear in a three-round exhibition, but he gets no mention in the press reports, so presumably did not show. With the preliminaries over, the crowd watched with bated breath as the tall, skinny figure of Pat, and the shorter, stockier, wavy-haired Oldfield each made their way to the ring.

From the outset, Pat made full use of his extra height and reach, snaking out his left with fine precision and nimbly darting in and out before Oldfield could counter. The Leeds man worked hard and fast with both hands when he managed to get in close, but for the most part he was out-speeded and kept at long range. Frequently he aimed vicious hooks at the Marylebone youth's head; but these invariably were blocked or ducked. 'The Leeds battler continued in his efforts to force his opponent into a fight,' observed *Boxing*, 'but Daly was always too clever for him, and the score sheet stood well in favour of the London lad when the half-distance was reached.' Opening the second half of the fight with a rush, however, Oldfield had more success with his hooks and managed to land one flush on Pat's jaw. But 'Daly then pulled out a deal of clever defensive work,' said *Boxing*, 'ducking and swaying away from punches in capital style, while at the same time never losing any opportunity for "pinking" his rival with a left to the face.' The last few rounds were fought at top speed with Pat still piling up the points, and appearing, as *Boxing* put it, 'to come past the winning post "as fresh as paint".'

It was another virtually punch-perfect performance and almost everyone in attendance – including Oldfield – believed a decision in Pat's favour to be imminent. 'When the referee, Mr. Jack Morris, declared in favour of Oldfield,' reported *Boxing*, 'there was a loud outburst of protestation in the shape of booing by the crowd.' So absurd seemed the decision, that when the announcement was made, Pat started to laugh. With a look of embarrassment, Oldfield turned to his opponent, patted him on the back and muttered sheepishly, 'I'm sorry, Nipper. There's nothing I can do.' 'Pat must be given credit for being a great-hearted little sportsman,' wrote *Boxing*, 'for although he must have felt keenly the injustice of the decision, he merely smiled his acknowledgement of the great hand he got when he left the ring.'

The Daily Express felt that 'Daly had won easily'. While *Boxing* concluded, 'So far as the registration of boxing points was concerned, there was only one in it in the majority of the rounds, and where and how Oldfield won must for ever be a puzzle... Harry Reeve, the old ex-cruiserweight champion expressed to us the opinion that the decision was "one of the worst ever", and "Reevo" is no bad judge.'

What the press did not know, or had failed to note, was that the referee, Jack Morris, was a relation of Oldfield's manager, Joe Morris – the same Premierland matchmaker to whose colt, Billy Boulger, Pat had suffered his only other points defeat; again under dubious circumstances. According to Pat's eldest son, John Daley, the Ilford show's promoter, Jack Greenstock, was also related to Morris – via marriage.

Naturally, the verdict was a disappointment but the outcome did not harm Pat's reputation. A picture of him on the cover of the next edition of *Boxing* was captioned, 'The Nipper's achievements speak for themselves... Don't forget Daly's contest with Dod Oldfield on Thursday last. The referee said Oldifeld had won, but no one else did.'

Efforts were made to stage a rematch with Oldfield. 'He is ready to meet Dod Oldfield again at any time and at any place and only hopes that Oldfield will not jib at the prospect of taking another trouncing,' announced *Boxing*, and over the ensuing weeks several appeals were made for a return to be staged. Two months drifted by without any word from Oldfield before *Boxing* finally declared, 'Nipper Pat Daly, weary of waiting for Dod Oldfield, is prepared to make a match with anyone in the country at 8st. 2lb. over either 12 (3 min) rounds or 15 (2 min) rounds.' But no one, it seems, came forward, for a week later the newspaper added, 'Professor Newton is still waiting to hear from 8 st. lads. Have all these run to earth?' When he did find a fight, it was not on English soil. He was matched for 29 September to meet the German flyweight champion, Ludwig Minow, on the latter's home turf.

Pat, Andy Newton and three other English boxers docked at Dortmund a few days before the fight. For Pat the trip offered a welcome break from the intense media scrutiny that surrounded him back home. He was embarrassed by the 'baby face' and 'boy wonder' tags the press heaped on him, as he felt that he had outgrown such epithets. He had never experienced a normal teenage life – the past six years had been ones of unremitting dedication and self-discipline. Now having beaten some of the best men at his weight, he did not feel like much of a boy. At least in Germany, he reckoned, nobody would know him and he'd be spared the embarrassing nicknames. But within hours of landing, he scanned the German press and saw his name in several papers. He noticed the phrase 'Kleiner Bube' used repeatedly, and so, pointing to the paper, asked a local what it meant. 'It means little baby,' they answered with a grin.

During the stay Pat made the mistake early one morning of entering Andy Newton's room unannounced. Inside he found Andy lying in bed with a naked woman whom he took for a chambermaid. 'I'm sorry,' he mumbled, edging back towards the door, his hand fumbling for the door handle. 'Wait a minute,' barked Andy as a knowing grin spread across his face. 'You can get into bed with her if you like.' Though never daunted by any ring encounter, this was one situation Pat was ill prepared to face. Red-cheeked and shocked by the suggestion, he bolted from the room.

Pat got into shape at the German gyms, which he later described as 'superb', and come the day of the fight, he had no doubts as to his chances. The contest was held at the Westfalenhalle, an impressive indoor arena built just three years earlier and, incidentally, the place where a 21-year-old Max Schmeling won the European light-heavyweight crown in 1927. Pat began by wowing the crowd with a demonstration of Professor Newton's system of training. Then over 10 clever rounds he defeated Ludwig Minow, whom he described as a 'worthy champion who lacked variety in his punching'. Pat received a tremendous ovation on being returned the winner. He was hoisted shoulder-high and carried around the ring to the tune of *Rule, Britannia*. 'Nipper Pat Daly electrified the Germans,' reported *Boxing*. As he left the ring the attendant German band 'struck up a triumphal march and played him to his dressing room'.

Elsewhere on the bill, Harry Jones of Hoxton and Jim Carr of Reading also beat their German opponents, but Harry Crossley of Mexborough (a future British light-heavyweight champion) lost to Ludwig Haymann, the German heavyweight champion who, interestingly enough, later qualified as a doctor. Of course the England versus Germany theme was nothing more than an arranged piece of good-natured sporting rivalry. Little did the fighters or fans realise, that 10 years later they would be enemies in a war that would see the Westfalenhalle destroyed and rebuilt.

No doubt delighted by their three wins out of four, the English team under the charge of Andy Newton sailed back to England.

★★★

At around this time Billy Pullum, son of the one-time world weightlifting champion W. A. Pullum, and then a 16-year-old amateur, paid a visit to Newton's gym. Decades later he wrote of the experience for the London Ex-Boxers' Association's journal, *Box On!*, offering a unique outsider's glimpse inside the famous gymnasium:

> 'Leaving school, I expressed a desire to enter the paid ranks, so my father consulted his old friend John Murray, the then Editor of *Boxing*. Murray's advice was "first put him in the ring for a trial with one of the best in the country and see how he performs." So towards the end of 1928, up to Professor Andrew Newton's "Empire School of Arms" in Marylebone I went with my father, John Murray, and a young man named Gilbert Odd, already showing his great love and attachment to the fistic art.*
>
> What a green mug I was! The upright and daunting figure of the old Professor appeared and gave me the "once-over". "So you want to be a pro fighter, do you? Then let's see what you can do with my boy here." The boy was "Nipper" Pat Daly! During the first round of the three round trial I had the misfortune to surprise the Nipper with a good left hook to the solar plexus. The Professor thundered "STOP! What the blank blank hell do you think you are doing letting a mug catch you with a punch like that after all I've taught you – BOX ON!" The next thing I knew, I had been knocked through the ropes. In rounds two and three I received every different punch in the book delivered in classic style, but I survived and did not visit the canvas. Everybody, including the Professor, seemed to think I had performed well, but myself, I was disgusted I could not clobber the Nipper. I was

---

* Gilbert Odd joined the staff of *Boxing* in 1922. He was later the Editor of the paper's successor, *Boxing News*, and the author of several boxing-related books. He was recognised as one of Britain's leading boxing historians and was elected into the International Boxing Hall of Fame in 1995. He died in 1996, aged 93.

so much a mug I just did not appreciate what a prodigy he was for his years. As I got out of the ring after a warm pat on the back from the Nipper a comment came from a figure on the side in dark glasses – "one thing anyway, the boy has a gooseberry tart".* At the time, being so young and new to the game, I did not realise this was a real compliment from a great and game fighter – Andy Newton.'

Billy Pullum of Camberwell did turn pro, and amassed a traceable record of 20 wins, four draws and four defeats. He was never knocked out or stopped and could boast a points win over the excellent George Daly of Blackfriars. He also became a successful fight promoter and later the owner and Editor of *Health & Strength* magazine. For Pullum the encounter was singularly significant – it marked the start of his love affair with pro boxing. For Pat, it was probably just another day at the gym.

---

* Rhyming slang for 'heart'.

12

Chasing a Championship

'Fly-weights and bantams are our soundest hopes these days. For some mysterious reason they are easily the most expert performers we have, and we are still of the opinion that Nipper Pat Daly is the best box-fighter of them all, for all that he is only 15½.'

Boxing, 11 September 1928

After a three-year absence, Pat returned to the Hackney Manor Hall on 21 October to oppose Siki Coulton of Leicester. Coulton, however, withdrew with an injured ear and was replaced by Billy 'KO' Yates of Mexborough, who as his nickname implies was something of a puncher. He had actually stopped Coulton two months earlier and in October 1929 would also force future British bantamweight champion Johnny King to chuck in the towel.

Yates was game enough but, as *Boxing* noted, 'he certainly was not good enough to hold Professor Newton's wonder'. Pat began by firing rapid straight lefts, then moved inside and landed some heavy body shots. Yates covered up fairly well but lacked judgment with his swinging counters. Pat continued to force the fight and in the third whipped in a right to Yates's body that floored the Mexborough lad for eight. He recovered and pegged away doggedly until the sixth, whereupon 'he took a rare hiding and was sent reeling across the ring by a heavy right to the belt. The referee visited the provincial's corner,' wrote *Boxing*, 'but though Bill elected to continue he was in a helpless condition when the affair was stopped during the 7th round.'

A fortnight later at Premierland Pat faced ex-Corporal Jack Connell of Aldershot (formerly of the 1st Cameronians). He'd won the 1928 Army Championships, plus the Imperial Services Championships, which made him the best flyweight in Britain's military. After reaching that year's ABA flyweight semi-finals, Connell decided to leave the Army and try his luck as a professional. His bout with Pat was his first pro outing, yet he no doubt believed that his tough Army conditioning would see him through the 15 rounds. 'Connell is game and clever, for an amateur,' remarked *Boxing*, 'but he was simply not in it when pitted against Daly.' Connell took a severe drubbing until the referee finally intervened at the end of the ninth. He had remained on his feet, but his eye was badly cut, and it is doubtful whether he could have carried on. The win, as ever, had been stunningly one-sided, but one newspaper alluded to a weakness in the Nipper's arsenal. 'Considering the number of rights he landed it was surprising that Daly could not put Connell down.' With his growing string of victories, it was becoming increasingly apparent that, as a growing boy fighting predominantly full-grown men, Pat did not yet hold a real knockout punch. When he did force a stoppage, it was usually the sheer volume of blows that he landed and the relentlessness of his attack that wore his man down. But this did not detract from his allure to his growing army of fans. They did not pay to see brute force, but rather his rare blend of pressure fighting and consummate ring craft.

The Ring at Blackfriars – perhaps the best-remembered pre-war fight venue – was the setting for Pat's next contest. Much like Premierland, The Ring attracted a predominantly working-class crowd but it was also common to see stars of screen and stage sat ringside. Situated on the Blackfriars Road at the junction with Union Street, the building had started as the non-conformist Surrey Chapel – built in 1783 and circular in design so that the devil had no corner to hide. Reverend Rowland Hill, its first pastor, was an eccentric revivalist who delivered his impassioned sermons from a raised pulpit at its centre. The building had lain empty for some time when former British lightweight champion Dick Burge converted it into a boxing arena in 1910. Thanks to its circular shape, every spectator had a fine view of the centre. The spot from where Reverend Hill had once harangued his flock was now occupied by a boxing ring. The fight hall quickly became and remained south London's leading palace of punch. Dick Burge died prematurely in 1918 and the reins then passed to his wife Bella, who continued to run the venue alongside manager and matchmaker Dan Sullivan.

Pat's opponent at The Ring was 25-year-old Cardiff veteran Frank Kestrell, who had boxed professionally since 1916 and twice fought for the Welsh flyweight title.* Kestrell had bags of know-how and experience and had once been strongly fancied for the British flyweight title. 'He knows the game, and was expected to test the boy's qualities pretty severely,' wrote *Boxing*, 'but the Nipper, even if he has still over three months to travel to his 16th birthday, was as good as a seasoned veteran. He had height and reach in his favour, and he refused to allow Kestrell a glimpse of victory. Try as he would, the Cardiffian could rarely get past that steady left, and when he did, he generally got met by the Nipper's right, and suffered some more. Daly took round after round, until, with Kestrell hopelessly behind on points, the referee intervened at the end of the 12th round.'

'Nipper Pat demonstrated to the entire satisfaction of all present that he is all that has been claimed for him,' concluded *Boxing*. Another one-sided win against top opposition had certainly not harmed his title prospects; but getting a shot at Johnny Hill's crown would not prove an easy feat. Having stayed unbeaten against the cream of Britain's flyweights and capturing a version of the world crown from the American Newsboy Brown earlier that year, Hill stood head and shoulders above the rest of Britain's eight-stone men, and was even ranked number three in the world by America's boxing Bible, *The Ring* magazine. There was one man, however, who stood out from the pack of aspirants to Hill's British title. As *Boxing* commented at the time, 'Here in England, Bert Kirby stands out as practically the sole opponent to be found for Hill at the weight.'

With an impressive run of wins Birmingham's Bert Kirby had caught the eye of renowned trainer Fred Dyer (real name Frederick O'Dwyer), a Welshman who'd once stayed the distance with legendary middleweight Les Darcy. Dyer was dubbed 'The Singing Boxer' in his ring days, for at the end of a gruelling fight, he would often entertain the crowd by performing a song in his rich baritone voice. In the mid-1920s he decided to open a gym and form a stable at The Strand in London, and enlisted Bert Kirby as one of its first members. With Dyer's erudite coaching, the naturally tough and hard-hitting Brum soon stormed his way through Britain's best flyweights. He'd beaten such notables as Dick Corbett, Billy James, Dod Oldfield, Harry Hill, George Greaves and Ernie Jarvis to

---

* It should be noted that Welsh championships then carried more kudos. In the 1920s the Welsh rings teemed with talent and a Welsh title win was a prestigious achievement.

establish himself as number one flyweight contender. And, given the chance, many believed that the Brum would dethrone Johnny Hill.

For Pat to get his own shot at Hill he first had to topple Bert Kirby. But he knew that he was racing against time to do so, for any month now he would outgrow the eight-stone class. For some time Pat had urged the Professor to get him a match with Kirby, and it was starting to seem as if the fight would never happen. But, suddenly, on 20 November *Boxing* announced the news that every fight fan wanted to hear. Pat would tackle Kirby on a 17 December charity bill at Birmingham's Alexandra Theatre. Facing the formidable Brum on his home turf was a tall order, but conceding home advantage did not concern Pat.

Top of the Birmingham bill was the gifted Len Harvey, an older, better-established performer.* But nonetheless *Boxing* predicted, 'the greatest and most thrilling as well as the most instructive item on the bill of fare will be provided by Bert Kirby and Nipper Pat Daly.' However, the trade paper gave Pat less chance than usual. For the first time it felt that the Marylebone boy may just have bitten off more than he could chew:

> 'Nipper Pat, even if beaten will still deserve to be rated as a prodigy, but in tackling Bert Kirby he will have been asked to do something and then some more... Young Daly will have height and reach in his favour, but he is still some two months short of 16 years of age, and Kirby's maturity, plus wider experience, will present a most serious handicap... Nevertheless, we venture the prophecy that whatever happens Kirby will know that he has been in a fight.'

In contrast to the predicament of a couple of months before, Pat was suddenly overwhelmed with prospective matches. In the run up to the Kirby fight he would have three fights in three weeks, leaving the Professor little choice but to decline several offers. With the big fight less than a month away, squeezing in so many bouts was a highly risky business. If he was cut or injured in one of these fights, he could well be forced to

---

* Harvey went on to win British and Empire titles at middleweight, light-heavyweight and heavyweight. He challenged Marcel Thil for the world middleweight title in 1932 and John Henry Lewis for the world light-heavyweight title in 1936, but lost on points on both occasions.

withdraw from the Kirby clash. And if he dropped a decision, his credibility as a title challenger could well suffer. The Professor, however, believed a busy boxer was a well-oiled one.

On 23 November at the Victoria Hall in Southend Pat boxed a three-round exhibition with one of his sparring partners, Tommy Cross. Then three days later at the Edmonton Alcazar he faced 27-year-old Johnny Murton: a Plymouth bantam who had beaten British and European bantamweight champion Harry 'Bugler' Lake, world flyweight title challenger Ernie Jarvis, and British featherweight champion Harry Corbett. In 1926 Murton sailed to America where he beat respected US bantams Lew Goldberg and Dodo Jackson. He had over 11 years' ring experience and was expected to prove a tough opponent for the Nipper. The fight was a money match at the 8 stone 6 lb bantamweight limit, which suggests that Pat was already burning off weight to get close to the 8-stone flyweight limit. He boxed rings round the seasoned Plymouthian, winning every round and even shaking the older man with a beautifully timed right in the fourth. In the fifth Murton's punches repeatedly strayed low, and after ignoring the referee's warning he was disqualified.

Pat's next assignment was at the Royal Albert Hall, where former Premierland and Wonderland 'guv'nor', Harry Jacobs (now fully recovered from bankruptcy), was promoting shows with his brother Ike. Appearing at the Albert Hall was every young fighter's dream. It signalled a step into Britain's top boxing echelon, and was often a launch pad to championship glory. Pat was booked to box George Garrard of Acton there over eight three-minute rounds on 6 December. The Acton man was a classy, experienced performer who'd been active since at least 1917. He boasted a fine record, including a stoppage win over Harry 'Bugler' Lake (two years before Lake won the British and European bantamweight titles), and a points defeat of future world bantamweight title challenger Gregorio Vidal (who then boxed as 'Young Marty'). After a two-year break from boxing, Garrard had recently re-launched his career, and since returning had remained unbeaten. His latest run of fights included wins over Dick Manning, Frank Maurier, Packey McFarland and Young Green, plus a draw with Pat's former rival, Dod Oldifield. By 1928 Garrard was probably a shade past his best, but he remained a skilful and dangerous foe all the same. If Pat felt anxious or awed looking out into the

Albert Hall's deep, spiralling crowd that evening, it in no way showed. *Boxing*'s report of the contest read:

> '[Garrard] pulled out all he knew to catch the youngster. He ducked and swayed cleverly, and with skilful "shifts" he got within range for hooks and jolts to the body, but he found himself opposed to an almost rock-like defence and was always compelled to play second fiddle to a lad who outspeeded him at every point. Daly made a great impression by his display of boxing, which was so good as to be almost flawless, and he had a good margin of points in hand at the close.'

Demonstrating that the crowd sometimes misses the hidden drama played out in a boxer's corner, Pat's enduring memory of the match was this:

> 'I came to my corner at the end of the 5th round and said to my manager, "I think he's broken my neck, the pain's terrible." "Your bloody neck is too thin – you should never have been a fighter," he replied. Just for the record I took a size 15½ collar, not bad for a 15-year-old. I forgot all about the pain [in] the next round, as I was too busy defending myself and offending my opponent for the rest of the bout and won by a fair margin of points... The purse was £12-10 shillings.'

The audience, and no doubt Garrard himself, had no idea that Pat had been hurt. 'He absolutely charmed the big crowd,' wrote the *Sunday Sportsman*. 'He hit Garrard from all angles with punishing shots, and although the Acton lad had experience on his side, he was unable to find any kind of defence for Daly's two hand hitting. I saw Garrard after the contest. His face was very badly bruised and he admitted having been well beaten. "What do you think of Daly?" I asked. Garrard said, "He is quite as good as he is made out to be and a bit better. He is one of the best youngsters I have ever seen." "How do you think he will shape against Kirby in a fortnight's time?" "He is as sure to beat him as I have this glass in my hand," replied Garrard, as he "wished him luck".'

Boxing proclaimed the Daly–Garrard bout, 'The Best of the Evening', saying that 'Garrard told us after he was dressed that Daly is the best boy he has ever met, and that is saying something, for George has met them in the real championship class.' Further up the bill Jack Kid Berg outpointed Notting Hill's Alf Mancini, and over 15 three-minute rounds

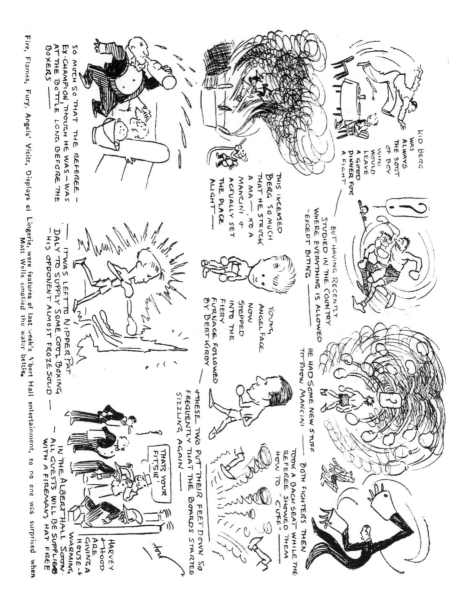

From *Boxing*, 12 Dec 1928.

Bert Kirby himself lost to the gifted Belgian champion, Petit Biquet. Kirby and Pat had no doubt sized each other up and perhaps devised a strategy for their forthcoming fight.

In the meantime, however, Pat had a West Country engagement to fulfil. A few weeks earlier a new boxing venture had started on the pier at Plymouth in Devon. Promoter Harry Jenkins was staging shows on the pier's pavilion (which held around 4,000 spectators) but had hit a serious snag in the shape of rival promoter Harry 'Bugler' Lake, who held shows of his own at the Arcadian Hall in the centre of town. Plymouth's fight-going fraternity had proven reluctant to trudge to the end of the pier in the wind and rain when a closer alternative was on offer. In order to compete, Jenkins realised he needed a big name to top his bill. And that was where Pat came in.

On the evening of Tuesday 11 December Pat was to box 15 rounds against leading local bantam Young McManus (real name Henry MacManus), a well-built 17-year-old later dubbed 'Lightning McManus' for his exceptional speed. Previewing the bout, local newspaper *The Western Independent* announced that 'another celebrity will be introduced to us... none other than Professor Newton's amazing pupil, Nipper Pat Daly... The selection of Young McManus as his opponent is to be commended, and if the latter reproduces the form, and boxes with that speed and vigour which led to his overwhelming Charlie Symonds at the Arcadian Hall recently, Nipper Pat will find that he cannot take any liberties.'

But the bout was a big step up in class for McManus and for once he was understandably unsure of his chances. He had read of the Londoner's exploits in the press but so far had not seen him in the flesh. Now in his 70s, Young McManus's son, Pat MacManus, recalls the story his father told him of the fight:

'That particular day his mate saw him down the town and said, "You've had it tonight Maccy." "Don't worry," my Dad said, "I'll be there when they're holding his hand up at the end of the fight" – meaning that Nipper Pat Daly wouldn't put him away. That evening he was sat in his dressing room getting ready for the fight, feeling dejected and a bit nervous about getting in the ring with him, when Professor Newton knocked at the door and said, "Daly would like to meet McManus". "Come in, by all means," my old man said. Daly came in and shook hands with him, then when he'd gone out my dad turned to his manager and said, "I don't care who is he, he won't go fucking 15 rounds with me tonight." You see Daly was a very slight boy and didn't look much like a fighter.'

When the action commenced, however, the Plymouth lad quickly realised he'd been badly mistaken. McManus 'did not fight in his customary manner,' wrote *Boxing*. 'There was altogether too much holding on his part. He sought to make a close-quarter fight of it, but Daly was as much his superior at in-fighting as he was at long range and consequently McManus came in for a lot of punishment without actually being knocked out... Daly's boxing was well nigh perfect, both in attack and defence.'

'My Dad went 15 rounds with him,' recalls Pat MacManus, 'and when it ended Professor Newton got up into the ring and asked him if he'd like a return. My Dad, who was a modest man, said, "No. I know my limits, and he's a far superior boxer to me." "I was quick," he told me, "but when I got out there I never seen him [Daly] from the first bell till the last one." My Dad never stopped talking about him and what a wonderful boxer he was. He was very, very complimentary about him – he thought he was brilliant. To be honest, I think it was the highlight of my father's career – even though he lost.'

Six days later, Pat arrived at Birmingham's Alexandra Theatre for the crunch match with 20-year-old Bert Kirby. The theatre had been loaned for the eighth successive year by owner Leon Salberg, with all proceeds going to Birmingham's 'Police-Aided Association for clothing destitute children'. It was a prestigious event attended by local dignitaries such as the city's Lord Mayor, Sir Percival Bower, and its Chief Constable, Sir Charles Rafter, and as Pat recalled, 'It was quite an honour to be on the bill.' The fight was over 12 three-minute rounds, officiated by the famous referee Eugene Corri, and at the agreed poundage of 8 stone 2 lb. At the weigh-in, it is believed that Pat was a pound and a half over, but the fight went ahead nonetheless. A defeat of Kirby promised to clear the way for a shot at Johnny Hill's title and seemingly endless possibilities thereafter. Pat recalled the occasion in his memoirs:

'When the match was made there was much consternation among the experts and others without expert knowledge. I was to fight the second best flyweight in Britain and all logic was against me.

We travelled to Birmingham via Paddington station, and as the train was leaving the platform a young man came running after it and just managed to scramble into our carriage. After I had helped him to get in and put his bag on the rack I looked at him and recognised Len Harvey, who was topping the same bill that I was on. After we had made ourselves comfortable, only naturally boxing became the main subject. We talked about my fight and Len said, "Don't worry Nipper, just you box as you can and I don't think you'll have any trouble with Kirby."

The story was around, boasted by Kirby, that he would KO Daly in the first round. He also said that little boys (I was two inches taller than Kirby) should not be allowed to fight a real man and that he would do him inside one round. And he nearly did too – as he rushed out of his corner in the first round and hit me with a terrific right swing. The whole theatre fell on top of me, or so it felt like it, but having had considerable experience in the ring (one hundred or so fights), I grabbed him to save myself from going down. The ref. said, "Stop boxing! Come here Daly. If you don't stop holding I will disqualify you." The few seconds he spent warning me was enough for me to recover and from the second to the twelfth round I gave Kirby a boxing lesson and a good hiding to go with it.'

'Kirby showed a tendency to lay on his opponent,' noted the *Birmingham Gazette*, 'whereas Daly was more at home in the open and landed with smart double lefts. Twice Kirby was told not to hold with his right. He was, however, obviously at a loss to guard against his opponent's straight lefts... Kirby was not in love with his task, for Daly was faster both on his feet and with his gloves... He fought on gamely, but had to be repeatedly told to refrain from holding with his right. This 15-year-old Londoner surprised both Kirby and the crowd, and displayed ringcraft, speed and a rare hitting power.'

'Nipper Pat Daly, who is not yet sixteen years old, flung a bomb into British boxing circles by easily outpointing Bert Kirby at Birmingham,' wrote boxing manager and journalist Charlie Rose in his *Daily Express* column. 'It is almost unbelievable that Kirby, whom we saw box so splendidly against Petit Biquet at the last Albert Hall show, has been beaten by a youngster of such slender years and experience.'

'It was assumed that Kirby would have a soft job on hand in his 15-year-old opponent,' reported *Boxing*, 'but the "old Professor's" pupil upset all the odds and left Birmingham rubbing its eyes in wonder... The "Nipper" won practically every round and practically walked home by the length of the whole journey from London to the Midlands... Owen Moran [who years earlier had held a version of the world bantamweight crown, beaten Battling Nelson and drawn with Abe Attell and Jim Driscoll] saw "the Nipper" in action at Birmingham, and well – you ought to hear the little marvel's eulogies.'

'When the verdict was announced it was well received,' recalled Pat, 'and the first to congratulate me was Len Harvey, who two bouts previously had KO'd his opponent in the first round. On catching the train for our return to London I told the Prof that I was tired and suggested that I have a sleeping berth, as I was fighting in London on Wednesday and would miss sleep that day Tuesday (the train left at 1 am and arrived in London at 4 am). He refused saying that "Money don't grow on trees. Anyway, it's only a short journey, we'll be home in no time".'

The Wednesday bout Pat refers to does not appear on his traceable record, but it's quite possible, given the volume and regularity of his London fights, that *Boxing*'s reporters simply weren't at the show. The front page of the newspaper's Christmas Eve edition was filled with praise for the rising star:

'He has still nearly two months to go before he attains his 16th birthday. Yet he has shown that he is not so very far away from World Championship class... We saw him before he even appeared in public and we then broadcast the news that a world beater had entered the game.'

Everything seemed on track for a British-title showdown with the elusive Johnny Hill. 'I'd done everything asked of me,' Pat recalled, 'why shouldn't I consider myself good enough to have a go at the title?' There was, however, one rather serious and uncontrollable hitch. 'He could not make the fly-weight or rather should not be permitted to make the attempt,' considered *Boxing*. 'Otherwise matched at catch-weights with Johnny Hill, we venture to believe that there are a few Midlands sportsmen who would provide any side-stakes in reason for Nipper Pat Daly.' The *Sunday Sportsman* noted that of late he had been fighting at around 8 stone 3 lb, and even at this weight, 'he carries no surplus. Daly is built along the same lines as Jimmy Wilde. He is all arms and legs, with a body like a matchstick. No one would think he was a fighter to see him stripped; indeed, many would feel sorry for him, and suggest the poor lad should be given some nourishing food. But to see Pat in action is another matter... Daly can be very little, if any, behind Johnny Hill.'

It seems that Pat was struggling to stay even three pounds above flyweight, so to boil down beneath eight stone would be an unhealthy and arduous task. Nevertheless, Pat and the Professor were willing to try, so long as Johnny Hill's people were also agreeable. They offered Pat an overweight non-championship match, but would not permit Hill to put his title at stake. Realising it was his final chance to contest the eight-stone crown and believing that he deserved a proper title fight, Pat declined their offer.

Bert Kirby, the man he comprehensively beat, got his own crack at the title 10 months later. Tragically, in the meantime, Johnny Hill had died of pneumonia, leaving Kirby and Manchester's Jackie Brown to contest the vacant crown. A third-round clash of heads left Kirby groggy, and Brown quickly capitalised by landing a right-hand follow-up, which stretched the Brum for the full count. Kirby was outraged and claimed that Brown had only won because of an illegal head-butt. In a rematch five months later he got his revenge by knocking out Brown in the very same round, and was thus crowned British flyweight champion himself. Pat, by then, was boxing up at lightweight.

13

Bantamweight Contender

'Has Britain another Jimmy Wilde in the making? A fighting phenomenon has been produced from the stable of that old boxing teacher, Professor Newton, in the person of a fifteen-year-old Marylebone boy who fights under the appropriate name of Nipper Pat Daly... Whether such a number of fights, while yet immature, will impair his career in later years is open to question... I hope that, in view of the wonderful talent and spirit the lad has shown, he will not be called upon to shoulder too many big handicaps before he grows into manhood.'

All Sports Weekly, 1 December 1928

The 60-mile River Wear slices through the heart of Sunderland and streams out into the North Sea. A short distance from its Wearside banks, for just over a decade, once stood the North East's finest palace of punch. A place where in the late '20s Wearsiders flocked in their droves to watch weekly boxing shows. The prevalence of Sunderland boxing – like its coal, engineering and shipbuilding industries – has long since faded, but the sheer number of men who once boxed there bears testament to the popularity the sport then enjoyed. Purpose-built just after the First World War, the 3,000-seater, dome-roofed Holmeside Stadium was the brainchild of brothers George and Alfred Black, who owned a lucrative chain of North East cinemas. With running water tapped to boxers' corners (reputably the first venue in the world to have this), a fully equipped gym and a shower room, by '20s standards it was cutting-edge. Though fundamentally a venue for the masses, all seconds were required to wear a collar and tie and unruly spectators were quickly shown the door. In an era characterised by shabby, makeshift venues, Sunderland's ultramodern Stadium possessed a touch of class.

Three days before Christmas in 1928 (and five days on from beating Kirby), Pat had one last job. Andy Newton had booked him to box at Sunderland's Stadium in the first of five appearances. The match had been arranged with the venue's matchmaker Fred Charlton, who was also the house referee. In addition, he was a freelance fight reporter and covered many of the North East's shows for *Boxing*, sometimes refereeing and writing about the same fight. Writing for the *Sunderland Echo* in 1975, he remembered Pat's five Sunderland appearances fondly:

'Nipper Pat Daly was the most talented teenage prizefighter I ever saw. He was baby faced, which accentuated his precocity. He was a well-built youngster, tall for his weight, with an unusually long reach. He boarded at Tom Richwood's home near Garrison Field in Sunderland. Few watching young Pat playing handball with young Tom Richwood in their Kingsley Street backyard could have visualised in him the skill and strength to acquire the name the "Wonder Boy".'

In his Saturday night Stadium debut Pat faced Sheffield's Tiny Smith (real name Elijah Smith), a tough but limited 26-year-old who had boxed since 1922. Smith actually lost more than he won, but nevertheless, on his day he was good enough to snatch draws from the likes of Kid Socks, Ernie Jarvis, Frankie Ash and flyweight kingpin Johnny Hill. In 1922 he had even beaten future British feather and lightweight champion Johnny Cuthbert, though at the time, it should be noted, both were raw novices.

To overcome Pat's superior height and reach, Smith tried his utmost to fight him in close. His strategy, it seems, was to wear the boy down with a prolonged body assault. When he got close, however, his blows were blocked by gloves and arms, and skilfully countered by well-timed uppercuts. Putting some distance between himself and the Sheffielder, Pat snapped his head back with a torrent of straight lefts. In the second Smith was twice warned for holding and in the third for 'unfair use of his head'. A cut left eye threatened to finish him in the tenth, but his gameness kept him in it and he lasted the distance. 'Daly was superior to his opponent all round, and won comfortably on points,' reported *Boxing*.

The arrival of 1929 brought a landmark restructure to the British Boxing Board of Control (BBB of C). The Board had actually existed since 1918, but being comprised chiefly of NSC members, many within the sport perceived it merely as an extension of the then ailing Club. The Board, therefore, had struggled for credibility, and had failed to assert any real authority over the sport. But on the insistence of the sport's figurehead, Lord Lonsdale, that was about to change. A radical restructure was now underway and the Board would soon begin to assume control. Initially, however, few gave the reformed Board any more credence than its predecessor, and *Boxing* mockingly called it the 'Board of Alleged Control'. But pretty soon it was patently clear that the new BBB of C was there to stay.

However, its proposal for a new set of rules and the introduction of paid-for licences for boxers, promoters and officials at first provoked scepticism if not outright hostility. The men who made a living from the sport had done so for decades without such a system. One Welsh *Boxing* correspondent claimed that 'in their eagerness to establish themselves, the "Contollers" are slowly but surely killing the sport in these parts. Their insistence on foisting their selected referees on West Wales promoters has created an unpleasant feeling among the fans.' The Board's retraction of the licence of a leading Welsh official without clear explanation prompted John Murray to comment, 'We have here a ready-made sample of the erratic tyranny we may expect should our conglomerated Board of Control ever be permitted to get into stride.'

The BBB of C's new proposals included setting the minimum age for a boxing licence to 17 and, in line with America, restricting boxers aged under 21 to contests of no more than six rounds, with British title fights reserved for those aged 21 and over. In the hope of reaching a compromise, a group of leading managers formed their own federation and drafted a list of requested amendments to the Board's proposed rules. Much to the chagrin of *Boxing*, however, they raised no objection to the proposed age restrictions:

> 'Nipper Pat will not reach his 16th birthday until the 17th of next month. This fact is well known. The managers cannot have forgotten his existence, since he has beaten so many of their own boxers, including several who are considered eligible to compete for championship titles... Is the Nipper to be debarred from public contests for over a year? Is he to be kept down to six round preliminaries for the next five years? The veteran Professor has produced the finest piece of fighting material this country has possessed since the days of Jim Driscoll. Are we to be denied the advantages and the prestige he would bestow on us merely because the managers have

been forgetful or selfish, that is to say, timorous where their own colts are concerned? We address these queries to the British boxing public.'
Boxing, 23 January 1929

The rules regarding the age of licence-holders and limiting those under 21 to six-round bouts never reached fruition, but to the dismay of Pat and the Professor, an age limit of 21 for British-title contestants (though later lifted) was brought into force. Pat's dream of becoming British champion while still in his mid-teens was instantly dashed. But the Board was still in its infancy and its rules were hardly set in stone, so he still held a hope that if he breezed through Britain's bantamweights with the same ease he had her flyweights, perhaps the 'controllers' could yet change their ruling and allow him to box for the title. It was a faint hope but it helped to raise his spirits.

On 2 January Pat made a return visit to Germany where the sporting public, after seeing him outbox their flyweight champion three months earlier, were keen to watch him again. Five days after landing he faced Willi Metzner (a future German champion at fly and bantamweight) at Rheinlandhalle in Cologne. A programme for the event called Pat 'Der Wunderknabe', meaning 'The Wonderboy'. The bout was scheduled for just six rounds and five-ounce gloves – rather than the British standard six-ounce – were to be used. To the disappointment of everyone, though, the fight ended early with Metzner ruled out for fouling in the second.

Back in England, two days later, Pat tackled 22-year-old Arthur Boddington of Wellingborough over 10 three-minute rounds at the NSC. Boddington began his career in 1923 and initially boxed in Northamptonshire to earn a degree of local fame. But to gain recognition on a national scale and to earn better money, Boddington quickly realised he must move his matches to London. He had amassed a decent record by the time he met Pat, including a well-earned points win over the legendary Nel Tarleton. Pat, however, fared better than Tarleton, and according to *Boxing*, 'had little difficulty in winning cleverly on points.' Later Boddington fought reigning world champions Frankie Genaro and Panama Al Brown, although both stopped him inside the distance.

Jimmy Rowbotham of Birmingham was next to enter the roped square with the Marylebone Nipper. They met five days after Pat's bout with Boddington, at the Edmonton Alcazar over 15 rounds. Jimmy, who was four years older than Pat, was an elder brother of Charlie Rowbotham, who Pat had whipped at Premierland in 1927. So when the chance arose to fight Pat himself, Jimmy did not hesitate, for family pride was at stake. Boxing for Aston ABC, he had been Midlands amateur bantamweight champion, and since turning pro in 1927, had lost only two of 26 bouts. He had already beaten decent men such as Sid Raiteri, Billy Cain, Johnny Quill, Jim Haddon and Jimmy Thornton, and was probably the best bantamweight in the Midlands.

Both tall and lean, Pat and Rowbotham were physically well matched, which meant the first few rounds became a battle of left leads. In the first couple, despite some lively exchanges, there was little to choose between them; but Pat gradually took over and by the halfway stage was bossing the fight. It seems the Brum expended much of his energy in those early exchanges, for as the fight wore on he repeatedly held, causing the referee to enter the ring in the thirteenth to prise him off of Pat. 'Never have we seen Daly so persistently aggressive,' wrote *Boxing*, 'and his tactics well paid, for he was a long way ahead on points at the close.'

Pat returned to Sunderland for his next fight, where he was matched against hot North East bantamweight prospect, 19-year-old Billy Smith. Third eldest of eight, Smith learnt the game from his father, Paddy, who before the war had fought regularly at The Star Music Hall in Sunderland's Sans Street. Keen for his sons to continue the family tradition, Paddy rigged up a makeshift gym in the attic of their High Street East home and trained Billy and his other sons in the evening and at weekends. Billy absorbed his father's lessons with zeal and, having learnt all that Paddy could teach him, continued to train under his own steam, recruiting his brothers and other locals as sparring partners. All the Smith boys boxed competitively at some level, and Billy's younger brother Tom (who was said to be less talented than Billy) in the '30s won the Northern Area featherweight title and fought Nel Tarleton for the British championship. Billy boxed pro from the age of 15, and by the time he met Pat had lost only six of 50 or more ring encounters. He was never once beaten inside the distance and, apart from a slip in a 1927 fight with Aberdeen's Sandy McEwan, was never floored either.

The clash between Pat and Smith was key to both boxers. It would be Pat's stiffest test yet as a bantamweight, and also a chance to further his claim as a British-title contender. For Smith, there was the chance to earn national recognition by defeating one of the game's rising stars. In recognition of the bout's significance, two judges – local businessman John Homes and leading Manchester middleweight Len Johnson – were appointed to give verdicts alongside referee Fred Charlton. Johnson, who had beaten top American Sunny Jim Williams four nights earlier, was Britain's uncrowned middleweight king. There was a widespread belief that he would easily capture the British title, if only he were allowed to fight for it. While Pat was barred from challenging for a title due to his age, Len was barred simply because his father was black. British boxing's 'colour bar', which wasn't lifted until Dick Turpin became a champion in 1948, meant that black or mixed-race fighters could not contest British titles. Johnson beat Len Harvey two years before Harvey became British middleweight champion. Harvey reversed the decision in a rematch five years later, but by then the Mancunian was well past his prime. Pat, who had seen both men in action, maintained that Johnson was the better fighter.

On the evening of Saturday 26 January hundreds of people were turned away from the Holmeside Stadium, as the venue was crammed to capacity. The 15-round fight between Pat and Smith was fought at a blistering pace and Pat, uncharacteristically, boxed on the defensive early on. Smith proved an extremely clever and ring-wise opponent and pulled out all he knew against the Londoner. Initially he made Pat's body his target, but then he switched to long range and aimed swift shots at his opponent's head. Pat blocked most of these and generally landed more than he took, but for the most part he contented himself to countering. From the tenth round, however, having 'taken Smith's measure' (*Boxing*), he elected to take the fight to the Wearsider and was the aggressor throughout the last five. 'Daly boxed with strength and confidence to the conclusion of the bout,' wrote *Boxing*, 'and won well on points.'

Two days after the fight, Smith came down with appendicitis. The subsequent operation kept him out of the ring for six months, but when he returned he stayed unbeaten for almost two years. He twice beat his North East rival Benny Sharkey, a man who went on to defeat five British champions, plus a reigning world bantamweight champion in Baltazar Sangchili. In October 1930 Smith also beat former British bantamweight champion Jim Higgins (who had won a Lonsdale belt outright). But unfortunately the Wearsider did not reach his full potential. Ongoing stomach trouble forced him to quit the sport in November 1931, when he was aged only 22. Had this not been the case, given the chance Billy Smith may just have made a champion.

The Smith win capped off a rather busy month for Pat – he had fought four times in as many weeks. 'Can young boxers be overworked? Professor Newton would seem to believe they cannot,' quipped *Boxing*. 'Catch them young and work them hard, would appear to be the Professor's motto.' Pat was supposed to box on the 7 and 10 February (at the Albert Hall and Premierland respectively), but both fights fell through, which gave him a rare three-week break in his schedule. Work at the gym, however, continued apace. And an extract from Pat's memoirs, entitled '1 week of my fighting life', reveals just how intense his regime was:

'I rose at 7am. Sometimes I had breakfast but if I was too heavy I went without. By too heavy I mean [not] within 4 lb of the next weigh-in. I used to go to the gym on a Sunday after I had been to Mass, and used to train for my next fight, which was usually that week, as I very seldom had a complete week off. I would probably start with five or 10 mins on the punch bag, have about 15 minutes with a team of four boxers throwing [a medicine ball] around the ring – one [boxer] in each corner. Then after that we would put the gloves on and I would take on one fighter from each corner, about three minutes each one. This would last for half an hour, sometimes longer, with about five minutes' rest. Then we'd start again for another half hour. This used to go on every day: Monday twice, Tuesday twice, Wednesday three times, Thursday twice, Friday three times, Saturday once, Sunday once.'

The Professor considered sparring by far the best activity for developing the skill and stamina needed for boxing. He did not place much faith in activities such as roadwork, shadow boxing and skipping, so sparring formed the core of Pat's gym work. Headguards and gumshields were never worn. Both contraptions were slow to catch on, and many British boxers – Pat included – did not even wear gumshields in actual fights.

***

On opening their breakfast newspapers on 15 February 1929, the British public were met by astonishing headlines from across the Atlantic. In an event later remembered as the 'St. Valentine's Day Massacre', seven American gangsters had been slain in cold blood on the orders of gangland boss Al Capone. The massacre and Capone himself were no doubt much discussed by gatherings of people across the world during the days and weeks that followed. And the large crowd that assembled to watch a boxing show at the Palais de Danse Athletic Club in West Bromwich three days after the event was probably no exception.

They were there to watch Pat, who was fighting a rematch with Jimmy Rowbotham, who since their first fight a month before had captured the Midlands bantamweight title, which made him worthy of a return in the eyes of the West Bromwich fans. But the Midlander was beaten even more soundly than in their first fight. 'From the first stage to last,' said *Boxing*, Pat 'always held the mastery, sailing home at the close a clever and comfortable points winner.' The Marylebone youth had double cause to celebrate that Sunday afternoon, for it was also the occasion of his sixteenth birthday. First to congratulate him was his stable-mate Arthur Norton, who on the same bill had outboxed Charlie Rowbotham over 10, setting the score at two to nothing for the Marylebone Road stable. Pat and Arthur boxed on the same bill many times, were regular sparring partners and stayed lifelong friends. Norton, who was nearly four years older than Pat, was perhaps then a little more street-wise, and on at least one occasion saved his friend from a rash altercation. One day, after the pair had walked past an Army barracks, a group of soldiers yelled derisive remarks about the large hat Pat was wearing. Incensed, the Nipper turned on his heels and started back towards the barracks, determined to teach the men a lesson. Sensing trouble, Arthur shot after his pal, grabbed him by the collar and tried his best to talk him round. 'It's not worth it, Pat. They don't know who you are,' he remonstrated. 'Why don't you let it go?' Luckily Pat took his friend's advice, no doubt realising that the potential legal trouble (if not the physical) of a brawl with a group of soldiers was something best avoided.*

It had been over three months since Pat last boxed at Premierland, and East End fans were itching to see their favourite west Londoner back

---

* In later years Arthur Norton and his wife often visited Pat and his family. Arthur retired to the Isle of Wight, where he died in 1990, aged 81. Pat's youngest son Terry remembers him as 'a mild-mannered man who you wouldn't have picked out as a former pro boxer'. He boxed professionally from 1927 until 1934 and had over 60 contests.

in a Whitechapel ring. A week after his return with Rowbotham, Pat was back at the East End fistic Mecca to take on Billy Boulger of Canning Town, the lad he had suffered a disputed points defeat to in a six-rounder back in 1925. Boulger, it will be remembered, was managed by Joe Morris to whose colt Dod Oldfield Pat had suffered his only other points loss in a verdict the press judged a travesty of refereeing. Since their first meeting four years earlier Boulger, like Pat, had grown in status. He had lost only eight of 45 recorded fights and had beaten such good men as Young Bill Lewis of Bethnal Green, Lew Pinkus of Mile End, Lud Abella, and had drawn with Bert Kirby and Kid Nicholson of Leeds. Foremost among his victories was a points win over the brilliant future British bantamweight champion Dick Corbett. Boulger had been at bantam longer than Pat and was already one of the division's top prospects. The match gave Pat a chance not only to send a message to Britain's other bantamweights, but to settle the score with Boulger, which must have been gratifying.

Boulger had his sparring partner Teddy Baldock in his corner, but no amount of advice from the 'Pride of Poplar' would help him this particular day. 'Daly was always on top, and scoring freely with both hands,' wrote *Boxing*. 'Despite a last fierce rally by Boulger, Daly was quite easily a points winner.'

It was only Pat's second month as an 8 stone 6 lb boxer, yet already he had beaten three of the country's best bantamweights. The two Newtons (father and son) were wasting no time finding him the matches that mattered. After the Boulger fight *Boxing* proclaimed Pat 'one of the best bantams in the country, if he is not actually the best.' In a division that boasted such talents as Teddy Baldock, Alf 'Kid' Pattenden, Dick Corbett and Nel Tarleton – not to mention a host of gifted prospects waiting in the wings – this was high praise indeed. 'Will the Board of Control adhere to the embargo which will keep Daly out of championship competition for another five years?' the trade paper pondered.

With a five-day break following the Boulger fight, Pat travelled to the Connaught Drill Hall at Portsmouth for a match on a special show staged in aid of the Old Contemptibles Association. A Royal Artillery band performed during the evening, and the Lord Mayor of Portsmouth (Councillor J. E. Smith), the Lord Lieutenant of Hampshire (Major-

General J. E. B. Seely) and Lord Lonsdale himself were in attendance. Pat's original opponent, Billy Cain of Birmingham, was unable to box because of doctor's orders, so he took on Archie Woodbine of Birmingham instead.

Woodbine, whose real name was Percy Oswin, was a far from typical pre-war pro boxer. He was a well-educated lad who had attended Ryland, an experimental boarding school specialising in art, music, mathematics and sport. Oswin had proven an able painter and pianist but, much to the chagrin of his family, boxing was his true passion and the thing at which he most excelled. He had boxed as an amateur while at the school and during school holidays snuck away to the Midland booths on which he boxed using aliases such as 'The Toff', 'Master Percival', 'Little Lord Percival' and other diminutives of Frances Hodgson Burnett's fictional character, 'Little Lord Fauntleroy'. The 'barker' dressed him in a sailor-suit collar and hat, and he was given a centre parting and obliged to adopt a matching lisp. His mother tried everything in her power to stop him boxing and eventually pulled him out of school. But he loved the thrill of a fight and secretly turned pro using the nom de guerre Archie Woodbine ('Archie' being First World War slang for anti-aircraft fire and 'Woodbine' a brand of fashionable cigarettes). Woodbine was the same age as Pat and went on to amass a traceable pro record of 85 wins, 44 losses and 20 draws, but at the time the pair met he was a little inexperienced. 'Daly, a wonderful lad, was far too good for his adversary,' wrote the Portsmouth *Evening News*. The Birmingham lad was floored several times, before retiring with a cut eye (thought to be caused by a clash of heads) in the fifth. His son, Johnathan Oswin, well remembers his father's recollections of Pat:

> 'He told me that "the Nipper" was a true sportsman and, due to the circumstances, took no pleasure in his win. He even apologised to my dad for the way it turned out; but dad acknowledged that he was getting the worse of the fight anyway and they parted friends with great respect for each other. My dad didn't mix with other boxers much, partly because he was fighting under an assumed name and partly because he didn't much care for many of his opponents. However, he genuinely liked Nipper and thought he was "an intelligent, considered boxer and a natural gentleman". I believe they travelled together part of the journey back home... Dad always pointed out Nipper's name to

me whenever he came across any mention of him, often in the *Black Country Bugle* boxing pages, and always with a genuine fondness.'

Eight days after the Woodbine fight, Pat returned to Sunderland's Holmeside Stadium to take on Salford's Tommy Brown over 15 rounds. The Salford lad had given Pat an extremely hard fight when they met the previous year in Blackburn and was expected to do so again. Early on the Marylebone lad boxed with caution, cleverly countering Brown and shooting out straight lefts as the northerner came to him. The Salford lad proved very game and attacked fiercely, giving Pat no rest for the first four rounds. But as the contest wore on, so Pat turned on the pressure, and in the twelfth he tore into Brown with a dynamite flurry of blows. The Salford lad dropped to the canvas, apparently out cold. But the bell came to his rescue and he was picked up and carried to his corner, where his seconds worked feverishly to bring him round. He could not meet the call for the thirteenth, however, so Pat was declared the winner.

Already he had stamped an authoritative mark on his new weight division and given the BBB of C considerable food for thought. Up next, however, was Pat's toughest test to date; a match that could either propel or derail his title ambitions. He was tackling the top-class 21-year-old champion of Belgium, the formidable Petit Biquet.

14

The Albert Hall Marvel

'I have a big opinion of 16-year-old Nipper Pat Daly. This clever youngster should be a future champion, if he stands the racket of big contests.'

Jimmy Wilde (former world flyweight champion),
The News of the World, 24 March 1929

Petit Biquet of Liège (real name Nicolas Biquet) had to fight from an early age simply to survive. Eldest of three boys, his father had died while Biquet was still a youngster, which instantly made him the breadwinner of the family. Being so young and small, he had struggled to find ordinary work, so instead turned to boxing to help pay the bills.

In February 1927 he won the Belgian flyweight title from former European champ Michel Montreuil, and a month later at the Albert Hall tackled Johnny Hill, who shortly afterwards became British flyweight champion. According to *Boxing*, Hill was outfought and out-generalled and then knocked out by a devastating eleventh-round body blow. The referee, however, saw the finish differently, and after dithering, tardily disqualified Biquet, saying that the finishing blow was low (much of the audience and many journalists disagreed). Hill managed to outpoint Biquet in a return match seven months later, but a rough Channel crossing had weakened the Belgian and may explain his poor showing.

Biquet beat top British flyweights such as Millwall's Ernie Jarvis, Aldgate's Phil Lolosky, Birmingham's Billy James, and of course Birmingham's Bert Kirby (twice). He also campaigned successfully in America, beating world bantamweight title challenger Johnny Erickson, and in Europe boxed draws with future world flyweight champion Emile Pladner, and Victor Ferrand, who in his own world-title bid drew with Frankie Genaro. In 1928 Biquet was ranked number 11 in the world in *The Ring* magazine's annual flyweight ratings, but by the time he faced Pat a year later he had moved up to bantamweight.

He had already captured the Belgian bantamweight title, and in his last fight, 11 days before he met Pat, had challenged the Italian Domenico Bernasconi for the European crown. The decision went to Bernasconi, but the bout had been fought in the Italian's home city of Milan. Undeterred, Biquet won the European crown himself in 1932. He successfully defended it six times, lost it in 1935, but then reclaimed it two years later. Recalling his two closely contested 1931 matches with Biquet, British bantamweight champion Johnny King, himself a first-rate boxer, candidly wrote:

> 'It was extremely difficult to pierce his excellent guard, while his eager counter-punching made my rights go astray. I would shoot a left at his face, over would come his right and he'd be banging in a left before I knew where I was. I also found he knew more about infighting… At the end of an interesting fifteen-rounder, the referee decided in my favour. It must have been a very close margin of points because a large number of spectators disagreed with the verdict… [The return fight] was another near thing, but again the referee decided in my favour. I learned a lot from those two contests with Petit Biquet…' *Boxing News*, 30 December 1953

In the mid-1930s the middle finger of one of Biquet's hands had to be amputated because of a sceptic cut, which occurred while opening a tin at the general store he owned in Liège. He feared his career was over, but when he got back in the ring he found, despite the handicap, that his knowledge and skill were still too much for most of Europe's best bantams. Remarkably, he continued to defend his European crown and boxed on for several years. That, of course, was all in the future. A contest with Pat lay in the present.

'From the moment I was matched with Petit Biquet,' Pat recalled, 'I realised that the fight might mean just everything in my climb to the top.' The newspapers were largely noncommittal in their forecasts. 'Petit Biquet will tell the British public the best and the worst about the Nipper,' wrote *The Sporting Life*; while *Boxing* feared that Pat's extraordinary run of success might have fooled him into thinking he was invincible. 'Should he enter the ring in any such frame of mind,' the paper admonished, 'he is liable to be disillusioned. Biquet packs a punch, and is one of the last recover.' Nevertheless, Pat also had backing of the highest order. Jimmy Wilde, in his column for *The News of The World*, was prepared to stick his neck out by saying, 'Daly is an exceptional youngster... In naming Daly as the probable winner, I am but re-echoing the opinion of many good judges.' Bombardier Billy Wells, the popular former British heavyweight champion who wrote for *The Topical Times*, was in agreement and added, 'The chief interest in this fight to me is that Daly's progress is worth watching at each stage.'

★★★

On the day of the fight the rain had started early. Pools of water dotted the pavement, the gutters overflowed. Rain trickled down off the majestic domed glass roof of the Royal Albert Hall, but below it thousands of men wrapped in soggy hats, Macs and mittens filed in through the entrance unperturbed. There was a general air of excitement among the gathering, but also a mood of sadness for some.

Harry Jacobs, the man who had arranged the star-studded bill, had not lived long enough to see it. The founder of Premierland, who at venues such as Olympia and the Royal Albert Hall had brought boxing promotion to new heights, had been seriously ill for some time. Against doctors' orders, on 31 January he had attended his last show just six days before he died. His astute matchmaking and bullish approach to business made him an unforgettable if not universally liked figure in the boxing world. His career – which had certainly had its low points – had ended in a blaze of glory with a regular and highly successful tenure at the Royal Albert Hall. Upon his passing, his brothers, Ike and Barney, had vowed to put on shows there for the dates Harry had already booked.

The gallery, orchestra stalls, balcony and ringside were all packed that evening in anticipation of a thrilling bill of fare. In an historic move, the top-line match between Johnny Hill and Ernie Jarvis was the first British title fight to be sanctioned by the BBB of C, and a Board official, Mr J. H. Lambert, had attended the weigh-in at *The Sporting Life* office the previous afternoon. (This, in itself, was unusual, as weigh-ins were generally held on the same day as the show.) Pat had registered 8 stone 6 lb exactly at the weigh-in, which suggests that he was already in danger of outgrowing the weight.

Pat's fight over 10 three-minute rounds was the second of the evening. As he strode through the great hall towards the ring, a volley of cheers shot up all around him. Cries of 'G' luck, Nipper' and 'Don't let the old country down' were loudly bellowed from the gallery.

When he had sat and watched Petit Biquet outbox Bert Kirby on the night that he had beaten George Garrard, Pat had thought the Belgian's nickname of 'Angel Face' wholly appropriate, for from a distance he resembled a miniature matinee idol. When they stood face-to-face, however, he noticed that Biquet had taken some pretty big whacks. The trademark cauliflower ear and flattened nose were well in evidence, but more striking than these was a large patch of scar tissue just above his left eye. Ironically, this had not been attained in the ring, but was the result of a fall from a horse during a boxers' cross-country race in Belgium, when he caught his head on a stone.

As the bell clanged for the start of round one, Biquet bustled forwards throwing shots with all his might. Pat quickly realised that the Belgian was the strongest man he had ever faced and wisely kept him on the end of a stiff straight left. He blocked most of Biquet's blows with his arms and elbows, but one right did land flush and shook Pat up. As the Belgian rushed in to finish him, Pat steadied his assailant with a right of his own, which raised a large lump above Biquet's eye. In the latter half of the fight, Pat sensed that his opponent was growing weaker and for the last few rounds he took the fight to him. 'There was not a phase of the game of boxing at which Daly was not superior,' noted *The Daily Chronicle*. When Pat chose to fight Biquet in close, the audience shouted warnings for him to get away. But when they realised that he was beating Biquet at Biquet's own game (infighting), they cheered for him to carry on. Pat had the faster hands, the better timing and pre-empted the Belgian's fight-plan throughout. 'Biquet did not know what to do,' remarked *The Daily Chronicle*. 'Whenever the gallant little Belgian advanced with a rush, he was met with a straight left. If he rushed and led with the left at the same time, his left was avoided, and he found himself the recipient of a thudding right to the front of his face.'

'During the eighth round, and the fight was going in my favour,' recalled Pat, 'Biquet threw three consecutive swings: left hook, right hook, followed by another left hook and I ducked the three punches. When a boxer is in the ring and the fight is on he goes deaf to all the crowd's cheering, booing or any remarks made outside the ring, but even I as one of the contestants heard and appreciated this applause.'

When the last gong sounded the referee, Matt Wells,* walked straight up to Pat and raised his arm. Above them the rain continued to batter the dome glass roof, but beneath it the fans were cheering loud enough to lift it clear off. Sportingly, Biquet smiled, patted his opponent's back and told him what a great fight he had given him. Pat returned the compliment, gestured towards the Belgian, who received a rare loser's roar from the crowd. To the boom of the Albert Hall organ and a prolonged storm of applause, Pat returned to his dressing room a hero. 'We know what Biquet has done to some of our best,' wrote *The Daily Chronicle*, 'and yet none of them did with Biquet what this 16-year-old boy did last night.' On a bill featuring such stars as Johnny Hill, Ernie Jarvis, Teddy Baldock and Fred Webster, against the odds Pat had outshone them all. 'It seemed to me that the world was at my feet,' he later recalled. 'With all the tough breaks in big boxing there are moments like that at the Albert Hall which more than make up for the heartbreaks.'

In a piece headed 'Pat Daly, a Boxer of the Future', *All Sports Weekly* commented, 'Daly – who looked what he is, a mere boy – boxed and fought with a cleverness that would have done credit to a fighter who knew all the tricks of the trade. He took a lot of vicious punches, most of them to the body, but so far as I could see, he did not blink an eyelash… I have marked him down as a boxer of the future. Newton does find them! He will make a champion of Daly if he does not ask the boy to attempt too much.' This last sentiment was echoed by Trevor C. Wignall of *The Daily Express*, who pondered, 'Here is a youngster with the most palpable fighting spirit; but is it wise to work him as he is being worked?'

'The Prof had several letters from Belgium with good purse offers for me to have a return with Biquet over six rounds,' recalled Pat, 'but he turned them all down despite the fact that the money was good for a six-round fight. It had to be six rounds or less as the IBU would not give permission for a longer fight, as I was 16 years old. I thought then that the IBU was doing its job as it should be done by "taking care of young

---

* Four times ABA lightweight champion (1904-1907), British and European lightweight champion (1911-1912), and British and world welterweight champion (1914-1915).

fighters" and saving them from being burned out too quickly.* Anyway, we did not go to Belgium as the Prof did not fancy the journey. He did not say so, but that was the reason. Also he refused several good money jobs as they were abroad or a long train ride away. I was acting as his secretary so I knew all his business, also I knew the man very well.'

This half-uttered criticism of his handling suggests that Pat was aware of the dangers of fighting so often and at the level he was. He may well have felt that he was being overworked – he need only have looked in the newspapers to get that impression – but no doubt his supreme self-belief combined with a reluctance to disappoint others (his mentor, his parents and his growing army of fans) helped to purge such thoughts from his mind. In spite of the demands made on his immature physique, boxing was still the love of Pat's young life. To be paid so well and receive widespread adoration for doing something that he loved, he counted himself very lucky.

As Pat's popularity grew steadily in London, his rise to fame was ardently followed elsewhere. In Wales, where Pat was born and had lived his early years, there was particular interest when he started regularly making the sporting headlines. His Welsh relatives were all extremely proud of his achievements and his maternal grandfather, Will Evans, was treated like a minor celebrity in his home village of Birchgrove. The morning after each of Pat's contests the locals rushed to the post office, eager to get their hands on that day's newspapers to discover how their boy had done. Word would then spread rapidly round the village that, 'Nipper's done it again!' In May 1929 the *South Wales Echo* ran a feature on Pat and, with the approval of Andy Newton, issued a challenge to the reigning Welsh bantamweight champion, Dan Dando of Merthyr, to defend his title against the London-based Nipper. 'Although Daly would receive a big welcome in Wales,' noted the paper's reporter, 'I do not think there is a promoter prepared to offer a suitable inducement, for Daly is at present drawing big money.'

Just over two weeks after his 8 stone 6 lb battle with Biquet, Pat faced Nottingham's Arthur Adkins up at 8 stone 10 lb at the Victoria Baths, with a 2 lb leeway on the weight to help Adkins who was a full-blown

---

* Formed in Paris in 1911, the International Boxing Union (IBU) was an attempt to create a unified international governing body for professional boxing. It also oversaw European title fights. The European Boxing Union (EBU) replaced the IBU in 1946.

featherweight. Dubbed 'The Fighting Butcher' on account of his day job, the Nottingham man had boxed since 1923 and lost just two of 39 recorded fights. On the afternoon of the match the 'Butcher' weighed in just inside 8 stone 12 lb, while Pat scaled just below 8 stone 11 lb. Alarmingly, he had piled on nearly 5 lb in a fortnight and was now nearer featherweight than bantam. But even with the added weight, a photo of the pair stripped shows a gaunt, stick-like Pat stood next to the shorter, thickset Adkins. From appearances it seems that the youngster was far from comfortable, even at 8 stone 11 lb. *Boxing* wrote that Adkins put up 'one of the best fights of his career [but] could neither keep out the way of the Nipper's varied assortment of punches, nor was he often able to penetrate Daly's singularly sound defence.' In the ninth, and again in the twelfth, Adkins dropped to his knees through sheer exhaustion to gain a vital eight-second breather. 'The London Jimmy Wilde never gave his man a moment's rest,' wrote *The Nottingham Guardian*, 'and punched with machine-like precision throughout.' At the end of 15 fast-paced rounds Pat was a clear winner.

For his next match, fixed for 8 stone 8 lb at the Connaught Drill Hall in Portsmouth, the Londoner would need to lose three pounds in just four days. He was facing an 18-year-old Irish lad called Patrick McFarland, who boxed under the alias Packey McFarland in tribute to the famous American fighter.* A couple of years earlier Patrick (or Packey), together with his friend Pat Casey, had scraped together just enough to pay for a passage from Dublin to Liverpool. Picking up scraps of food along the way, the pair tramped to London and wandered in to Fred Dyer's gym at The Strand to ask for work. The two by now malnourished lads vowed, in exchange for food or money, to fight anyone who Dyer cared to put in front of them. The trainer was somewhat taken aback, but when he found that the lads fought as well as they talked, he naturally took them under his wing. 'There is no need to be told that he is of Ireland,' *All Sports Weekly* wrote when profiling McFarland, 'the map of his country is stamped all over him. And if he was not intended for fighting, no boy ever was. He has a fighter's head, a fighter's mug, a fighter's mind, a fighter's ways. In physical make-up and general appearances he is the most blatant advertisement of his trade ever... I am

---

* The original Packey McFarland, who boxed from 1904 until 1915, was a world-class lightweight and welterweight contender who many consider an all-time great.

not going to predict that McFarland is a sure champion of the future, but you may be assured that he fights like blazes.'

Since his first pro outing the previous November, McFarland had suffered only one defeat in 18 fights. He had beaten Jimmy Thornton, Young Bill Lewis of Bethnal Green, Billy Housego of Paddington, Billy Pritchard of Treherbert, Joe Bull of Blackfriars and in his last two fights drew with and beat the brilliant Dick Corbett. This placed him among the top bantamweight prospects, and made him someone Pat had to beat to prove his own worth at the weight.

One look at the diminutive Irish lad's powerful physique was enough to convince Pat that it would be foolhardy to allow him in close. So he shot out his left and kept him at long range, as all the while McFarland battled to gain the inside position. When he got inside, Pat defended smartly, gave back more than he took, then got away and continued to box at range. Pat was a long way ahead coming into the tenth, but in that round McFarland tore in with vicious intent and caught Pat cleanly with a hard right. Before the round had ended, however, Pat floored McFarland with a beautifully timed right cross of his own, but the Irish lad was up at once and continued to bustle forwards. He fought furiously for the last five rounds in which Pat, knowing he was well ahead on points, boxed chiefly on the defensive to earn referee Ted Broadribb's verdict.

Afterwards, Pat had a rare three-week break in his fight schedule. Rather than a deliberate attempt to rest the boy, however, it seems that this was forced on the Professor. A few days before his fight in Nottingham, Pat had cut a finger on some glass while cleaning windows at the Marylebone Road gym. Initially, neither he nor Newton paid the injury much attention; but he ended his fight with Arthur Adkins with a right glove full of blood. By the time he fought McFarland four days later the cut had turned sceptic. At one stage it was feared that the finger might even have to be amputated, and by the time of his next fight – at the Royal Albert Hall on 2 May – it had yet to fully heal.

The man he was due to face over 10 three-minute rounds, Dick Corbett, was later described by Gilbert Odd as 'one of the greatest bantam titleholders we ever had... a superlative exponent of the Noble Art.' Corbett's real name was Richard Truman Coleman and he was born in the renowned East End fight district of Bethnal Green on 28 September 1908. He recalled that his first big fight happened when he worked as a van boy on a railway truck, earning just 35 shillings a week. Another youth, far heavier than Dick, had taunted him about his red hair, a brawl erupted and Dick taught the impertinent lad a harsh lesson. As an amateur he boxed for the East End's famous Repton Boys' Club, reached the flyweight final of the London Federation Championships, and won the Railways Championship. In 1926 Dick's elder brother, British featherweight champion Harry Corbett, introduced him to pro boxing and to manager Ted Broadribb. Harry had started his own ring career using the pseudonym Young Corbett – in tribute to his boyhood hero, 'Gentleman' Jim Corbett, and so that his family wouldn't discover he was boxing.* As he progressed he kept the name, and as he grew older 'Young Corbett' gave rise to 'Harry Corbett'. Quite naturally, when Dick Coleman turned professional he borrowed his famous brother's ring name.

The one fighting asset that Dick Corbett lacked was a hurtful punch, but he more than compensated with his remarkable skill. 'It was his straight left and almost impregnable defence coupled with the complete mastery of the art of in-fighting,' wrote author Peter McInnes, 'which enabled him to beat the best.' When British bantamweight champion Johnny King later spoke of his five battles with Dick, he described them as 'like fighting a shadow'. In a career spanning at least 185 fights Dick Corbett was never knocked out. At the time he met Pat – save two disqualifications – he had lost only nine of 65 recorded bouts, mostly against top opposition.

At the weigh-in on the afternoon of the fight Pat scaled 8 stone 5¼ lb – over five pounds lighter than his weight for the Adkins fight the previous month. Corbett tipped the scales at a half-pound over the agreed 8 stone 6 lb limit, so the Professor insisted he take it off. A run-round shifted the excess and apparently did not mar his performance. *The Topical Times* pundit Bombardier Billy Wells would note afterwards, 'Dick Corbett fought twice as well as I have ever seen him fight.'

Pat's only worry was for the sceptic right-hand finger. Few then knew about the injury, but one man who did was Corbett's manager, Ted Broadribb. 'You'll need more than one hand to beat my boy,' he scoffed at Pat before they went on. But Pat was less worried than he might be, for the Professor, drawing on years of first aid experience, had bandaged the

---

* 'Gentleman' Jim Corbett was world heavyweight champion from 1892 until 1897.

hand so he could punch with less pain. And as Broadribb had pointed out, against a boxer like Corbett he would certainly need both hands.

During the early rounds Pat ducked and slipped his opponent's leads, all the while piling up the points with his own lightning lefts. In the second Corbett managed to land a couple of well-timed right-hand counters; but Pat retaliated with a beautifully timed right cross of his own, which raised a large lump on Corbett's cheek. He used the right sparingly, but as *Boxing* noted 'this handicap cannot have been suspected by the average spectator, as Daly's work was, as is invariably the case with him, positively brilliant. His flashing left found Corbett time and again and the rapidity with which he used this was an object lesson for the older professionals present.'

In the minute's rest between the fourth and the fifth Newton muttered into Pat's ear, 'He's keeping his left hand high when he leads. How's that right of yours for a punch to the heart?' 'It feels all right,' Pat replied and immediately knew what to do in the next round. When the opening came, Pat hooked heavily on Corbett's heart and the Bethnal Green man collapsed in a heap. He staggered up at 'eight' but the grimace on his face and the shakiness in his legs told Pat that he was 'all in'. Before Pat could finish the job, however, the bell came to Corbett's rescue. Immediately he realised the mistake he had made and did not give Pat the same opening again.

The standard of boxing from both fighters was exemplary; but through it all Pat was the faster, the cleverer and the better ring general. Coming into the tenth and final round Corbett knew he needed a knockout. In a last ditch effort he threw caution to the wind and tore into Pat with savage intent. Pat stood and traded with him for a few seconds, but after taking a couple of rights he heard Newton scream, 'Get away Pat, get away...' He soaked up several more stinging lefts before he managed to break free of Corbett's onslaught. As the Bethnal Green man rushed after him, Pat kept him off with a volley of straight lefts. Knowing now that the fight was almost over, in the last minute he again stood toe-to-toe with Corbett, giving the crowd a grandstand finish. As the two left-hand stylists threw technique aside to trade blows, the audience were on their feet, passionately cheering them on.

At the bell, referee Matt Wells immediately made Pat the winner, and a long flurry of cheers, claps and stamping followed. What impressed Pat most that evening was the sportsmanlike attitude of his opponent. Corbett crossed the ring with a beaming smile and warmly gave him a congratulatory slap on the back. As he left the ring the Bethnal Green man looked over at the front row of pressmen and called out, 'Some boy this – he's a cert for a title!' This sporting gesture was immortalised by *Daily Mail* cartoonist Tom Webster, who drew illustrations of the fight two days later. (Ironically, two years later it was Corbett who won a British title, which he made his own property for much of the 1930s; by which time Pat had hung up his gloves.)

Pat's father pushed his way to the ringside to congratulate his son (his mother had stayed home with his two younger brothers) and the German heavyweight champion Ludwig Haymann, who was also on the bill, came round to Pat's dressing room to say how impressed he was.* When the noise and excitement subsided, up loomed a grim-faced Professor Newton. If Pat expected praise from him, he would soon be disillusioned. 'Why did you go in and make a fight of it in that last round?' he growled. 'Just what Corbett wanted – he had nothing to lose. And I can tell you, my son, I've seen men big and little, a street ahead on points just like you were, get smacked right out with a fight already in their pockets.' Pat explained that he had got a bit carried away, and having already tasted Corbett's best shots, felt there was no risk of a knockout. 'You did box very well,' the Professor finally conceded. 'I only wish I could put an older head on those young shoulders of yours.'

The winner's end of the purse that evening – split between the Newtons and Pat – was £50. By then they were getting between £50 and £100 per match, and between £10 and £20 for each of Pat's exhibitions.

His display against Corbett had staggered the critics and the next day's papers were filled with praise. 'He possesses the inherent ring-craft of a boxer twice his age,' wrote the *Daily Herald*. 'He is the most promising bantamweight we have,' said the *Daily Sketch*. While Norman Hurst of *The Sporting Chronicle* concluded that he was 'in a class all by himself'. *Boxing*'s John Murray, meanwhile, paid him this tribute:

---

*   Haymann lost on points that night to British and Empire heavyweight champion Phil Scott.

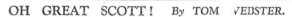

SATURDAY, The Daily Mail MAY 4, 1929.

OH GREAT SCOTT! By TOM WEBSTER.

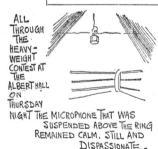

ALL THROUGH THE HEAVY-WEIGHT CONTEST AT THE ALBERT HALL ON THURSDAY NIGHT THE MICROPHONE THAT WAS SUSPENDED ABOVE THE RING REMAINED CALM, STILL AND DISPASSIONATE.

BUT THERE — THAT MICROPHONE HAD NOTHING TO SHAKE ITS LITTLE WIRES ABOUT — ON PREVIOUS OCCASIONS GREAT MEN HAD SUNG INTO IT PROMINENT MEN HAD SPOKEN INTO IT WONDERFUL MUSICIANS HAD PLAYED INTO IT

BUT IT TOOK THE WHOLE OF THE HEAVY-WEIGHTS 15 ROUNDS ON THURSDAY NIGHT WITH COMPLETE INDIFFERENCE.

I THINK IT MUST HAVE BEEN ON ITS HOLIDAYS.

WE MUST NOW RAISE GENT'S STETSON TO NIPPER PAT DALY

MARYLEBONE'S 16 YEAR OLD CHILD.

MASTER DALY HAS HAD SUCH A CONVINCING ARRAY OF VICTORIES LATELY THAT MARYLEBONE'S FIRST THOUGHT ON RISING IN THE MORNING IS FOR THE NURSING HOMES TO GET AN EXTRA BED PREPARED — READY TO TAKE MASTER DALY'S PATIENT OF THE NIGHT BEFORE.

MASTER DALY'S OPPONENT ON THIS OCCASION WAS

DICK CORBETT OF BETHNAL GREEN

YOUNG DICK IS A GREAT LITTLE BATTLER TOO AND I LIKED HIM MORE THAN EVER WHEN, AS HE LEFT THE RING-SIDE HAVING BEEN DECLARED THE LOSER, HE

GAVE A BACKWARD JERK OF HIS THUMB TOWARDS DALY AND SAID "HE'S A GOOD BOY."

THAT LADIES AND GENTLEMEN IS THE SPIRIT WHICH NEARLY MADE FRANK GODDARD WHAT HE IS TO-DAY.

APART FROM THE EPIC SLAM BETWEEN DALY AND CORBETT WE ALSO SAW THE LIGHT-WEIGHT TITLE CHANGE HANDS AS THE RESULT OF A FIGHT BETWEEN — SAM STEWARD - AND FRED WEBSTER

NOT AN UNSUCCESSFUL EVENING — THE ORGAN BLEW ITS LOUDEST — THE CROWD WERE AT THEIR WITTIEST AND

PHIL SCOTT AND LUDWIG HAYMANN WERE ALSO PRESENT.

'A certain press critic when eulogising his performance against Dick Corbett, stated that Daly appeared to know all there is to know about the boxing game already and went on to express a certain curiosity as to his future. This, of course, on the lap of the gods, but we can well believe that Daly will go a very long way indeed... He has all the assets a boxer can need, as enumerated by Mr George Bernard Shaw in a recent pronouncement... He has the fastest left hand seen anywhere since the days of Tom McCormick, while the jabs and shots he deals out with it are of snappier and consequently more effective quality.*
He has the ability to select almost instantaneously the right move to make at the right time. He can get an opponent "guessing" in that he can and does think more speedily than the average boxer. And finally he can and does adapt himself to varying situations. He may lack the killing force of the great fighters, but this will develop in due course. Mr Bernard Shaw cited all the above qualities as being instinctive, but he has more than these and has them, uncannily, in one so young.'

On the evening of 3 March 1944 – 14 years, 10 months and one day after the Daly–Corbett match – there was a full air raid on London. Hearing the sirens, Dick Corbett rushed home to his wife and children but found the house empty. He realised they had gone to the nearest air-raid shelter – Bethnal Green tube station – so he headed there himself. He arrived to find people – hundreds of them – pouring in to the narrow station entrance bound for the sanctuary 78 feet below. As a Civil Defence volunteer, Corbett did his best to maintain order amid the throng. He was close to the bottom of the long flight of steps when he saw a young mother carrying a tiny baby trip and fall. The former champion scooped up the child in his arms and tried to stem the oncoming surge as the woman regained her feet. At that very moment, however, a bomb fell in the street outside. There was a loud bang and a blinding flash as a stampede of terrified people rushed for the stairs. Those at the rear pushed those further down off their feet, causing a landslide of bodies to tumble down the steps. Men, women and children – 173 of them – lost their lives, while a great many more were injured. Near the bottom of the stairs they found Dick Corbett who, like many others, had

---

* McCormick (a British, Empire and world welterweight champion) was killed in action in France in 1916.

been crushed to death. But beneath his body, still clutched in his arms, was the tiny baby, miraculously still alive. Corbett was just 35 and still fighting professionally. The man who had outfought and outthought the best of Britain's bantamweights had, at the crucial moment, given no thought to his own safety. Richard Truman Coleman was a hero.

15

Great Young Hope

'Pat promises to eclipse even Jimmy Wilde in the affections of the British public, to say nothing of Teddy Baldock, whose popularity is more recent. Daly has won most of his fights in such a fashion as to convince the most sceptical that he is something approaching the wonder of the age.'

Charlie Rose, *The Daily Express*, 12 April 1929

The departure of Jimmy Wilde and Jim Driscoll, and the decline of Ted Kid Lewis as a world-class force, left a void in British boxing. Although there were some excellent prospects, none of the new crop of British fighters had managed to match the precedent set a decade before by Wilde, Driscoll, Lewis, Owen Moran, Matt Wells and Freddie Welsh – all of whom conquered America. Teddy Baldock and Johnny Hill had beaten top-class Americans for British versions of world titles, but neither received his full due across the water.

The hunt was on for a talent who might restore Britain's once high place in the boxing world; a fighter who possessed that extra sparkle that had made Wilde and Driscoll so singularly special. Fans and writers were starting to believe that they had found such a saviour in the person of Nipper Pat Daly. With each new brilliant victory, their conviction grew stronger. To say expectations were high would be an understatement. 'Being what he is today,' wrote *Boxing* in May 1929, 'we may hope with increasing confidence, to live to see the day when he is acknowledged as "absolutely the best and greatest there has ever been".'

Pat was now known in a circle wider than boxing. People who didn't follow the sport knew his name and round west London they would shout it and wish him luck wherever he went. Schoolboys – ironically, some not much younger than he was – followed him around and asked him questions – 'Who ya fighting next, Nipper?' 'D'you think you can lick Teddy Baldock?' – and he was now bombarded regularly for his autograph. What endeared him to people – besides his talent – was his genial, unassuming manner. 'Despite the amazing and it can be said unparalleled success which has pursued him at such a very young age,' noted *Boxing*, 'there isn't a suspicion of any swollen-headedness about him.' Pat went about the business of boxing in a focused, workmanlike fashion. He was never 'flash' and would never attempt to humiliate an opponent or make a point of the ease with which he could beat one by playing to the gallery. Outside of the ring, though supremely confident of his own ability, he was a modest lad of few words. 'Anyone seeing him in ordinary clothes would be astounded if told that he was a professional boxer,' noted one newspaper. 'Yet Daly, despite his innocent air and modest behaviour outside the ring, becomes a different person when the gloves are on and the gong clangs.' An *Evening Standard* journalist who attempted to interview him found this modesty stood in the way of a newsworthy quote. 'Daly the conversationalist is unlike Daly the boxer,' wrote the bemused scribe. 'When talking he leaves the "leads" to the other fellow.'

Nonetheless, many fans of the sport were eager to meet him and to be around him, and Newton's gym was besieged like never before with visitors. Wannabe fighters wanted to be trained by the man who had produced Nipper Pat, and a host of others who held no fistic ambitions, simply wanted to get within the gym to see the 'wonder boy' up close. One such man who visited the gym on the pretext of training, one day remarked to Pat, 'I want you to cauliflower my ear.' 'You want me to do what?' he replied incredulously, and the man explained that he wanted to find film work as a 'tough guy' and believed that a cauliflower ear would increase his chances. He would be honoured, he added, if Pat would administer it. Initially he declined, but on the other's insistence eventually agreed. As requested he hit the man repeatedly on the ear and sure enough the ear swelled up, giving the wannabe 'tough guy' his wish. Whether the disfigurement got him the film work he craved is unknown.

Although some may have viewed a cauliflower ear as a symbol of toughness, many boxers went to great lengths to avoid receiving one. Jack Kid Berg described the feeling of having his ear pierced by a doctor to drain off blood in an attempt to avoid a cauliflower as 'like someone swinging on your ear'. Essentially a cauliflower occurs when the skin of the ear is separated from the cartilage. In boxing this is usually due to a blood clot caused by a trauma to the ear. Deprived of the nutrients and oxygen normally supplied by the flow of blood, the cartilage contracts and causes the outer ear to shrivel. If the blood flow isn't restored, the cartilage dies and the structure of the ear collapses – a complete cauliflower being the result. Professor Newton had his own method for preventing cauliflower ears, which was recalled by '20s boxer Johnny Hicks in his autobiography *Sparring For Luck*:

> 'The ear should not be allowed to harden, and an outlet should be made to let the blood flow freely, otherwise it will congeal. So while the ear was still ripe I got my young niece to bathe it for me with hot milk and soda water. On the Professor's advice, although it was painful, I got a piece of boracic lint soaked in surgical spirits and laid it on the ear. I had a 'stiffener' of cardboard or plywood handy and bandaged it with the lint to my ear. When going to bed I had to lay on the ear, which was the left one. It was very painful of course but by the next morning it was almost back to its normal size, although it was still tender to the touch. But it had to be bathed again the next day with boiling water and surgical spirits.'

Cauliflower ears are seldom seen in boxing today, but a glance at the mug shots of many pre-war boxers indicates that they were then fairly common. According to founding London Ex-Boxers' Association member Peter Kent (who knew Pat in later life), the reason for the current absence of cauliflower ears in boxing is 'they don't have enough fights nowadays and aren't taught how to slip punches'. Pat had a slight cauliflower on his left ear, which was evident in photos from at least the age of 14 and grew more marked as his career progressed. When asked, he explained that this had indeed formed due to an accumulation of the blows he slipped. His reactions were fast enough to allow him to avoid shots with a quick shift of the head while on the advance, enabling him to land snappy counters to his opponent's exposed head or body. Few boxers can carry this carefully learnt skill from the gym into actual combat, and the ability to do so set Pat apart from most.

Following his win over Dick Corbett, Pat faced another fighter who hailed from the same East London district. Eldest of six, Kid Socks was born in Ramsey Street, Bethnal Green on 14 August 1904 with the unlikely given name of George Joseph Stockings. He was often billed as the 'Wrecker of Champions', for although he never won a title himself, he was highly adept at embarrassing title-holders. During his distinguished career he beat the reigning flyweight champions of Europe, Britain, France, Belgium and Ireland, plus the reigning bantamweight champions of Britain and France. He also boxed draws with world flyweight champion Emile Pladner, European bantamweight champion Domenico Bernasconi, and in 1924 was the first to spoil Teddy Baldock's long run of victories, when he held the Poplar man to a draw in a match which Baldock later confessed he feared he had lost. In 1925 Socks beat the renowned Ernie Jarvis plus the reigning British and European flyweight champion, Elky Clark. The Clark win earned Socks a shot at both of Elky's titles – the only title shot he ever received. They met in April 1926 and, although Socks managed to make it a close run thing, he was stopped in the twentieth and final round. Pat remembered reading about the fight in a newspaper as a 13-year-old schoolboy. Scarcely could he have imagined that he would fight Socks three years later.

At the time of their fight, at almost 25, Socks was a little past his prime but far from 'over the hill'. Now a bantamweight, in his last four fights he had beaten Con Lewis and Lew Pinkus and boxed draws with Young Bill Lewis and Len Fowler – all top-class men – and in his next would outpoint Packey McFarland. Although very small, even for a fly or bantam, Socks was uncanny at anticipating his rival's moves, smart at countering, and exceptionally fast on his feet and with his fists. 'He was one of the cleverest fighters that I ever met,' Pat recalled, 'but he lacked a KO punch.' Despite Socks's cleverness, Pat had a relatively easy time with him. His chief tactic was to crowd Socks, bombard him with leather and give him no room to manoeuvre. 'Daly won every round by a wide margin,' wrote *Boxing*. 'It was a monotonous contest, however, for in each round Daly was there, using both hands like piston rods to the face and body, with Socks doing his job as manfully as he could in the circumstances.' Studying the fight, an observant *All Sports Weekly* reporter noted:

'I watched Daly closely during the minute breathers. His calm is a study; he sits with closed eyes, and always under Newton's watchful eyes will take two spells of deep breathing. Serenely he listens to any words that may be spoken to him, but many of the intervals passed without a word being spoken. He gives the impression of wanting to get the most out of his rest, the closed eye and tranquil pose never being departed from… We must regard him as the biggest drawing card at the moment. He received a tremendous welcome from the house. I have not seen such a number of fight fans disappointed at their efforts to get into a show since the night Carpentier fought Beckett at the Holborn Stadium.'

The usually taciturn Professor was uncharacteristically emotional following the victory. 'The boy's too good,' he told the *All Sports Weekly* reporter. 'Sometimes I can hardly believe it can all be true.' Thanks to Pat's burgeoning success, Newton had now reached a level of repute he had never known before. After a visit to the Marylebone Road gym earlier that month, *Topical Times* columnist Bombardier Billy Wells remarked, 'when I saw "Professor" Andrew himself teaching Daly the "tricks of the trade" I knew the reason why the youngster goes on from victory to victory… the relations of teacher and pupil, both in the school and at the ringside, reminded me inevitably of my friend and opponent, Georges Carpentier and [his manager] Francois Descamps.'

The week of the Socks fight the formidably moustached Professor made a bold and very public challenge on behalf of his young fighter. It was issued through *Boxing* to Britain's two best bantamweights, Teddy Baldock and Alf 'Kid' Pattenden, and to the European champion, Domenico Bernasconi. Pat, he said, would meet any or all of them for side-stakes of up to £200. 'It will be agreed that the challenge is as bold as it is sweeping,' wrote *Boxing*. 'One thing is certain. The Nipper has so many enthusiastic admirers that any promoter would be safe in bidding for the contest or contests since there must be several thousand fans who will be satisfied that the Nipper would hold a real chance… it will remain to be seen whether this boxing excellence [of Pat's] will suffice to offset that deficiency in punch, which even "the Professor" would acknowledge would prove his heaviest handicap in any contest with such men as Baldock and Pattenden. Either or both of these heroes might hesitate to own that the 16-year-old boy possesses a sounder all-round equipment.'

On 16 May (four days after the Socks fight) the Professor and Pat watched a show at Olympia, where for once, instead of fighting, they were studying potential opponents. Teddy Baldock and Kid Pattenden – from the neighbouring East End districts of Poplar and Bethnal Green – were meeting to settle a dispute over bantamweight supremacy. Their quarrel over who was the true British king had started the previous year and was partly owed to the division's previous champion, Johnny Brown of St. George's.

After winning enough title defences to make the Lonsdale belt his own property, Brown had left Britain on a yearlong worldwide tour. He returned in 1927 to find a long queue of hopefuls, eager to wrench his title from him. The NSC proposed several matches to Brown, but with its meagre capacity, the venue could not hope to generate enough revenue to tempt him into fighting there, so he instead took matches offered by other promoters with deeper pockets. He also kept his weight just above 8 stone 6 lb to ensure that if he lost, he kept his title. By June 1928 the NSC (backed by the BBB of C) had grown tired of waiting for Brown and so declared his title vacant. Initially they chose Teddy Baldock and Kid Pattenden to box for the vacant crown, but when their purse proved too low for Baldock, they drafted in Leeds-based Kid Nicholson to replace him. Subsequently Pattenden knocked out Nicholson to become new champion and belt-holder, but Brown, who had not lost his title in the ring, maintained that he was still champion. And so, when Baldock demolished Brown inside two rounds that August, the Poplar man claimed that he was the rightful champion. Naturally, Pattenden resented this, especially since he had also beaten Brown, in a non-title fight back in 1927. Baldock and Pattenden remained at loggerheads for some months until a match was finally arranged to settle their dispute.

The resultant fight was described by Gilbert Odd in 1979 as 'one of the greatest battles ever seen in any division. I shall remember it as long as I live'. Pat was in concurrence, saying that the fight stood comparison with any held in Britain. There were twists, there were knockdowns, there was blood and valour, yet also moments of great skill from two men who could not countenance losing. Three British titles changed hands that night: Len Harvey knocked out Alex Ireland to gain the middleweight crown, Johnny Cuthbert beat Harry Corbett for the featherweight belt, and Teddy Baldock was crowned king of the bantams after 15 blazing rounds with Pattenden. For the first time in history Lord Lonsdale presented the new champions with their belts from inside the ring. Sat in the crowd, Pat must have looked longingly at those magnificent trophies, knowing he could not win one because of the Board's new age regulations. According to *Boxing*, Pat's challenge to Pattenden and Baldock was the hot topic at ringside. After the presentations, Professor Newton turned to Pat and asked him how he thought he would do against Pattenden or Baldock. He replied that he felt confident he could beat either man. He would not have long to wait to test his mettle against one of them.

Pat's next outing – two nights after his trip to Olympia – was at Sunderland's Holmeside Stadium against Bolton's Joe Greenwood, one of the best bantams in the north of England. Greenwood had fought 80 recorded fights, of which he had lost 18. Among the top men he had beaten were George Greaves of Manchester, Billy Smith of Sunderland, Harry Hill of Birmingham, Frankie Ash of Plymouth, Kid Socks and Lew Pinkus. The contest was scheduled for 15 two-minute rounds, but only eight of them were needed. In the eighth 'Daly was so far ahead of his opponent and had him in such a state of subjection,' wrote *Boxing*, 'that the referee stopped the contest.' As Pat left the ring, a fierce-faced little man emerged from the crowd and in a broad Aberdeenshire accent challenged him to a match for side-stakes of up to £100 a side. Andy Newton, who accompanied Pat, promptly accepted, and the terms for this match with one Douglas Parker were fixed with Fred Charlton, who would act as referee. The contracts were then signed and the fight was fixed for 8 June.

Pat and Andy returned home, but en route stopped off at Blackpool, Preston and Nottingham, where Pat boxed exhibitions. He returned to the north five days after fighting Greenwood to take on Jim Crawford of Wrexham at the Liverpool Stadium. Since Pat's last Liverpool appearance, 14 months earlier, control of the venue had passed to Johnny Best, a promoter who was later nationally renowned. Although he hailed from North Wales, Jim Crawford was very popular in Liverpool, where he had fought most of his contests. He had lost six of his 32 recorded fights, but three of these defeats were to future world flyweight champion Jackie Brown. Crawford was only 18, but he possessed a powerful punch and plenty of know-how. There was a dispute over bandages before they went on, so referee Ben Green ordered both fighters to remove them, which meant, despite the risk of injury, that they fought without hand wraps. The Wrexham lad fought his heart out through each of the 15 rounds, while the crowd, particularly a large Wrexham contingent, cheered his every effort. The noise was almost deafening when he staggered Pat with a shot to the jaw in the third, and again when he rocked him with a right cross in the tenth, but cleverly Pat evaded Crawford's efforts to follow up.

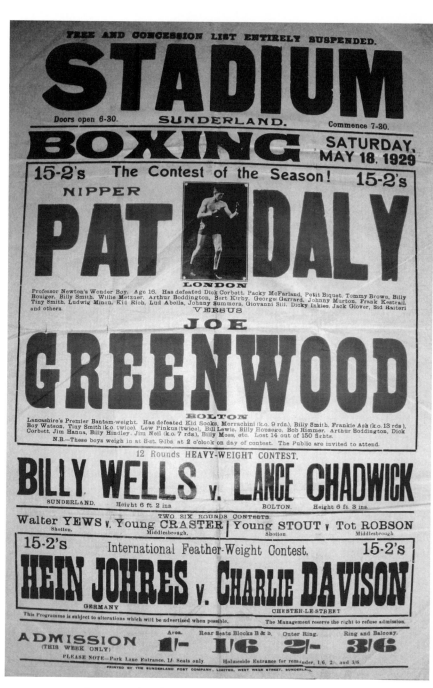

A poster advertising Pat's fight with Joe Greenwood.

'Crawford worried him considerably with constant forcing tactics,' wrote *Boxing*, 'but Daly was quite cool, and his left was going with machine-like movement.' At the end of what the trade paper called 'a real fistic treat', Pat was a clear winner, but Crawford's great effort had earned him a return – same venue, same terms, scheduled for three weeks' time.

It had been a busy week, even by Pat's standards. He had fought two 15-round contests, boxed three exhibitions, and travelled the length of the country within the previous five days. Reluctantly, the Professor conceded it was time to give him a couple of days off. With his mentor's blessing, Pat took his mother and younger brothers to Southend for a weekend holiday. In the '20s holidays abroad were beyond the reach of most working-class families, so for millions the next best thing each summer was a week at the seaside. Typically a family could only afford one trip a year, so it became an event that they saved for and dreamed of during the other 51 weeks. Coastal resorts such as Southend, Blackpool, Great Yarmouth, Skegness and Margate were the places to go. When the trains rolled into the stations and the masses descended, they found each town amply equipped to cater to their every whim. Outdoor swimming, brass bands, boat rides, amusements and sun bathing were an integral part of the holiday experience. The local businesses were run off their feet but delighted by the extra income, as fish 'n' chips, ice creams, jellied eels and pie and mash were all devoured by the bucket-load. In 1929 Southend boasted the longest pier in the world (and still does). The last time Pat had set foot on one was to fight Young McManus on an icy December night in Plymouth. But this time, in the hazy May sunshine, he could enjoy its many attractions at his leisure. For two days he could laze on the beach, swim in the sea and spend rare quality time with his family. The break was the perfect antidote to the strain of constant fighting and training, but like any quick fix it could not last.

On 4 June 'to thunderous applause' (*Boxing*), Pat boxed a three-round exhibition at Gillingham with a fighter called Jimmy Turner from nearby Chatham, billed as the bantamweight champion of Kent. 'The youthful Daly handled Jimmy very easily,' wrote the *Chatham, Rochester and Gillingham News*, 'and introduced him to a straight left that resembled the lightning that flashed over the town earlier in the day. The Nipper is certainly a wonder boxer...' Four days afterwards he returned to Sunderland to meet the challenge laid down by 21-year-old Douglas Parker.

Originally from Aberdeen, Parker left Scotland in 1927 after two pro fights to tour Britain as part of a boxing booth. After a couple of months on the road he decided to stop off at Sunderland, where he met a local girl called Elizabeth Conlon, whom he married. Wearside fight fans were thrilled by the Scot's all-action style; and when he started appearing regularly in the local rings, were happy to adopt him as one of their own. Though certainly no mere brawler, Parker was not the most skilful or subtle of practitioners. But what he lacked in boxing finesse he more than made up for with unbelievable power, for nature had given Parker a knockout punch in each hand. Some 40 years later Fred Charlton, an expert on North East boxing, described him as 'by far the heftiest puncher, pound for pound, ever to appear in North East rings'. At first sight Parker's record before meeting Pat does not look especially impressive. He had lost almost half of his recorded fights, but 14 of his 24 wins had arrived via stoppage or knockout. He maintained an impressive stoppage ratio throughout his career, and in 170 recorded fights scored 60 per cent of his wins inside the distance – this, of course, in an era when opponents were seldom hand-picked. The little Scot turned out to be a phenomenal causer of upsets, and in 1931 knocked out the reigning featherweight champion, Johnny Cuthbert, in a non-title affair. Other top men he stopped would include Dom Volante, Benny Sharkey, Kid Pattenden, Kid Nicholson, Phineas John, Kid Farlo and Len Wickwar. In early June of 1929, however, few outside the North East had even heard of Douglas Parker. But that was about to change.

When Pat stepped in the ring that evening he certainly had no idea of the calibre of puncher he would face, but even if he had, it would not have dented his confidence. Since being stopped by Young Siki 14 months earlier, he had won all 27 of his fights, apart from the dubious points defeat to Dod Oldfield. He was beating Britain and Europe's best bantamweights with relative ease, but what troubled him more than any opponent was the constant strain of keeping off weight. Under the Professor's directions his food and fluid intake was now strictly rationed. In place of a meal, he was given steaks to chew but not swallow, and had to spit them out after the nutrients were absorbed. Oranges, similarly, had to be sucked piece by piece until the flavour had gone and then spat out so as not to digest any extra calories. (As a result, Pat developed a lifelong dislike of oranges.) He was told to drink liquids only when he needed them and when he did to take only small sips – just enough to quench his thirst, the Professor insisted. His special diet left him constantly thirsty and sometimes weak, but he trusted his erudite mentor and was of course bound by contract to regularly make set weights. At the weigh-in on the afternoon of the Parker fight Pat was a pound over the agreed 8 stone 9 lb limit and was obliged to burn it off. With nowhere else to do roadwork, he ran repeatedly round the ring. After countless laps and several weight checks the surplus finally shifted, but the effort left him weak and lethargic.

Come ring time he still felt decidedly below par, while the man across the ring from him by contrast was brimming with adrenaline, pacing the canvas, and raring to be let loose by the bell. Parker was about to enter the fight of his life and knew full well that a win over the Londoner would earn him national exposure. He realised he could not match the boy for skill or speed, but knew that his powerful fists and the element of surprise were both on his side. With this in mind, he tore from his corner at the chime of the first bell, racing towards his opponent with both fists flying. The attack was wild and slightly crude, but it caught Pat completely off guard. A crunching left hook dropped the Londoner to the boards and prompted referee Fred Charlton to start the count. From that punch onwards Pat had no memory of the fight, yet he rose on instinct at nine and stabbed off Parker with his left until the Scot was back in his own corner. Pat's legs were gone, however, and he had not recovered his senses; so when Parker landed another left hook he went down immediately. Frantically, Andy Newton rushed to the side of the ring where Pat had fallen and banged his fist on the ring apron to rouse him. Charlton reprimanded Andy for this intrusion, but it had the desired effect, for at 'eight' Pat staggered up gamely. But he was now an easy target for the merciless Sunderland Scot, and a single, murderous punch – a right uppercut to the chin – put him down again. This time Pat did not get up. His body lay sprawled without a flicker of movement. For the second time in over 80 pro fights the teenager was out cold. Parker had put him away inside 90 seconds and the noise inside the Sunderland arena was deafening. According to *Boxing* Parker 'was cheered again and again, and it is a long time since such a scene of enthusiasm was witnessed in the Stadium.' Mercifully perhaps, Pat heard none of this. He was carried from the ring unconscious and did not come round for several minutes. When he awoke he would ask what had happened.

'Practically the sole topic of conversation in fistic circles these last few days has been the sensational defeat of Nipper Pat Daly,' wrote *Boxing* in its next edition. Andy Newton, who had arranged the match and accompanied Pat, had a case to answer but insisted the defeat was purely Pat's own making. 'It was really tragic,' Andy told *Boxing*. 'Still Daly has only himself to blame. He has been told times out of number that he should be super-careful when coming out of a clinch, and before this fight with Parker I gave him another special warning.' The trade paper, which had once been highly critical of Pat's handlers, now raised no objection. Instead of criticising his managers, it chose to admonish the boy himself. 'These successes have somewhat naturally made him over-confident and consequently inclined to believe that no opponent could present any real danger... I am sure it will prove to have been one of the best things which could have happened to him.' Pat, noted the newspaper, was eager to have a rematch with Parker, but it doubted whether he could keep his weight down long enough. Showing more concern for the boy's condition, *Daily Express* columnist Charlie Rose commented, 'I do hope this knockout will not seriously affect Daly's future, as it might well do in one so young... I should be greatly surprised if Parker were able to repeat the feat in a return battle.'

The aura of invincibility that had surrounded Pat since he joined the top contenders had taken a hefty battering. As James Butler (father of renowned sportswriter, Frank Butler) wrote in *The Sporting Chronicle*, the defeat 'proved that the boy is human'. He may have proven to be something less than superhuman, but after only one such defeat in so many regular fights, his box office value would prevail. There was still no other fighter remotely like him and the public would be just as keen – perhaps more keen given the defeat – to discover the next twist in this captivating saga.

16

A Fight to Remember

'When I heard Mr. Eugene Corri, the renowned referee, solemnly assert that this 16-year-old boxer belonged to the "greatest ever" class at his age, it became incumbent on me to visit Professor Newton and hear what he should say about Nipper Pat Daly... Boxers thrived best on boxing, the Professor said, as we discussed the question of overworking growing boys and giving them fights of too long duration.'

Clyde Foster, *The Evening Standard*, 10 July 1929

With the ink barely settled on the press reports of the Parker defeat, five days later Pat was in Liverpool for his return 15-rounder with Jim Crawford. The pressure was on to put on a good performance, but just days after the knockout, and with the added burden of staying at 8 stone 9 lb, he did not feel in the best of shape. Under the circumstances he boxed well, while Crawford according to *Boxing*, 'fought the fight of his life'. It was another fierce battle and left Pat with a split eyebrow. Referee Ben Green called it 'the best contest he had refereed for years' and declared it a draw. Pat had seemed decidedly off form, but nonetheless much of the crowd still felt he had won. 'The spectators who have written us,' noted *Boxing*, 'one and all protest against the verdict, stating that according to their tally of the points Daly won at least nine of the fifteen rounds, while three were even. One gentleman writes to say that if Daly and Crawford were rematched over ten "threes" he would willingly wager £25 on the Nipper.' At the end of the fight Tommy Rose, a fighter from Bolton, climbed into the ring and challenged Pat. As ever, the two Newtons accepted and the match was added to his roster of fights.

That week – shortly before the Parker fight – some excellent news had reached the camp of Newton and Daly. Recently dethroned British champion, Kid Pattenden, had finally accepted Pat's challenge to a match. Before their Olympia battle neither Pattenden nor Baldock had seemed willing to face the boy. A win over a 16-year-old would hardly have enhanced the reputations of two men who were already world-renowned (both were in *The Ring* magazine's last top-10 annual ratings for bantamweights); but defeat to an adolescent, however talented, could seriously harm their credibility. There was still no word from Baldock, but with his title gone, the fight suddenly made sense to Pattenden and his manager, Victor Berliner (the Premierland promoter). By now Pat lay just behind Baldock and Pattenden in the bantamweight pecking order, so a win over the Nipper would help smooth the way for a return title fight with Baldock. Kid Pattenden had demolished leading contenders such as Kid Nicholson and Young Johnny Brown – clever fighters who were also grown men – so could this mere slip of a lad realistically fare any better? Berliner and Pattenden were satisfied he could not, so the fight was fixed for 7 July. In the meantime – while Pattenden went into serious training – Pat had more fights arranged.

Each summer, as temperatures soared, the number of boxing promotions across Britain dwindled. When the weather was warm promoters found fans were reluctant to crowd inside their cramped, sweaty halls. Fight shows continued but were less frequent, and to compensate for lost earnings, many fighters signed up with boxing booths and toured the country for two or three months. But the lack of indoor promotions also created a gap in the market for a small clutch of wealthy or heavily backed promoters. These intrepid entrepreneurs hired vast venues such as football grounds and greyhound tracks and adapted them for open-air boxing shows. A temporary ring was erected in the middle of the pitch or track, rows of chairs were placed round it for pressmen and more affluent spectators, while the stadium's inbuilt seating, which was generally a long way back, was available to the rank and file. The extra seating capacity inevitably meant larger gate receipts, but the hire costs of these vast venues was huge, and a day of bad weather or a badly planned event would see the attendance plummet along with the profits. Financial disaster was in store for any promoter who failed to do his maths. The previously mentioned example of Major James Arnold Wilson, who booked Wembley Stadium for a fight show but was spectacularly bankrupted back in 1924, is a case in point.

Two days after the Crawford rematch, Pat gave a boxing and training exhibition on a fight bill at Brentford FC's ground, Griffin Park, in front of around 4,000 fans. The event was organised by the multifaceted extrovert Captain Albert Prince-Cox who, apart from boxing promoting,

Pat preparing to spar in an outside ring
at grounds off Highgate Road,
Kentish Town.

Pat aged four.

Professor Newton's gym in the mid-1920s. Pat is second from left on the steps.

Pat with the Professor's son, Andy, a leading welter and middleweight of the 1920s.

Pat aged only 12, but already making a name for himself as a pro fighter.

Pat (aged 12) spars with the Professor's niece, Annie, the self-styled 'Women's Boxing Champion of the World'. The Professor looks on.

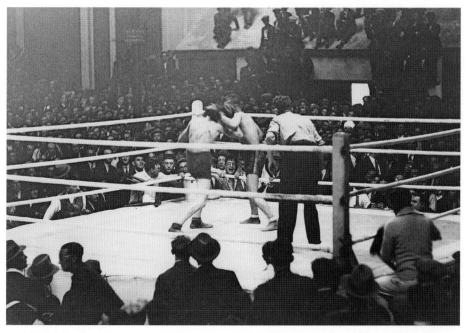

Pat (plain shorts) evades a left hook from Jack Garland, Premierland, 11 Aug 1929.

Showing the strain of weight-making. An emaciated-looking Nipper (aged 16) weighs in opposite the Midlands featherweight champion, 28-year-old Ted Cullen, 11 Nov 1929.

Professor Newton with his prize pupil, June 1928.

Pat (left, aged 14) and Boy Sharpe weigh in
for their fight at Nottingham, 2 Jan 1928.

Bert Kirby proudly displays the
Lonsdale belt he won by knocking out
future world flyweight champion
Jackie Brown.

Bert Kirby and Pat after weighing in for their fight on 17 Dec 1928.

Pat (centre), Charlie McCleave (right) and one of Pat's seconds (left) in Hyde Park.

30 Sep 1929 – not an ounce of fat to spare as Pat trains for his fight with reigning British featherweight champion Johnny Cuthbert. He later called making the contracted weight 'one of the hardest jobs of my life'.

British bantamweight champion Dick Corbett, who Pat fought in May 1929.

Pat (aged 15) at the
Marylebone Road gym.

Pat at the seaside (thought to be
Southend) in 1929.

Pat (back to camera) vs. Kid Socks, Premierland, 12 May 1929.

Pat in Hyde Park.

Pat (second from right) in Blackpool, July 1929. The woman shaking hands
with the Professor is the dancer Violet Kaye, victim of the infamous
1934 Brighton 'trunk murder'.

The tough, clever European bantamweight
champion Petit Biquet, who Pat faced in
March 1929.

Pat and a friend with two young women in
Blackpool, July 1929.

The rugged, hard-hitting British bantamweight champion Alf 'Kid' Pattenden.

Pat pictured at around the time of his fight with Pattenden.

Kid Pattenden strolls to a neutral corner after flooring Pat in the twelfth round of their 15-round fight, Premierland, 7 July 1929.

A picture of Pat with a signed dedication to Miss Anita Leslie, daughter of Sir Shane Leslie.

The phenomenally hard-hitting Douglas Parker, who Pat faced in June 1929.

Professor Newton puts Pat through his paces.

Jack Garland, who had two terrific fights with Pat in 1929.

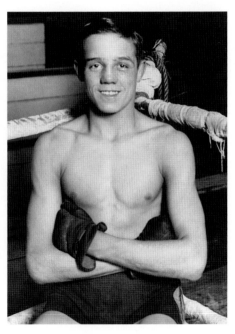

Pat pictured in May 1929.

With his pals. Left to right: Mike McGrath, Davey John Daley, Pat and Leonard Daley.

British champion and world title challenger Seaman Tommy Watson, who Pat fought in April 1930.

Reigning British featherweight champion
Johnny Cuthbert and Pat after weighing
in for their 9 Oct 1929 fight.

Cuthbert returns home to Sheffield after a
successful title defence in London – the
leading boxers were treated like film stars in
'20s Britain.

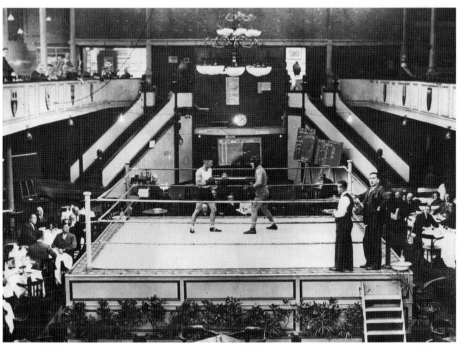

A lunchtime sparring session at the Holborn Stadium, site of the Cuthbert-Daly contest
(the American Dave Shade wears the head guard).

Pat (aged 21) with younger brother Bobby, on a family holiday at Margate, 1934.

A wrestling publicity photo of Pat, aged about 23.

10 July 1937, Pat (aged 24) marries Mary Newrick, pictured here at Elliott's Row, Elephant and Castle.

Pat at his Irish dance hall in Peckham, mid-1950s.

Pat puts a pupil through his paces, New North Road, 1950.

Nipper's New North Road, Shoreditch gym, 1950.

The exterior of Premierland in Whitechapel (1928), one of Britian's leading pre-World War Two fight venues.

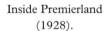

Inside Premierland (1928).

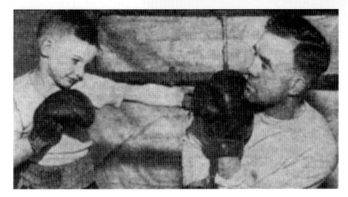

Early 1953, Pat coaching his youngest son Terry, who wrote the foreword to this book.

Left to right: Pat, LEBA member 'Goffy' Phillips and Pat's friend and
Newton stable-mate Arthur Norton, early 1970s.

Pat with the author, circa 1982.

served at various times as an international football referee, a circus and aqua show organiser, a music hall performer, and manager-secretary of Bristol Rovers FC. Though the attendance was lower than expected, Pat's exhibition proved a roaring success, and Prince-Cox eagerly booked him for a real fight – a 15-round headliner – at Griffin Park later that month.

In the meantime, six days after the first Griffin Park job, Pat had another open-air engagement; this time at the Clapton Stadium, a venue used for greyhound racing and home to Clapton Orient FC. The match, unlike his last, was no mere exhibition. His opponent, 21-year-old Jack Garland, was a highly dangerous proposition. Born in Belfast on 2 January 1908, Garland started boxing as an amateur while working as a caulker at the city's shipyard. During this time he won a local 7 stone 4 lb title, but when work at the shipyard dried up, he joined the Second Battalion Gordon Highlanders Army regiment, which kept him in tip-top condition and helped to develop his boxing. In 1927 he won both the Army and Imperial Services championships and reached the ABA bantamweight quarterfinals. The next year he went one better and again won both military titles, but also captured the ABA bantamweight title too. As ABA champion he was Great Britain's sole bantamweight hope at the 1928 Olympic Games held in Amsterdam that August. He had the misfortune to meet the eventual gold medallist, Vittorio Tamagnini of Italy, in the second phase of the Games and was duly eliminated. A few months later, with the financial help of a publican friend of his father's, Garland bought his discharge from the Army and was taken in hand by the experienced duo of Jack Goodwin (trainer) and Syd Hulls (manager), who brought him to London where he turned pro in January 1929. As a former ABA champion big things were expected of him, and his very first contest was a 15-rounder. He had won each of his eight pro fights, defeating top men in Kid Socks, Con Lewis, André Regis of France and Young Jackie Brown of St. George's, and was already widely tipped as a future British champion. Garland, it seems, was being developed with relative care – in the same five and a half month period Pat had fought 17 times. 'Only one thing worried me,' he recalled in his memoirs, 'that we had to weigh in at 8 stone 9 lb, which would mean more starving and sweating for me to make it.'

The promotion had been arranged by the entrepreneurial Ted Broadribb, who then managed an impressive array of stars, including Nel

Tarleton, Alf Mancini, Jack Hood, Dom Volante, and Dick and Harry Corbett. He is probably best remembered today for his role in later years as the manager of Tommy Farr and Freddie Mills, but in his boxing days – fighting as 'Young Snowball' – he earned the distinction of being the only Brit to defeat the legendary Georges Carpentier, although it should be noted that Broadribb was then 21 and the Frenchman just 16. For the Clapton event, Broadribb secured the backing of Billy Chandler, Garland Wells and Charlie Luper, with whom he formed a company called British Sporting Promotions. In addition to Pat, the bill boasted top men such as Manchester middleweight Len Johnson, British lightweight champion Fred Webster and future featherweight champion Nel Tarleton. Inspired by American-style matchmaking, Broadribb decided to limit each contest to no more than 10 rounds, and thereby fit more short, fast-paced fights onto the bill. At the weigh-ins, at The Ring, Blackfriars on the afternoon of the show, the boxers picked names out of a hat to decide the referee for each fight. Pat and Garland drew Bombardier Billy Wells as their 'third man'.

That evening the promoters had the luck of the weather but were less lucky with the turnout. 'With such an interesting, well-varied, and thoroughly good-class programme to tempt the public, it was surprising to find that a far greater number did not seize the opportunity of seeing a lot of excellent sport,' wrote A. J. Daniels of *The Sporting Life*. Accommodation had been provided for over 30,000 but only just over 5,000 attended, leaving large pockets of empty seats. 'Chandler insisted on running it on Ascot Friday,' wrote Broadribb in his autobiography. 'Experience through the years suggested that it would be the wrong night, because many people have often lost a great deal of money over the four days of the Royal meeting, and I cannot say that I was surprised that we lost about £1,500.'

'It was a very big bill and several contests had to be shortened to allow the management to show all the contests advertised,' remembered Pat. 'My contest with Jack Garland was not altered so we met over eight three-minute rounds as arranged.' Newspaper forecasts were noncommittal, but a victory for the unbeaten former Olympian and ABA champion was not ruled out. '[Daly] may get beaten by Jack Garland,' wrote the *Daily Herald*'s reporter. '...it is just possible that [Garland] may catch "the real wonder" boxer napping,' agreed *Boxing*. 'It would be difficult, if not impossible, to name any contest between any conceivable pair of boxers in the country which is so brimful of a promise of interest as this one, which we have not hesitated to label as the 'tit-bit' on the menu.'

The show started at 8pm sharp and in the first two fights – which were cut from eight to six rounds – two former opponents of Pat's, Moe Mizler and Packey McFarland, respectively outpointed Bud Wally of Singapore and Gonzalez of Barcelona. Third on the bill of fare was Pat's clash with Garland. 'He was very strong and was a heavy puncher,' recalled Pat, 'as he twice shook me up with right hand punches in the first round, and he also had an accurate left lead, which was nearly as fast as mine, but when it connected it was heavier.'

In the early rounds two rights and a left hook left Pat visibly shaken, but as *The Sporting Life's* A. J. Daniels noted 'he boxed with the skilled defence of a veteran until he pulled round'. Garland used his superior strength to good effect in the clinches, but Pat regained a foothold with a steady stream of straight lefts, and by the end of the second blood flowed freely from the Irishman's nose and mouth. Garland, though, continued to press forwards and in the fourth shook Pat again, with a vicious left hook. He tried to finish it there and then, but found the two rights he threw next were neatly parried. Several clinches followed, with both boxers admonished by Billy Wells for pulling on the neck. The action was fast and fierce, but for the most part Pat kept his man on the end of his long left, causing further damage to an already liberally blood-soaked nose and mouth. When the Irishman did get inside Pat's left, he was time and again knocked back by a rasping right uppercut. In the seventh Garland again had some success, but in the eighth and final round, despite a slip to the canvas, Pat 'boxed brilliantly to the end to win a most popular decision,' wrote A. J. Daniels. And in contrast to Garland's blood-smeared face, 'he left the ring without a mark on him'.

'The verdict was very well received by the audience,' remembered Pat, 'but loud protests came from the opposing corner.' Garland's backers, who had no doubt wagered a fair sum on their hitherto unbeaten fighter, were adamant he had won. 'Garland and his seconds were sure that the referee had made a mistake,' wrote James Butler in *The Sporting Chronicle*. 'Said Jack Goodwin after the contest, "Garland ought to have had the verdict. Daly was holding most of the time, and the referee never cautioned him about it." Well as I saw the bout Daly was not guiltless. At the same time it was my opinion that Daly thoroughly earned the decision that rightly went his way.'

The newspapers mostly agreed with Billy Wells's verdict, although the *Daily Sketch* and the *Sunday Sportsman* felt a draw would have been fairer. 'The small minority who seemed to imagine that Garland should have got the verdict from me,' wrote Billy Wells in *The Topical Times*, 'should bear in mind that a mere hitting out at an opponent does not constitute points. It is the blows that land that count. The closed glove blows which get legitimately to the vital spots. I should say that for every six punches delivered by Garland, five were taken by Nipper Pat on the forearms or shoulders. No: Daly won. But he did not win by a mile, nor did he, in my opinion, box as well as I have seen him do previously.'

Boxing felt that some reporters were seated too far back to observe whether Garland's blows were landed or blocked. Their own journalists had left their designated press seats to take up chairs near the ring, which afforded a much better view. 'As we saw the exchanges,' said the trade paper, 'the "boy" won by a very comfortable margin. Yet we have to say, we have never seen him box so badly.'

This last sentiment was something most of the reports agreed upon. Though Pat had beaten the man put before him, he had done so with far less ease than usual. His opponent, of course, was a classy fighter, but something of Pat's usual polish was absent from the performance. Had they known of the arduous training and dietary regime that had got him to 8 stone 9 lb, they might not have been surprised.

In truth, Pat was no longer a bantamweight and the chances of him ever making 8 stone 6 lb, should the Board allow him a title match with Baldock, were now extremely slim. But not everyone was aware of this. 'Garland demanded a return fight, which the Prof agreed to,' remembered Pat, 'and the Premierland promoters offered a purse which was accepted by both sides. Garland's advisers insisted on the bout being 12 three-minute rounds [with a] weigh-in at 9 stone at 11am. Jack and his manager were very pleased as they thought that the new weight (9 stone instead of 8 stone 9 lb) would be decidedly to his advantage.' They of course had no idea that the extra weight would also suit Pat. 'Let's have a "monkey" on it,' snarled Garland's manager, meaning of course £500. 'All right,' retorted the Professor to the amusement of bystanders. 'I'm going to the zoo tomorrow. I'll get you one.'

Pat's next engagement was supposed to have been a 15-rounder against Frenchman Rene Gabes at Brentford FC's ground, Griffin Park, on Saturday 29 June. But Pat wasn't well enough to box and had to withdraw, and without his star attraction promoter Prince-Cox cancelled the whole show. 'His indisposition,' reported *Boxing*, 'was due to a slight reoccurrence of trouble resulting from some low punches received in a recent contest.' Another paper was equally vague and said he was 'suffering from internal injuries'. Whatever the ailment, according to *Boxing* he was 'now wonderfully fit and well' and 'passed O.K.' when examined by a doctor on 2 July. This, of course, was just as well, for he was fighting the recently dethroned British bantamweight champion, Kid Pattenden, in five days' time.

The man the boxing world called 'Kid' was born Alfred Edward Pattenden on 21 November 1907. He first saw the light of day in Clerkenwell, but the family soon moved to East London, where he grew up. A natural athlete, he won certificates for swimming and medals for cross country, but was always best at boxing. Early on he joined one of the East End's many amateur clubs and at 14 was a Federation of Boys' Clubs champion (a title he won three times). At 18 he beat Fred Webster in the season that Webster won the first of his three ABA titles. Convinced that he had the stuff of champions, shortly afterwards Pattenden quit his job at a boot and shoe factory to become a professional. Fighting mostly at Premierland, within two years he stormed his way to a British title victory. Nel Tarleton, Kid Nicholson, Frankie Ash, Kid Socks, Johnny Brown (British champion at the time), and Young Johnny Brown (the champion's younger brother) were all Pattenden victims, while he held top American Archie Bell and all-time bantamweight great Panama Al Brown to draws. Gilbert Odd, who sat ringside for many Pattenden fights, later recalled:

'Pattenden's style of boxing could not be termed orthodox. He paid little heed to defence, but relied upon his hustling tactics to stop the man in front of him from scoring points. There is a boxing adage that "attack is the best form of defence". Pattenden believed in this to the last letter, and he made his rise to fame with the whirlwind way in which he used both hands, and kept them going in non-stop fashion from first gong to last... Pattenden was unbelievably tough. He could absorb punches that would knock the average fighter cold; he could trade blows with harder hitters than himself and be the last to break off a rally. Only twice was he stopped and that was when he was nearing the end of his tremendous career. His jaw had a granite streak in it; his body was trained to the texture of teak; he had the fighting heart of a tiger.'

The Pattenden fight promised to be Pat's toughest and most contentious match to date. Over half of the 21-year-old Bethnal Green man's wins had arrived inside the distance, so Pattenden could certainly punch as well as take a punch. 'It really looks as though Nipper Pat Daly is running the risk of having his career ruined before he has reached his best by being rushed along at too great a pace,' wrote the *Daily Mirror*'s boxing columnist days before the fight. 'His advisers ought to bear in mind the fact that he is not strong enough to oppose boxers who are fully matured and exceptionally strong for the weight.' *The Daily Herald*'s correspondent was equally dubious about Pat's chances. '...Clever as Daly is,' he wrote, 'I cannot imagine him escaping scot free from punishment... although Daly beat Petit Biquet, I cannot think he will account for Pattenden.' Jimmy Wilde, writing in his *News of the World* column, was in agreement. 'I must confess that Daly's chances are not particularly rosy. Should Daly rise to the occasion and outpoint Pattenden, I sincerely hope he will be given a long holiday.'

Usually Pat entered a contest without specific instructions – the Professor would trust him to make the necessary adjustments in the ring to handle the style of each opponent. This time, however, perhaps concerned by recent press criticism, Newton insisted that they hold a pre-fight conference. The Professor told Pat to take it easy for the first few rounds – he should box with caution and at all costs avoid mixing it. But to his mentor's surprise, Pat had a different plan of attack. 'I'm gonna take the fight to him,' he said. 'Pattenden likes to get on top, and if I can cramp his style and put him out of his stride, I think I can win easily.' Shaking his head, the Professor told his colt he must be mad. But on the boy's vehement insistence that he knew just how to beat the ex-champion, Newton finally agreed to let him box as he saw fit.

***

Deep within a maze of grimy, worn-out Whitechapel Streets, on an otherwise insignificant byway called Back Church Lane, in what was then the Jewish East End, once stood Premierland. Just one road away, 41 years before Pat's fight with Pattenden, on Berner Street (today called

Henriques Street), Jack the Ripper took the life of his third victim, Elizabeth Stride. His macabre reign of terror lived long in the minds of Whitechapel folk, and no doubt some who lived through it were seated at Premierland that afternoon. (A 23 year-old Professor Newton, incidentally, won his first ABA title in 1888, the year of the Berner Street murder.) The streets had changed very little since the poverty-stricken days of the Whitechapel killings, although some four decades on, people from outside the area now had a reason to flock to it. As the author Thomas Burke would write, a Premierland Sunday matinee 'was one of the sights of London'. Thousands of fight-loving Londoners were drawn there from every corner of 'the Smoke', and they weren't all of the bloodthirsty, spit and sawdust variety. 'I went to see ballet,' wrote Burke in his 1932 social study *The Real East End*, 'which, to me, was more beautiful than any formal stage ballet.'

On this particular Sunday in July 1929 the top-line bout promised the Premierland event of the year – the combatants were two of the best in the country and both huge East End favourites. 'It will surprise me if all the people who want to get into Premierland on Sunday afternoon will be able to do so,' predicted A.J. Daniels in *The Sporting Life*, 'for it would be difficult to recall an event here with as much pulling power as the meeting of Alf (Kid) Pattenden and Nipper Pat Daly in a 15 round contest.'

At the 11am weigh-in 'you could not buy a seat for love or money,' recalled Andy Newton. 'The shrewd judges had bought a lot of tickets up and were getting as much as a pound for a five-shilling ticket. The odds against Daly winning were 4 to 1, and in some places, before the contest commenced, 5 to 1 could be obtained. My friend and I had backed Daly to win £400 at these odds.' The contracted weight was 8 stone 10 lb, and Pat came in a half-pound inside. Pattenden, however, had to burn off a few ounces and be re-weighed.

The 'house full' signs were up early that day, with every thinkable space beneath Premierland's steel-girdered roof adapted for customer use. A sea of faces – mostly men, but also the occasional female – covered the hall on all sides. Many men wore cloth caps, especially those stood or sat farther out, while closer to the ring hats were more common. The air, as always, was filled with chatter and cockney banter, blue with tobacco smoke and thick with its stench. Near ringside, bookmakers bawled out odds and wrote down bets, journalists leafed through notebooks, and the tobacco smell was masked by the more pungent aroma of resin and embrocation. 'Get yer chocolates!', 'Fine orange!', and 'Ices!' rang the cries of the hawkers with their trays, as a man gingerly hoisted the number of the first round – which he would update between rounds – aloft a high wooden pole in readiness for the afternoon's first fight. At the very centre, lit by dazzling electric bulbs, was a raised, roped, bright-white square which split the dingy hall four ways. The crowd's chatter continued, and then, as Thomas Burke remembered it:

> 'The thing opened with no parade. The referee would appear from some obscure hiding-place, and take a raised seat at the ring-side. The time-keeper would follow him. Two or three stout fellows in sweaters would appear with pails. And then the M.C. [Lew ('Buster') Cohen] would climb through the ropes and take the centre of the ring, and the thing would be on. With his appearance the babble was suddenly arrested. He would lift an arm with air of prelude to a mighty drama. In the tones of a town-crier he would announce forthcoming events, and then turn to the business of the afternoon.'

That particular afternoon, besides the 15-round main event, the bill comprised three 10-rounders and some shorter, unspecified fights billed only as 'other special contests between picked lads', which probably meant whoever could be found at short notice to fill the time. After the MC's introductions each fight began with the timekeeper's bark of 'Seconds *out!*' and the clang of the bell. The boxers sprung from their stools then, as Burke noted, 'For some seconds you would hear nothing but the thud of soft feet and the pad-pad of glove on body.' But the crowd's silence was only momentary:

> 'It was broken by a skilful blow or a mighty swipe, or by the absence of either... Every good blow received recognition from one section and every slogging mix-up received it from another section. If nothing happened in the first few seconds a voice would float out of the violet cloud above: "Come on, there! Come on. Show us something." Other voices, having been started by a Leader, formed a Chorus. "Use that left. Come on, Bill. Come on. Now! Now you got him." At first these voices would be conversational; and the M.C.'s monotonous "Keep quiet, there!" could still be heard. But once one of the boys had started something, the voices merged in a roar and the M.C. would give up.'

'Event would follow event,' wrote Burke, 'up to the middle of the afternoon, when "the big 'un" was staged – a fifteen or twenty-round affair. This was what the crowd had come to see, and this indeed moved them.' After the last of the ten-rounders had ended, the ring was cleared for Pattenden and Daly, who then made their way through the crowd towards the ring. 'My Mum and Dad had a box near the ringside,' remembered Pat. 'To me they stood out a mile, as did Teddy Brown the famous music hall performer, who attended all my Premierland fights.'

Both boxers sat in their corners, shuffled their feet in a resin tray (to prevent them slipping on the canvas), and were then called to centre ring. 'Order there! Silence!' yelled the hefty house MC, Lew Cohen. Then syllable by syllable he bellowed, 'Eight-stone 10 pound contest of 15 two-minute rounds, between Nipper *Pat Daly*, Marylebone, and Alf Kid *Pattenden*, Bethnal Green. On my r-ight – DALY. On my l-eft – PATTENDEN." There was a spot of applause, to which both nodded their heads in appreciation as Lew Cohen left the ring. From his ringside chair the referee warned both contestants to break clean and keep their punches up, then both returned to their corners. Finally came the cry of 'Seconds *out*!', followed by the clang of the bell, and they both leapt from their stools.

Pattenden crossed the ring to find Pat already upon him. Two jolting straight lefts smashed into his mouth before he could block, and as his guard went up a punch to the body put him onto the back foot. Pat pursued him across the ring and crowded him onto the ropes. Pattenden broke free from the onslaught and charged back at Pat, but as he came forwards the Nipper sidestepped and hooked him neatly to the ear. 'Pattenden tried to bring his man down with right swings very early,' noted *The Evening News*, 'but his judgement of distance left something to be desired and he was made to miss rather badly by Daly's habit of just moving his head sufficiently to avoid.' To the surprise of everyone, 'Not only was Daly much superior as a boxer – his left-hand work was splendid – but he did not appear to mind going in to have a fight.' Unrelentingly Pat crowded into his man, out speeded and outboxed him in a series of blazing exchanges that whipped the large crowd into a frenzy. The first five rounds were his by a mile, and left the ex-champion utterly bamboozled. Wrote *The Daily Chronicle*'s reporter:

'I have never seen cleaner close fighting, and through it all the lost sheep was Pattenden. He could not discover what Daly was after or where he could be found. Daly worried Pattenden so much that the latter must have wondered whether he was in a boxing ring or a threshing machine, so many and varied were the punches that set his left eye bleeding, caused his lips to swell and bleed, and which would have demoralised a boxer less determined and plucky than he. Daly seemed to have at least six moves to Pattenden's three. Daly gave a great exposition of how to use the left feint and the right follow... Many times Daly repeated this move.'

The ringside betting, which had opened at two to one against Pat, soon swung wildly around. 'No sooner had the match opened than there was a wild scurry to lay the odds on Daly,' noted *The Evening Standard*. Pat was just conscious of the ballyhoo, and would remember a wildly excited Jewish-looking merchant at ringside shouting, 'It's a turn-up for the book!' The Professor, usually like ice in his man's corner, could barely contain his excitement. But Pat, noted *Boxing*'s correspondent, remained as composed as ever:

'One thing struck me very much, and that was the cool way Daly acted during the minute's rest. He sat with eyes closed while the two Newtons ministered to him. He merely nodded acknowledgment of their remarks, but whether he was absorbing advice or not I cannot say.'

Pattenden came after Pat like a whirlwind at the start of the sixth. He tore into him with both fists and for a moment the boy looked in trouble. But suddenly, much to the crowd's delight, Pat flew back at Pattenden, who according to *Boxing*:

'was caught by everything bar the post. It was a toe-to-toe fight in the seventh round, with Pattenden all out to do or die, and he was very good with some hard jolts to the body. He made good use of a snappy uppercut to the chin, but the weedy looking youth from Marylebone took them all and gave more in return... Pat's main asset was the way he crowded into Pattenden. He never let him go a foot away from him, and banged away at Alf's head and ribs with two hands.'

Pattenden tried all sorts of moves and pulled out every trick he knew; but to his dismay he found his 16-year-old adversary wise to them all. 'Daly is like an eel to hit,' wrote the *Sunday Sportsman*'s reporter, 'he wriggles, ducks, and dives, and side steps like a toe dancer.' 'The repeated efforts of Pattenden kept Daly at full stretch,' said *The Evening News*, 'and the result was that, although the last named was practically always having the better of the scoring, the fight was good to watch throughout.'

Coming into the twelfth, the Professor told Pat to take things easy; he had won every round so far and now need only protect his lead. As advised, Pat eased off and boxed on the defensive, but he soon discovered that this was a mistake. A right cross from Pattenden sped towards his chin; there was no time to block but he managed to sway backwards, which lessened the blow's impact. Nonetheless, it sent him sprawling to the canvas, and a photograph taken that moment shows a scene of pandemonium. Men are shouting with arms raised high; a dour-faced Pattenden strolls to a neutral corner, while the referee counts over Pat, who is down but propped up by his outstretched arms. Outside the ring on either side of him are the Professor and Andy Newton. The Professor's arms rest on the canvas as he pleads with Pat to 'Stay down, son. Don't get up yet...' Pat rose at nine and as Pattenden rushed in to finish him, though badly shaken, he fenced him off with a volley of stinging straight lefts and forced him around the ring for the rest of the round.

'For the remainder of the contest,' wrote *The Daily Chronicle*, 'it was a case of constant lefts being pushed into Pattenden's face... [But] those lefts were always followed by something useful from the right.' In sheer desperation to land a telling punch, Pattenden rushed at Pat wildly. 'When that was done,' said *The Daily Chronicle*, 'Daly either guarded, ducked or shifted his head the necessary few inches to avoid, and then always remained so close that, before Pattenden could bring his guard into proper position again, he would receive anything from one to four rapid punches.' The ex-champion was utterly bewildered. He'd never been in with an opponent like this one, and never before nor afterwards was he beaten in such a one-sided fashion.

In the fourteenth Pat nearly nailed him. A left feint set up a perfect right cross to Pattenden's jaw, the former champ was sent reeling, and groggily crashed into the ropes. As *The Evening Standard* had it:

'The ropes prevented him falling to the floor, but he was hurt, and was then staggered by a tattoo of punches to the head and body that made him fight fiercely to avoid being put down. It was a wonderful fight, a feast of boxing in every round, and when the last session came up Daly was unmarked and much fresher than Pattenden. The last round was a thriller. Both lads went all out for a decisive punch, but Pattenden was up against a master boxer and a better fighter than himself.'

Pattenden did not need to be told the winner. As the last bell sounded he embraced his young opponent and congratulated him on a great show of boxing. When the verdict was officially rendered the East End hall erupted with a prolongued storm of stamping, cheering and heartfelt applause. Professor Newton was nearly overcome. 'Well done, my boy, well done,' he kept murmuring, while his son, Andy, threw his arms around Pat and kissed him. All three were mobbed as they left the ring and it was some time before Pat could get to his dressing room. 'During this journey,' remembered Andy, 'Daly received more slaps on his head, back and body from the cheering crowd than he had received from Pattenden during the whole 15 rounds.' After a quick change into his street clothes, Pat proudly took his mother on his arm and the entourage made for Newton's gym for a celebration. There were beers aplenty that evening, but only a celebratory steak and chips for the Nipper who, though old enough to conquer champions, was still too young for alcohol.

The doubts brought on by the recent below par performances – and in particular the shadow of the Parker defeat – had all been laid to rest. The Nipper was back to his brilliant best.

17

Can Daly Last?

'London, it is said, has begotten an astounding fighter, Pat Daly, not yet 17 years of age. And it is declared that before long he will go to war against and beat a world's champion. Bold prediction: yet it may come true... The dramatic leap to something like notoriety by this boy with a roguish Irish name interests me vastly; he is of the same age as I was when I dared to dream and believe that I would achieve international renown... Advice I would tender – the risk of over-leaping oneself is very real... That he should ache for a place among world beaters is very natural: no youth should embark upon the trade of pugilism unless determined to win the highest position, but there must always be danger that comes from over keenness and impatience.'

Georges Carpentier (former world light-heavyweight champion),
The Advertiser, Adelaide, Australia, 26 September 1929

Pat's one-sided win over Pattenden brought him greater adulation and wider recognition than ever before. Against expectations, not only had he defeated the highly ranked ex-champion, but in doing so he had supplied a display of boxing that stood comparison with any. The Premierland crowd had seen an exhibition of the noble art that would stay etched in their minds for years to come. It had been breathtaking, and all the more so given his youth. As Steve Boston, writing for The London Ex-Boxers' Association journal *Box On!*, decades later declared, 'They had seen an exhibition of boxing worthy of the greatest – a fight not easy to forget.'

Newspaper commentary in the days after the fight was duly flattering. 'Probably the greatest bout witnessed at Premierland since its early days... It was an extraordinary performance... Daly's boxing was perfect,' wrote the *Daily Herald*. While James Butler, writing for *The Sporting Chronicle*, affirmed, 'Daly is really a wonder for his years. I do not suppose we have a more accomplished boxer in Europe.' Several papers drew comparisons with Teddy Baldock's fight with Pattenden and decided that Pat had won in far better fashion. 'To Daly's credit it can be said that he punched

Pattenden more frequently in each round than Baldock had done, and took far less punishment than Baldock took in the championship contest,' wrote *The Daily Chronicle*. Inevitably, the prospect of a Daly–Baldock match was raised again by *Boxing*. 'It must surely be on the cards,' said the trade paper. 'Nipper Pat Daly may not be considered to be qualified to fight for a title for another four years; but there isn't a doubt he would find a host of supporters were Baldock to consent to venture his luck.'

After the fight, the *Sunday Sportsman*'s columnist wrote, 'Like many other critics, I was amazed by Daly's performance, and so I sought the Professor for an interview.' When he caught up with the boy's mentor, Newton seized his chance to reproach his detractors:

> 'Being the oldest trainer of boxers in this country, I must be given credit for experience... Daly's victory this afternoon is not only a triumph over Pattenden, but also over most of the critics, who have been telling me for months past that I have been overworking young Pat, and that I should sap all his strength before he reached his best. Now, let me tell you I have had Daly under my charge since he was ten years of age, and I ought, and do, know the boy's little peculiarities and the best way to keep him at concert pitch.
>
> The fact of the matter is this. Daly only shows at his best when he is kept busy. As soon as he takes a holiday or a few days off he goes stale, and that was why he was beaten by Douglas Parker in the North recently. It came about like this. After he beat that clever boxer Joe Greenwood, he had a three days' holiday, and then went on to Liverpool, where he only boxed very moderately to beat Jim Crawford, of Wrexham. From there he went on to Preston to box an exhibition bout, and then returned to town to have a week-end at Southend with his mother. I did not have the chance to rub the rust off him before he went to Sunderland, where Parker knocked him out. When he returned, after travelling all night, I gave him a test in the ring and half-an-hour's training. I put him up against a clever featherweight – a dark horse, by the way – and Pat gave him a real hiding. From that time I kept him in good work, with the result that he has beaten Jack Garland, and now Pattenden.'

But the criticism of Newton did not abate. 'Daly's manager, Professor Andrew Newton, disagrees with me that the lad is being rather overworked,' wrote James Butler in *The Sporting Chronicle*. He went on to cite the case of an unnamed boxer from Yorkshire, once chasing title honours, who 'was worked too hard when in his early teens', and whose career was consequently ruined. 'Daly probably will not feel the effect so much as the man I have mentioned, for the reason that Daly is infinitely more clever, and has a formidable defence. This means that he is not going to end up "punch drunk" like some of the so-called tough fighters, whose damaged faces and ears bear testament of their easily penetrated guard.' But even so, he concluded with a warning that 'nature takes its toll for the liberties which are taken on the constitution – whether young or old.' Trevor C. Wignall, one of sports reporting's earliest star columnists, wrote in a similar but more direct vein for the *Daily Express*:

'His trainer and mentor, Andrew Newton… states that the boy thrives on plenty of fights, and that his make-up is such that his development would be retarded if he were not given the maximum of employment. I do not find it easy to support this view… it does seem feasible that the claim that he is heading for a world's championship is well founded, but he should be intelligently nursed and matched until he is a year or so older. The long history of boxing proves conclusively that the average prodigy flickers out just when manhood is reached, all because he is rushed too swiftly. This must not happen to Daly, who is unquestionably the most promising youth in the country.'

All was quiet from the Newton stable in the days after the Pattenden fight. Pat had not been seen, and this, according to *The Sporting Life*, had 'given rise to a storm of rumours'. One was that he had set sail for the United States, and another that he was directly preparing to face Teddy Baldock for the British title. But neither was true. He had in fact – at long last – been sent on an extended holiday. The Professor's reasons for giving his colt a break, however, were far from benevolent, as Pat recalled in his memoirs:

'The critics and other people still clamoured that I should have a rest and the Professor had to do something about it. At this time (July) I had several invitations to spend a holiday at various resorts, [but] the Prof picked an address in Blackpool, so that's where I had to go.'

Pat stayed with an old friend and former pupil of the Professor's who, according to *Boxing*, cut a formidable figure at over 16½ stone. 'I shall have to slip plenty of work into him when he returns to tune him up again,' Newton remarked to the *Sunday Sportsman*'s reporter.

Blackpool's population had rocketed in the few years since the Great War, and by 1930 it would draw around seven million visitors per year: three times as many as its nearest British rivals. When Pat visited, in July 1929, the annual holiday season was in full swing. The writer Charles Graves, in a piece printed in *The Daily Mail* that month, sung the town's praises as a leisure resort:

> 'I have never seen so many people having so grand a time at the same moment and in the same place... Blackpool is overpowering. Its air is so strong, its places of amusement so gigantic, its enjoyment of life so terrific, its colours so bright that you grope for phrases to describe it adequately.'

Two pence in Blackpool went as far as one shilling would in London, claimed Graves, and with your shillings and pence there was no shortage of things to do. Blackpool boasted the famous Pleasure Beach, an enormous bathing pool, a rare-fish aquarium, a menagerie, the Winter Garden theatre, ballrooms and dance halls, sideshows and rides, and an incredible 18 cinemas. Pat was a fan of the flicks, so it's quite likely he watched a film or two, and photographic evidence suggests he may have had a companion. A photo taken in a Blackpool promenade studio shows Pat and another young boxer posing affectionately with a pair of young women, whom they had met on holiday, and the pair reappear in another photograph. How well they knew one another is unclear, but as Pat's memoirs reveal, the trip wasn't all fun and games. Although neither Pat nor the Professor were short of money, perhaps to ensure that Pat stayed in at night, the old man had insisted on a working holiday:

> 'After I had finished cleaning and taking the eyes out of five sacks of potatoes – it was a fish restaurant, which meant I was working until 11pm – I was free to have my holiday. So in between peeling potatoes I had some sun, had a few swimming excursions, and in general enjoyed myself. When my two weeks' holiday was over I returned home to London and went into strict training for a fight in Blackpool against Tommy Rose (Bolton), who had a big following in the north of England, having defeated all the top north country bantams.'

On 29 July *The Sporting Life* reported that Pat had returned from Blackpool and was back in training at Marylebone Road. 'He trains from 11 to 12 am and from 7 to 8 pm daily at Prof. Newton's,' noted the newspaper, 'and the public are cordially invited to see him at work.' The fight with Tommy Rose, set for the August Bank Holiday Monday, was part of an annual boxing show staged at Blackpool FC's Bloomfield Road ground. Top of the bill was Teddy Baldock, who opposed the leading Belgian bantam, Gideon Potteau. 'It would be difficult, not to say impossible, to imagine a more attractive bill-of-fare,' proclaimed *Boxing*. 'Two of the most magnetic box-fighters in the country will be on view in different contests, and as there has been a recent demand that Teddy Baldock and Nipper Pat Daly should be matched, there will be intense curiosity to inspect the two little fellows with a view to compare their respective merits... They will be able further to compare their recollections of Jimmy Wilde with the appreciation of the new star which has arisen, to wit, Nipper Pat Daly.' Tommy Rose had challenged Pat by entering the ring at the end of his return fight with Jim Crawford at the Liverpool Stadium. On that showing (the fight ended in a draw), which came a few days after the knockout defeat to Parker, Rose, who possessed a decent dig, must have fancied he had a chance.

Heavy rain in the early morning gave way to bright rays of sunshine that afternoon, and between 10,000 and 12,000 people flocked to Bloomfield Road. The ring, which was decorated in red, white and blue, was erected in front of the football ground's main stand. 'The crowd seemed well satisfied,' wrote *The Sporting Chronicle*'s reporter, 'but the intimate atmosphere of the boxing hall was missing. The boxers were too far away for the exact consequences of a blow to be noted.' In the first two bouts Eric Rolinson of Blackpool cleverly outpointed Jack Flynn of London over 10 rounds, and Fred Cookson (Oldham) outscored Fred Chandler (London) in a close 12-rounder. At 4:30pm Baldock and Potteau entered the ring, accompanied by an army of seconds. Their bout went 11 of the scheduled 15 rounds, whereupon the Belgian's seconds threw in the towel to save their man from being knocked out. Pat's fight with Rose – the penultimate on the programme – was up next, and this is how he remembered it:

'On coming out for the first round against Tommy Rose, he caught me with his favourite right hand punch, which not only shook me but left me with a pain in my head as if something was broken, and I had the pain for the rest of the fight. Rose knew he had hurt me and he took the initiative, only to run onto my straight left hand punches, and I just about held my own in the first round. On coming out for round two Rose was full of confidence and threw his right hand, which I ducked under making him miss completely, but when [in the third round] he repeated the punch, this time I just advanced on him and got inside his right swing with a short left hook which not only floored him but knocked him completely through the ropes onto the grass verge.'

According to *The Sporting Chronicle* it was 'a rapid right hook' that finished the contest, while *Boxing* remembered it as a 'short right to the point', both of which suggest Pat's recollection of a left hook may be wrong. But whatever the punch, it had the desired effect on Rose. 'Someone pushed him back into the ring,' wrote *The Sporting Chronicle*, 'but he rolled over and was unable to rise and was counted out.' British rings of the 1920s lacked the vertical cord that today holds the horizontal ropes in place, and reduces the chances of a fighter falling from the ring. (Teddy Baldock, in the previous contest, had at one stage punched his opponent through the ropes too, so that particular ring may have had especially slack ropes.) Although Pat had been hurt early, in customary fashion he had kept his cool and given no outward indication. The reports, anyway, made no mention of it:

'He took Tommy Rose's measure quite early, out-speeded the heavier and older man, stabbed him repeatedly with the left and had him shaken by an early stage with the crispness and accuracy of his right hand hitting. Rose was literally outclassed and when the K.O. came along in the 3rd round there was a consensus of opinion that the Nipper is clearly the fastest, neatest, and most effective box-fighter for his years, who has been seen anywhere for a very long time... Teddy Baldock, billed as Bantam Champion of the World, was presumably the main attraction, but from the general conversation of those present as the crowds dispersed, it was The Nipper who had created the deeper impression.' *Boxing*

Trevor C. Wignall in his *Daily Express* column was in agreement, saying, 'Teddy Baldock will have to look to his laurels. Not only did he disappoint the majority of the ten thousand spectators at Blackpool on Monday, but he caused the same big section loudly to exclaim that the best fighter on the programme was Pat Daly.' After the fight Pat returned to London to train for his return contest with Jack Garland, which was booked for six days hence. During this time, an increasingly intrigued Clyde Foster, of *The Evening Standard*, paid a visit to Marylebone Road to watch him train:

'Nipper Pat Daly is growing into a world champion, "the Professor" believes, and I am half inclined to agree with him... I wanted to see the Nipper at his work and to chat with him. I saw enough to prove that he is far above the ordinary boy boxer. But as for a chat, I am afraid I have little to write in that line. This boy boxer was so completely engrossed in his training that he found little time for conversation, and I let him alone while he evinced the utmost willingness to box the breath out of his body to oblige me. The ring seemed to be in a whirl with his fists, and those of his young comrades who threw themselves at the Nipper. The school was all fun and fury. It suggested to me a sort of clearing of the decks for action. There was not a still moment. The only time Daly could find for talking was when he came over to me for a moment to say that he hoped he would beat Teddy Baldock if they ever met.'

That same week the boxing correspondent at *The Star* echoed Foster's admiration for Pat, but also in no uncertain terms showed grave concern at the way he was being handled. Although Pat's arduous dietary regime was not public knowledge, the writer seems to have deduced its existence from his ability to consistently make weight:

'His clean-cut defeat of Kid Pattenden marked Daly as a most formidable opponent for Baldock, who had a great deal more difficulty in getting the verdict over Pattenden, and there is no doubt that Professor Newton's protégé gives promise of being as great a force in British boxing when he reaches maturity as Jimmy Wilde was. So good, indeed, is this child that it seems a pity a syndicate of sportsmen cannot be formed to let him lie fallow for a couple of years. He should be allowed to eat and drink just what he likes, and not have his physique taxed by training for and meeting grown men. Who cares whether he grows even into a welterweight so long as when he is really ready, he brings a world's championship home to England?'

His appeal, of course, fell on deaf ears. There were plenty more Goliaths for this young David to topple and a great deal more money could be made. Berliner and Lyttlestone, the Premierland promoters, were working hard to ensure a large turnout for their opening show of the new boxing season. But with as mouth-watering a headliner as the return between Pat and Jack Garland, they need not have tried too hard. 'Greatest Controversy Return Contest of the Year!' promised an advert in *Boxing*, which in bold letters pondered, 'CAN DALY LAST?' This was a question Garland's camp were sure they knew the answer to. Their man had troubled the youngster in no small measure over eight three-minute rounds, so in a contest of 12 three-minute rounds, 36 minutes of actual fighting, the boy's chances, they reasoned, should be slim. Buoyed by the assurances of his handlers and friends that the verdict at Clapton had been unjust, and also by a thirst for revenge against the youth who had inflicted his first professional defeat, Garland was certain he would defeat the boy, most probably inside the distance. 'Garland was supremely confident,' recalled Pat, 'as the weight (9 stone) suited him as he, aged 20 years [he was in fact 21], was still growing.' But unknown to Garland, Pat was equally glad that the agreed weight was 5 lb heavier than when they first met. 'The weight suited me,' he remembered, 'as I was able to have a light breakfast, which normally I never had before a weight match. At the weigh-in neither of us moved the beam at 9 stone.'

The purse at stake was £200, which probably would have been split 60 per cent winner, 40 per cent loser. This was that rare type of contest that all sports fans crave – a genuine 'needle' match between top-class practitioners – and they flocked in their thousands to see it. 'I heard men say that a chance was missed yesterday of doubling the charge for admission,' wrote Clyde Foster in *The Evening Standard*. 'An official told me that hundreds were turned away. There was a long, deep queue in the street after the house was full.' 'Premierland was literally crowded to the roof,' recalled Pat, 'the doors being shut at 3pm and nobody else was admitted.' A photograph of the event shows a sea of heads crammed together like sardines; men have crowded onto a sloping structure above the entrance, where a half-open door provides much-needed ventilation.

Before the action commenced there was a financial appeal made for ex-British featherweight champion Johnny Curley, who had recently been injured in a motor accident. Boxers who suffered misfortune were often assisted by the fight fraternity in this way. Curley entered the ring and received an ovation, plus £32 in donations from the crowd. This spectacle offered a poignant reminder of how the wealth attained through boxing could vanish as fast as it arrived. With the Curley appeal and the preliminary contests over, it was time for the main event.

Garland opened in forceful fashion. Early on he caught Pat with some jolting lefts that forced him onto the back foot, then followed these up with some stinging body blows. A right to the body, said *The Sporting Life*, was Garland's best punch, and these evidently hurt, for Pat was careful to avoid them for the rest of the fight. The first five rounds were closely contested, and unrelentingly furious, but Pat's startling speed and superior skill gave him the ascendancy. 'He kept up a speed which was even faster than many of Teddy Baldock's best moves, and that is saying something,' remarked *Boxing*. 'Garland appeared slow at times compared with him.' Garland's left did some damage to Pat's face and the Irishman landed occasionally with his right; but only occasionally. For, on the whole, as *The Daily Chronicle* noted:

'The precocious child knew more tricks than Garland. His number of guards for well-anticipated blows was uncountable. Similar versatility in the art of punching was shown by Daly. He seemed to have the correct punch for every situation whether it was straight left, straight right, left or right hook or any other kind of punch one can think of, this young Daly delivered it in this contest.'

The referee cautioned Garland for holding and hitting, but *Boxing* thought Pat was equally guilty. 'He is very clever at this part of the game, and knows how to do a bit of the rough stuff when he gets inside… [but] there is really no need for it from a lad of Daly's cleverness, the sooner the Marylebone lad drops it the better for himself.' *The Daily Chronicle* noticed this too, remarking, 'It was the only un-pretty thing he was responsible for in an otherwise excellent display.'

Though clearly behind, Garland had shown great skill and held his own during the first few rounds. But in the seventh the fight changed dramatically, as Pat started boxing as if suddenly possessed. 'To look at Daly's smooth, whiskerless face,' wrote *The Daily Chronicle*, 'one would find it hard to think that he could be so cruel. For the last half-minute of that round he banged punches at Garland with a speed and ferocity that would have looked positively brutal had not those qualities been displayed by a boy.'

From then on the fight was all Pat's. Garland fought back gamely, but was altogether bewildered and exhausted by the youngster's speed, skill and ceaseless persistency. 'This remarkable boy, Daly, set a pace that few boxers could have lived at,' wrote *The Daily Chronicle*. 'The result was that, by judicious choice of the time to make a rally, he on several occasions hit Garland so frequently that the game and clever Irish boy could do nothing but submit to the blows.' Garland strove vainly in the last few rounds to catch Pat with a knockout punch. Far from fading, as Garland's camp had hoped would happen, Pat seemed only to grow stronger and fought with more vigour as the contest progressed. At the close Garland was exhausted, while his opponent looked ready to go another 12 rounds. The verdict could only conceivably go to Pat, and this time not a single newspaper, nor Garland's handlers, would dispute it.

'It was Daly's amazing speed which beat Garland,' concluded *The Daily Herald*. 'Daly was very fast, indeed,' agreed Bombardier Billy Wells in *The Topical Times*, 'so fast that reports about his being overworked seem to be discounted on the face of it.' On this last point the ex-heavyweight champion was contradicted by *The Star*. Having criticised Pat's handlers the previous week, its columnist had been rebuked in a letter from a Captain F.B.H. of the United Services Club. 'Too much stupid gossip of this nature regarding Daly has appeared in the papers,' wrote the Captain, 'and it is time such ill-founded advice was stopped and more attention given to encouraging one of England's real boxing hopes.' *The Star*'s reporter, having quoted part of the letter, then replied to it:

'I quite agree with the Captain that Nipper Pat Daly is one of England's real boxing hopes and a potential world's champion. No doubt he is the best boy boxer we have had since Jimmy Wilde – but I have already written in this strain. This is the sole reason for my interest in his future. As he is still only 16½ I contend that for the next two years at least he should box at his natural weight, without having to reduce a single ounce to pass the scales, and not take part in long and strenuous contests. To be fighting in the ring for the best part of an hour at a time is too great a call on Nature for a boy of Daly's years. He may win fight after fight now, but I am afraid that exchanging punches with mature men will eventually sap his strength... My correspondent talks about encouraging Daly. He is already getting too much encouragement! What he wants is nursing... Nipper Pat Daly is growing all the time now. Let him grow. And let us sit-down and wait patiently for the time when he has matured. Properly handled, he may be the boxing wonder of the world.'

The writer was entirely right about Pat's rapid growth. For the second Garland fight he had weighed dead on the featherweight limit of 9 stone. The possibility of his making 8 stone 6 lb and challenging Baldock for the British bantamweight title (if the BBB of C would allow it) was all but lost. Pat would, decades later, recall the frustration he felt at having to grow. Even Newton's extreme measures could only halt his growth for so long:

'Despite all the training and fighting I was doing, nature would not be denied, I was still growing and putting on weight. Every mouthful I ate was making me weigh heavier and I used to get very depressed, because as I was outgrowing the various weight limits it seemed that I would never stop growing. As soon as I would be eligible to fight for a title at one weight I would grow into the next weight, and so on. There were so many good fighters about in those days to contest the eligibility of a new-comer into a new weight sphere, that it would take too long, and I would have to go into the next weight.'

There was still the question of whether the BBB of C would revoke its age restriction to allow Pat to box for a title, but as long as he continued to outgrow each weight class it was unlikely to be an issue. He was now, anyway, effectively a featherweight.

BOXING, RACING, AND FOOTBALL, SEPTEMBER 18, 1929.

WHEN I WON £300 IN JIG TIME, BY TED "KID" LEWIS

2D BOXING RACING & FOOTBALL

(With which is Incorporated "DOG RACING.")

VOL. XXXVIII, No. 1,045.   WEDNESDAY, SEPTEMBER 18, 1929.   Registered at the G.P.O. as a Newspaper and for Canadian Magazine Post.

UNNECESSARY RISKS RUN BY BOXERS.

WILL THESE SPOIL THE MARKET?

COMPETITION BESTOWS BENEFITS.

LAST week was not one of the brightest in British boxing annals. Americans had occasion to jubilate, as triumphs were registered over Europeans generally, while even in Australia one of our leading representatives suffered a setback. Finally, and this is a matter for real regret, our Board of Control has been put to heavy, unexpected, even if unavoidable expense.

Charlie Smith, who had made a somewhat impressive debut in the United States, and for whom really high honours were prophesied, has had a distinct setback. Teddy Sandwina, who figured on the same bill, was also beaten, while Ludwig Haymann suffered a technical k.o., in that he was stopped in four rounds by an American heavyweight, who is variously known as "Pussy" and as "Tuffy" Griffiths. Personally, we incline to the belief that the "Tuffy," is correct since we note that an American critic has credited him with being really "tuff."

Then Harry Corbett, who engaged in his second Australian contest on Saturday, was declared by the referee to have lost to an Australian, one Norman Gillespie, after fifteen rounds.

Teddy Baldock will not now be meeting Al Brown before October 2nd, so Mr. Donmall's visit to America will be still further protracted, while his expense account will be swollen. We do not know how deeply this inevitability will wring the sensitive soul of the Control Board's energetic and enthusiastic secretary, but we do fear that there will ensue some confusion in the engineering or whatever other industry claims Mr. Donmall's attention in such times as he is able to spare from his secretarial duties. He may even have commenced to ask himself whether his presence at the Baldock-Brown ringside has been, or will be, so absolutely necessary.

Smith and Sandwina Run Risks.

As for the defeats which have been registered, it is possible to say that there were excuses. Smith, we learn, went into the ring with boils and an abscess under the arm, and was weakened by these. Sandwina, we learn, had been further informed, met Harold Mays with a damaged arm, was unable to employ this and so lost a contest he should otherwise have won. There would not seem to have been any excuse for Haymann's defeat, while Corbett's was far from being popular, Harry, of Bethnal Green, had won his first contest "down under" when he beat Lou Bloom, of America, on points. In this second battle, for which both he and Gillespie weighed in at 9st. 7lb., we are told that "Corbett used his left with his usual speed and skill, and that the fighting was fast and clean throughout. Further details state that "many of the spectators thought the Englishman had won the verdict," and that "the decision in Gillespie's favour was greeted with a storm of hoots and boos.

It is a trifle consoling, also, to learn that the verdict which went to Paul Cavalier over Charlie Smith was not fully endorsed by the attendance at Madison Square Garden. Still, we have to say that both Smith and Sandwina shouldered risks they need not have taken, and had to pay the penalties.

Setting a Standard to the Americans.

It is all very well to display a reckless and a sporting spirit, but the policy rarely pays and we must confess that the managers of the two men were singularly reckless. When our boxers visit the States and get matched with American opponents, we usually notice that the Americans, or other opponents, possibly of foreign origin, are readily able to demand and to secure postponements whenever they may fancy they are in need of such.

Phil Scott went to the States on the first occasion expressly to tackle Paolino, only to learn that the Basque had injured his back, and then did it again, with the result that Phil had to see others. On the present trip, Max Schmeling decided that Scott should be given a wide berth, while Vittorio Campolo, who has consented to take the chance, has since sustained some minor injury which has necessitated a postponement.

These things will happen. Sandwina has been sidestepped several times. Teddy Baldock has had to wait in idleness, and at his own expense to suit the convenience of Al Brown. Yet here we have Smith and Sandwina, practically reduced to the state of one-armed cripples, yet willing to keep their appointments, yet willing to set an example to American boxers, which these gentry may—or, on the other hand, may not imitate.

Will There Be any Silver Linings?

It will remain to be seen whether Smith's prospects in the States will suffer from this setback. We learn that he started out like a champion, and that in the very first round he floored his opponent, Paul Cavalier, for a count of "nine," and that he then proceeded to pound the man from New Jersey most unmercifully with left hooks for four rounds.

Smith, in fact, was shaping all over like a real winner, but in the fifth round he began to tire and towards the end was "receiver general," taking heavy blows to the stomach and on the jaw with wonderful grit and endurance. He evidently did well enough to enlist the sympathies of the spectators, since they are told that the verdict in Cavalier's favour was not entirely a popular one.

It has been said that Americans will not accept excuses for beaten foreign boxers, however willing they may be to grant even to discover them for the home-grown article. Yet it is just possible that Smith may be able to readjust his standing in American opinion. His American manager, Mr. Tom O'Rourke, is shrewd and is by no means unpopular. He should be able to keep Smith going, but the Deptford man will be wise to insist that he should not be sent again into a ring under any such handicap.

Read "Sandown" Pages.
Last year placed the first three. This year the only racing correspondent to ★ ★ ★ nap the winner.

How Nipper Pat Daly learns his punches.
Note the position and the Professor's smile of satisfaction at his pupil's digestion of instruction.

Proprietors: Athletic Publications Ltd., 4-8 Greville Street, London, E.C.1
TELEGRAMS AND CABLES: AVICULTURE, HOLB, LONDON. TELEPHONE: CHANCERY 8601 (5 lines).

18

His Big Chance

'We have heard that the one and only Professor has been pressed to take his protégé to the United States. Every American critic who has seen him in action is satisfied that he would create a perfect furore in the States. The only reason for his continued stay at home has been the New York restriction on his championship qualifications on account of his age. This restriction would have to be lifted should the Nipper enter into a world title. And this event may not be so distant as some persons may suppose.'

Boxing, 15 May 1929

With his frequent top-line fights, Pat was amassing a great deal of money by working-class standards. If he had chosen or had the freedom to enjoy it, his celebrity status and bank balance would have afforded him quite a social life. At a similar age, though not then as famous as Pat, Kid Berg had made a name for himself around the London rings, on which, by his own account, he hadn't failed to capitalise. As a popular and high-salaried boxer he found the doors of the West End's clubs, bars and restaurants suddenly opened wide for him. With pockets stuffed full of cash, he hung out at establishments such as the Savoy, The 43 Club, The Ivy and the Kit Kat Club in the Haymarket until the early hours, dancing to jazz bands and picking up girls, before sauntering home to east London as the sun came up. For a young Berg, life outside of boxing was a perpetual parade of wine, women and song. Pat, however, was a different animal. By his own admission, Berg was a wild and unruly youngster, whereas Pat was unusually disciplined and mature for his years. The self-control and sacrifices needed for boxing had been ingrained in him since the age of nine. There was no room for teenage high jinks in the Professor's regime. If he were ever tempted to venture into the West End at night, the thought of the scolding he would get from Newton if the old man found out, would surely have dampened the idea. At any rate, boxing was his raison d'être; his goal was to become champion of the world, and any extramural activity that might undermine it he could certainly do without.

When he did find time to socialise, Pat mostly spent it among a close circle of friends, unconnected with boxing. His cousins Leonard and Davey John Daley – to whom he was related both maternally and paternally (his father's brother, it will be remembered, married his mother's sister) – were his closest pals, while two other good friends were Mike McGrath and a lad called 'Mac', who later died in the Second World War while serving in the RAF.

Fulltime training and fighting left Pat little time for girlfriends, but in around 1930, a certain aristocratic young lady took a decided shine to the young boxer. A year younger than Pat, Miss Anita Leslie was the only daughter of Sir Shane Leslie, a member of the landed gentry who was also a first cousin to Winston Churchill. The main Leslie family home was a castle in Ireland, but they also owned a house at 10 Talbot Square in Bayswater, just a stone's throw from Pat's house in Hatton Street. As a teenager, Anita Leslie appears to have had a rebellious streak and, unbeknown to her parents, was something of a boxing fan. According to his younger brother Ken, Pat brought Miss Leslie back to the family home a number of times and also took her on trips to the cinema. Ordinarily a lad of Pat's humble background could not hope to mix in such exalted company, but his ring fame bridged the social divide. It is unknown whether the relationship was platonic or of a more serious turn. Anita Leslie's son, Tarka King, recalls that his mother was concerned about the mistreatment of boxers and in her youth campaigned for better conditions and fairer contracts for them. She later became a writer and penned several books.*

A few days after Pat's spectacular return with Jack Garland, he and the Professor set sail for Germany, where he was to fight the latest flyweight champion, 22-year-old Karl Schulze – nicknamed 'KO Schulze' for obvious reasons. As an amateur, Schulze had won the German flyweight title in 1925 and '26 and was flyweight bronze medallist at the 1925 European championships. Upon entering the paid ranks, he knocked out Erich Köhler of Berlin to win the German flyweight crown

---

* These included biographies of her great-aunt Lady Randolph Churchill (Sir Winston Churchill's mother); her great-grandfather Leonard Jerome (Sir Winston Churchill's grandfather); her great-uncle, the writer and MP Moreton Frewen; and her father's cousin, the sculptress and writer Clare Sheridan. Anita Leslie died in 1985, aged 70.

in January 1929. By the time he fought Pat seven months later, he had grown into a bantamweight but retained the flyweight title.

More daunting than facing 'KO' Schulze on the German's home turf was the task of sweating down to the requisite weight. Having recently moved up from flyweight to bantam, Schulze naturally insisted that the match be made close to bantamweight. He was not interested in a fight at 9 stone, so they met over 10 three-minute rounds at the agreed poundage of 8 stone 7 lb; meaning Pat had to lose half a stone in 12 days. At the weigh-in (held, as usual, on the day of the fight), Schulze made 8 stone 7 lb with ease, while Pat was two pounds too heavy. He had already gone without food that day, but in an effort to shed the excess he spent the next three hours running around a local park. The extra pounds eventually shifted, but the effort left him weak.

The fight took place on Friday 23 August, at Germany's leading sports arena, The Sportpalast in Berlin. Built in 1910, the venue held around 10,000 spectators and was later notorious as a base for Nazi Party rallies. Joseph Goebbels is said to have called it 'Unsere großen politischen Tribüne' – 'our big political grandstand', and he and Adolf Hitler delivered many key speeches from within its walls. After the fall of the Nazis, The Sportpalast was used to stage rock concerts held by such stars as Jimi Hendrix, The Beach Boys, Pink Floyd and Bill Haley, before it was demolished in 1973.

As the action commenced, both fighters came out cagily. Pat had figured the German's nickname was probably well earned, while Schulze likewise thought better of rushing straight at Britain's wonder boy without first weighing him up. But in the second, the fight was all Pat's. The German could find no antidote for the Britisher's stabbing left leads and was uncharacteristically being boxed silly. Thoroughly frustrated, he decided to rush at Pat, and as he did so their heads collided with an almighty thud. Pat immediately felt his left eye swell up like a penny balloon, and when he returned to his corner the look on Newton's face confirmed his worst fears. 'Finish him off quick,' the Professor muttered. 'If he lands a punch on that 'e'll burst it, and then you'll really be in the wars.'

Spurred on by his mentor's advice, Pat charged from his corner at the clang of the third bell, intent on ending the fight quickly. But Schulze, who had first-class footwork, neatly sidestepped and crossed a hard right to his jaw. Pat went down with a smack that felt like the floor had risen up and struck him, and the German crowd rose to their feet as the referee started to count. They had heard that when Schulze floored a man he stayed floored… but not this time.

Pat staggered up at nine and managed to stall for the rest of the round. During the interval the Professor worked like a man possessed, putting a lifetime's worth of knowledge into helping his colt recover. Pat went out for the fourth somewhat improved but still unsteady. He spent much of the round evading Schulze's efforts to finish him off and protecting his damaged left eye. This time he returned to his corner feeling utterly dejected. For the first time in his career he was convinced he had fallen behind on points, and with each passing minute the injured eye grew worse. But to his astonishment, the Professor greeted the boy with a large grin. 'You're gonna win in the next round, Pat,' he crowed. 'A knockout for my little baby.' 'What are you talking about?' Pat snapped back. 'I'm not in the mood for jokes.' 'I'm not kidding,' replied the Professor. 'Watch him when he comes out of a corner – he always jumps to the left. Wait for him to start moving, then crack him one on the chin with your right hand.'

At the start of the fifth, Pat deliberately crowded Schulze into a corner and found that the German moved to his left in the manner Newton had said. Pat was so surprised that he hadn't time to connect, but immediately he knew just what he would do next. Charging Schulze into a corner again, Pat rained blows on him with both fists, then suddenly stepped back, giving the German enough room to make a quick jump to the left. Schulze moved fast but Pat's right hand was faster – the German ran straight onto the punch, his own momentum and Pat's swift shot combining to devastating effect. The smash it made against his jaw echoed around the hall. The referee counted to 10 but needn't have bothered. Schulze did not move. The poleaxed fighter was carried to his corner by his seconds, as Pat returned triumphantly to his dressing room. A glance in the mirror left him horrified by his enormous jet-black eye. 'I'd never seen one like it,' he recalled, 'and never have since.' The Professor's advice had no doubt saved him from defeat, but the eye would take some time to heal. Schulze soon recovered from the knockout and within two months officially vacated his flyweight crown and won the bantamweight title by stopping Berlin's Otto Ziemdorf. Six years later, in 1935, the boxing fraternity was stunned and saddened when Schulze drowned while swimming in the River Elbe.

A German newspaper cartoon depicting Pat's knockout of Karl Schulze.

Pat returned home the following evening, and two days later was seconding Jim Carr (another Newton fighter) at the Edmonton Alcazar, where he received a terrific hand from the crowd. The damaged eye was glaringly evident, and journalists grilled him about how he received it and how he scored his spectacular knockout. 'The contest would seem to have been a hectic affair,' wrote *Boxing*, 'as the Nipper states that Schulze's head was more dangerous than his fists.'

The Marylebone lad's next engagement was at a venue he'd never boxed at before, but one where he was assured a hearty welcome. The Vale Hall, which housed 3,000-4,000 fans, stood on Kilburn High Road in an area where Pat was considered a local. 'When he arrived with his mentor and friends in a taxi,' noted *Boxing*, 'he was surrounded by a big crowd of supporters. The Marylebone youth's genial Irish expression acts like magic, and if the elder Newton had not pushed away the crowd Pat would have gone into action with a tired right hand.' Nine days after his fight with Schulze, he was facing Bethnal Green's Con Lewis at the hall. The contest was scheduled for 15 rounds but less than half were needed:

'The bout was a real thriller while it lasted, and round after round was tolled off at a fast pace. Towards the end of the fourth Lewis looked a tired man, but he stuck manfully to Pat, and swapped blows with him at every opportunity. Although Lewis was well behind where points were concerned, he did not let Daly have all the argument. He realised, however, that Pat was more than a match for him, and wisely retired at the end of the seventh round. Lewis deserved the big applause that he received when he was leaving the ring.' *Boxing*

The next night, at Rochester Casino, a dance hall that doubled as a boxing arena, Pat boxed a three-round exhibition with Tommy Lye of Acton, and followed it with a demonstration of the Professor's unique system of training. In spite of some torrid weather, Pat's appearance drew a larger crowd than usual to the Casino. 'It was a show to the liking of the crowd, which was most enthusiastic over the Nipper's clever work,' wrote *The Evening News*. Pat no doubt was in high spirits, since earlier that day the reigning British featherweight champion, Johnny Cuthbert, had accepted a challenge to fight him. The next day (3 September) the relevant articles were signed, and the Daly–Cuthbert match was fixed for London's Holborn Stadium on 9 October. Andy Newton had pressed for the weight to be 8 stone 12 lb, but Cuthbert, wanting an assurance that, come what may, his title would stay intact, insisted it be fixed at 9 stone 1 lb: a pound above the featherweight limit. Pat immediately knew that this was the biggest fight of his career. If he beat Cuthbert, there were few who would dispute him as the best featherweight in Britain, if not Europe. There would be much debate, however, as to the wisdom of pitting a 16-year-old against a seasoned champion of 25.

Exactly a week after Pat's easy win at the Vale Hall, he made his debut at another London venue – one with a rich theatrical background. Collins's Music Hall opened in 1863 and stood towards the northern end of Islington Green. Charlie Chaplin, Marie Lloyd, Gracie Fields, George Robey and Tommy Trinder all performed there, but in 1958 the hall's interior was gutted by fire, causing the curtain to fall on its life as a theatrical establishment. The building still stands, however, and a blue plaque commemorates its star-studded past. From July 1929, promoter Maxwell Stein, with Ted Kid Lewis as his matchmaker, hired the venue for regular boxing shows. With its grand Victorian decor it made a change from the shabby halls most '20s fight fans were used to.

Pat's opponent for his Collins's debut was Lew Pinkus, a Jewish lad from Mile End who was then a week shy of his twenty-first birthday. Pinkus, who was stopped only three times in 107 recorded fights, was extremely tough and game. At times he would box with style and skill, but he was better known for discarding his boxing to have a tear-up. In July 1928 he had upset the odds by outpointing Dick Corbett (although Corbett beat him twice in return fights), and earlier in 1929 had held Kid Pattenden to a draw while Pattenden was still British champion. In sweltering afternoon heat, a large crowd crammed in to Collins's Music Hall to witness the Daly–Pinkus 15-round topliner – a match sure to entertain. In Pinkus's corner to give advice were manager Nick Cavalli and legendary former world bantamweight champion (and fellow East Ender), Pedlar Palmer. The referee was Sidney W. Ackland, Deputy Editor of *Boxing*.★

Lew Pinkus was a man in peak condition, as he proved by the merciless way he waded in throughout the contest. 'Pinkus could never get on even

---

★   Ackland became Editor of *Boxing* in 1936.

terms with his opponent for sheer skill and craft,' wrote *Boxing*, 'but by his indomitable spirit and amazing courage he fought an uphill struggle in amazing fashion to the bitter end.' The fight was filled with action and, as one report had it, Pat 'won every one of the fifteen rounds, but he had to go at top speed and all out to do so.' The verdict, of course, went to Pat, but the spectators got their money's worth and appreciatively cheered the roof off as both combatants left the ring. 'It is really astonishing how calm the Marylebone boy keeps even when hard pressed,' observed Billy Wells in the *Topical Times*. 'I can't help wondering if he has his trainer's brain somewhere on his shoulders.'

A week later, at the Rink Athletic Club on Paradise Street in West Bromwich, Pat took on Billy Cain of Birmingham before a crowd of nearly 10,000. Cain, a future Midlands featherweight champion, had already had more than 70 fights, of which he had lost just 15. Billy Boulger, Jimmy Rowbotham, Len Fowler and Willi Metzner of Germany were among the top men he had beaten. 'Cain appealed to me as a boxer from tip to toe,' wrote *All Sports Weekly*'s fight reporter the previous year, having watched Cain for the first time. 'A regular Bobby Dazzler... no end of tricks... he boxed and fought better than I have known many a champion do.'

Undaunted by his opponent's reputation, Cain flew at Pat with ferocious hooks from the first bell, making that round and the second fairly close. Pat had a slight pull in height and reach, which he used to full advantage in the third, firing out lefts, and shaking up Cain with short right uppercuts when the Brum got in close. Cain may have shaded the fourth with a sustained attack of straight lefts and swings. This roused the Midlander's many supporters, but Pat defended cleverly and quickly responded with an onslaught of his own. According to Boxing, the fourth was the last round in which Cain made any impact:

'In the fifth Daly attacked with vigour and handed out some terrific punishment. Cain's face soon bore evidence of the accuracy and power of these punches. The sixth was a bad round for Cain, who fought back as well as he was able, but Daly never left him and cornered him several times near the ropes to paste him well on head and body. The gong came as a welcome relief to the game Birmingham lad. Coming out for the seventh, Daly tore into his opponent with heavy hooks and jabs. He penned him in the opposite corner, and while Cain made every effort to smother up, he was taking so much punishment that his seconds wisely skied the towel in. Cain protested, but it was certainly the best thing to do...'

It was another spectacular win against a highly ranked opponent. 'A feature of the contest,' said *The Daily Express*, 'was Daly's clever footwork, which caused Cain to miss repeatedly. His long left fought the Birmingham lad to the ropes again and again.' 'It [was] obvious,' wrote the *Birmingham Gazette*, 'that the Birmingham boxer was no match for Daly, who proved a class in himself.'

At around this time Professor Newton received a letter from a team of doctors with a scientific interest in his prodigy. What piqued their interest was not his talent but his seemingly tireless stamina. As *Boxing* marvelled earlier that year, 'At the end of even 15-round contests he is as fresh as paint, even when he has engaged in two or three contests in a week.' Pat's ability to fight at top speed throughout a long and arduous fight was phenomenal. This apparent genetic gift to go 15 rounds without tiring, while other fighters, given any amount of conditioning, faded in the latter stages, set him apart. The doctors offered Newton £10 for the privilege of thoroughly examining him to try to determine the source of his staying power. 'Old Newton took me down to see the specialists,' remembered Pat, '[which was] his contribution for earning the £10 cheque (I did not get my 50 per cent).' The doctors no doubt hoped that a physical peculiarity would account for the boy's incredible stamina. But despite some thorough tests, they failed to find one, although they did find that his heartbeat, even for an athlete, was exceptionally slow. As a favour for attending, Pat was invited back:

'I continued going there as they said that I had a slight turn in my right eye and if I continued attending they would correct it free of charge. I started to attend and went there three times for my treatment, which consisted of exercises with various instruments. It used to take about three hours including travelling time, but the Prof said I was wasting my bloody time and would not give me permission to go any more. In my contract with the Prof I was working for him from 9am till 6pm, for which he paid me 10 shillings per week. I wear spectacles now.'

Since earlier in the year reports of the exploits of Britain's wonder boy had been steadily crossing the Atlantic. As early as May, *Boxing* had noted that the Professor had turned down several offers to take Pat to America, and was discussing him as a viable world-title challenger. By September things had moved up a gear. That month *The Ring* magazine ranked Pat at number 10 in the world (at bantamweight), and there were sure signs of interest from the non-sporting US press too:

'British boxing fans believe that in Nipper Pat Daly they have unearthed the finest fighter England has produced since Jimmy Wilde. [Wilde, the writer fails to realise, was Welsh]... It is in his fighting methods that he is so reminiscent of Jimmy Wilde. He has a born ability to land punches from every conceivable angle, especially at close-quarters, and his speed is amazing. Recently he has shown himself possessed of a flashing right-hand punch which has put a number of opponents to sleep, but whether he has the knockout blow of a world's champion only time can show...' *The Montana Standard*, 22 September 1929

In the US, the New York State Athletic Commission restricted boxers aged under 21 to a limit of six rounds per fight, which made the precocious development of a fighter like Pat an impossibility. And so, the existence of such a fighter elsewhere had added piquancy in a country that held novelty and individualism in high esteem. Just who was this youngster handing out hidings to Europe's best little-men? His rare blend of science with an attacking style, together with his youth, was an ideal composite for the American market, which was used to the idea – not altogether warranted – of the dull, defensive-minded Brit. When profiling Pat's career in July 1956, a journalist at *The Weekly News* would write, 'I remember Mickey Walker telling me what a sensation Daly would have been in America. He had it all. A punch and boxing ability to attract the men. A baby face to appeal to the women.'

But the US fans could only make an informed judgement if they saw the lad first-hand. Although Newton had so far resisted all attempts to bring Pat to America, an offer seemingly too good to turn down would now arrive. It nonchalantly fell through the letterbox of 241 Marylebone Road one morning in a plain brown envelope. The only clue that its contents were in some way special came from the USA postmark on the front. One of Pat's duties through his employment with Newton was to open, read and answer much of his post. Once he had read this particular letter – which he hurriedly relayed to his mentor – the normally laidback lad was fit to burst with excitement.

The letter had been dispatched in the wake of recent events overseas. An Italian-American called Christopher Battaglia, known to fight fans as 'Battling Battalino', had on 23 September wrested the world featherweight championship from the Frenchman André Routis, in a 15-round clash at Hartford, Connecticut. The American, renowned for his come-forward style and a penchant for fierce infighting, had proved too tough for the ageing Frenchman, which was grim news for Europeans. America now possessed the world title at every weight class – from fly through to heavyweight – and the glory days of Wilde, Lewis and Carpentier seemed more distant than ever. But the letter in Pat's hand threatened to change all that. It was an offer for a world title fight with Battalino. The writer, a noted American, had attained the agreement of Battalino's handlers, who were keen for the champ to meet the wonder boy in his first defence. The match would be held in America, where the problem posed by Pat's age had already been overcome. They had found a US state willing to stage a six-round world title fight, and had the blessing of the requisite authorities. Battalino, said the letter, took a while to get into a fight – he was a slow starter, whereas Pat got going from the very first gong. In a full-length 15 round fight there would doubtless be a danger of Battalino stopping or knocking out the Nipper; but over six rounds he should comfortably outbox the slower, less skilful champion. 'Whatever the outcome,' it concluded, 'we'll all make a lot of money.'

The letter is mentioned in a 1939 *Topical Times* article and is also recalled by several of Pat's family members. None, however, remembers the precise identity of the letter-writer. This valuable detail has been lost with the passing of time, although there are two plausible candidates. Jack Kearns (manager of Mickey Walker) had wanted to bring Pat to the States back in 1927, after the way he'd shaped up against Walker in sparring. No doubt two years on, Pat's reputation having spread, he'd be just as eager to bring the kid to the States. Another possibility is the top American manager Tom O'Rourke. In a *Boxing* article in 1941 Andy Newton mentioned that O'Rourke had offered his father £1,000 for Pat's contract.*

So what were Pat's chances in a fight with Battalino? The 21-year-old American was terrifically tough and could certainly punch, but ironically he was significantly less experienced than Pat. In his two years as a pro Battalino had fought just 22 times, over half his fights were six-rounders, two had been draws, and one a points loss. Pat, by contrast, had had over 90 bouts, boxed innumerable 15-rounders, and suffered six defeats. (Incidentally, Battalino had only 88 fights throughout his whole career, which lasted another 10 years. This gulf in frequency of fights speaks volumes about the difference in the treatment of British and American boxers during the period.) If the claim made in the letter is accurate, that Battalino was a slow starter, then Pat, with his superior boxing, would stand a good chance of staying six rounds and taking the title. But if the match were to happen, it would need to take place quickly, as Pat's ability to make featherweight would soon pass. If he were to win the title, he would almost certainly outgrow the nine-stone limit before he could defend it.

But this level of detail and analysis was by the by. A once in a lifetime offer had been extended, and to Pat's mind it would be crazy not to accept. 'When do we pack, Professor?' he asked, grinning from ear to ear. To his surprise, there was a pause, through which his mentor maintained a sombre face. 'We're not going, Pat,' came the answer, and a longer pause followed. 'I'm sorry, son. Forget about America.' In a state of exasperation and disbelief, Pat pressed the Professor for an explanation. All he got, however, was a sharper response than before. 'You're staying 'ere,' Newton snapped. 'You're not going to America. That's the end of it, and I'll hear nothing more about it.' With these words Pat's dreams of world-title glory were summarily dismissed. '16-year-old Nipper Pat Daly, featherweight champion of the world' – he had already imagined the newspaper headlines, but it wasn't to be. Newton never told him why he had stopped him going to America, but Pat believed he feared losing him to an American manager. The Newton–Daly contract, it later transpired, was legally unsound – something Newton might already have suspected.

---

* This offer, it seems, was rather too low. In October 1929 *Boxing* stated that the Professor had set a price tag of £2,000 for prospective purchasers of the contract.

Although the prospect of fighting in America had vanished, another similarly lucrative offer was laid down in the run-up to the Cuthbert fight. Fidel LaBarba, a former world flyweight champion now fighting at featherweight, had arrived in Europe from the States to take on the France-based Italian Kid Francis, in Paris three nights after Pat's fight with Cuthbert. It was widely reported that, if Pat was successful over Cuthbert, the eminent Europe-based American promoter Jeff Dickson would match him with LaBarba in November or December at the Royal Albert Hall. LaBarba, whose list of victories reads like a who's who of '20s and '30s boxing, was already a legend, and even today is still regarded among the all-time greats. Although a title wasn't at stake, a match with LaBarba would propel Pat into world boxing's top echelon. 'A contest between Daly and LaBarba would be a genuine bill topper in every respect,' wrote *Boxing*. 'It would be of a world wide importance, and would, we imagine, command a commensurate purse.' On the last point, certainly, the trade paper was not mistaken. As Andy Newton wrote in *Boxing* in 1940, after a meeting at the Savoy Hotel Jeff Dickson paid him £100 as an option for Pat to face LaBarba, should he beat Cuthbert. 'The purse he offered me,' Andy recalled, 'went into four figures.'

The stage was set for a super-fight between the legendary LaBarba and the boy hero. All that stood in the way was a man named Johnny Cuthbert.

Left: A 1929 newspaper ad for a training device endorsed by Pat.

Below: Pat (aged 16) ranked number 10 bantamweight in the world by *The Ring* magazine.

Heavyweights	Light-heavyweights	Middleweights	Welterweights	Junior Welterweights
1—Max Schmeling	Tommy Loughran	Mickey Walker	Jackie Fields	Mushy Callahan
2—George Godfrey	Leo Lomski	Ace Hudkins	Y'g Jack Thompson	Baby Joe Gans
—Jack Sharkey	Fred Lenhart	Dave Shade	Bucky Lawless	Ruby Goldstein
4—Young Stribling	Jimmy Braddock	George Courtney	Gorilla Jones	Manuel Quintero
5—Otto Von Porat	Maxey Rosenbloom	Rene De Vos	Tommy Freeman	Andy Callahan
6—Tuffy Griffiths	Billy Jones	Len Harvey	Sammy Baker	Jimmy Goodrich
7—Johnny Risko	Jimmy Slattery	Johnny Burns	Young Corbett	Joe Glick
8—George Hoffman	Rosy Rosales	Jack McVey	My Sullivan	Lope Tenorio
9—Babe Hunt	Cuban Bobby Brown	Haakon Hansen	Vince Dundee	Stanislaus Loayza
10—Salvatore Rug- gierello	Lew Scozza	Vincent Forgione	Johnny Indrisano	Jackie Brady

Lightweights	Junior Lightweights	Featherweights	Bantamweights	Flyweights
1—Sammy Mandell	Tod Morgan	Andre Routis	Bushy Graham	Izzy Schwartz
2—Billy Petrolle	Goldie Hess	Benny Bass	Al Brown	Midget Wolgast
3—Louis Kid Kaplan	Al Singer	Kid Chocolate	Teddy Baldock	Frankie Genaro
4—Billy Wallace	Jakie Zeramby	Earl Mastro	Kid Francis	Johnny Hill
5—Ray Miller	Pete Nebo	Fidel La Barba	Tommy Paul	Newsboy Brown
6—Jack Kid Berg	Sammy Dorfman	Andy Martin	Pete Sanstol	Willie Davies
7—King Tut	Johnny Dundee	Johnny Datto	Archie Bell	Black Bill
8—Tony Canzoneri	Davey Abad	Steve Smith	Vidal Gregario	Frenchy Bellanger
9—Joe Medill	Johnny Farr	Eddie Shea	Joe Scalfaro	Steve Rocco
10—Tommy Grogan	Harry Blitman	Bud Taylor	Nipper Pat Daley	Speedy Dado

19

Fight with the Champion

'There is a deal of curiosity concerning the actual weight of the wonderful little boxer, Nipper Pat Daly... though he has worked harder than any other youngster in the game, he jumped into and out of the bantamweight division so quickly that there was no opportunity for him to figure in a belt contest. He is to meet Johnny Cuthbert at 1 lb over the limit, and there is surprise at his temerity in presuming to give weight to a champion. Far from giving weight, however, it may well be Daly will have more trouble than Cuthbert to pass the scale at 9 st. 1 lb. Daly is growing so fast that his first championship bout may be in the welterweight class.'

The Daily Express, 18 September 1929

Rats roaming in cellars; cockroaches crawling from cracks in the walls; several households to a single outside lavatory; air thick with factory smoke and streets black with industrial soot – these things were all part of life in the slums of early twentieth-century Brightside in Sheffield, the place where Johnny Cuthbert grew up. Eldest of 11 children born to John and Elizabeth Cuthbert (only three of whom reached adulthood), living in such a setting imbued an unbreakable spirit in Johnny, who Gilbert Odd later hailed 'one of the best featherweights this country ever produced'.

Short, strong, cagey and an excellent ring general, Cuthbert's performances were workmanlike and measured, but seldom spectacular to watch. Even so, he possessed a very fast pair of hands, an intricate knowledge of boxing, and a style which, though quintessentially English and built around an excellent straight left, was rather unorthodox with quirks, such as an unusual side-on stance, that made him an awkward man to fight. His greatest asset, he would years later say, was his ability to 'box a fighter and fight a boxer'. Although often disadvantaged in height and reach, he boxed taller, longer-limbed men as if such disparities meant nothing, as his performances against rangy fighters such as Teddy Baldock, Nel Tarleton and Panama Al Brown all proved.

British Champions in the 1920s were hero-worshipped by the public, and when Cuthbert rolled in to Sheffield's Midland station fresh from winning his first title in London, he was mobbed by thousands of well-wishers. The streets were decked out with flags and decorations and the great throng cheered, shouted and threw streamers as he strode through town. But Johnny was a humble man who refused to bask in such extreme adulation. To celebrate, he took over a friend's chip shop and served free fish and chips to local youngsters all evening. The kids, in their enthusiasm, accidentally smashed one of the shop's windows, but amid the jubilation nobody seemed to mind. This quiet, unassuming manner would characterise Cuthbert throughout his career, as one journalist later noted:

'The little Yorkshireman was among the most unpretentious men I have met, almost as shy as a girl, and invariably unobtrusively dressed. So different from many members of the "cauliflower industry" who pursue the life and laughter of Bohemia.

Cuthbert never had a bunch of "hangers-on" in his camp. For big fights in London or abroad the quiet little man, always wearing a bowler hat and carrying a small handbag, travelled alone. Once I boarded a crowded 'bus at Piccadilly Circus to reach the Royal Albert Hall, where Cuthbert was the "star" attraction. I managed to find standing-room near the conductor's platform, and listened to the passengers discussing the big fight prospects. Suddenly I had a view of the front seats. In the front row sat Johnny all-alone looking more like a stock exchange clerk going home after a day in the office than a famous British boxing champion on his way to a job of work. None of the other passengers recognised him!'

Some newspaper articles record Cuthbert's birth-year as 1905, but the official indexes reveal he was actually born on 9 July 1904, making him 25 when he met Pat. His first taste of pugilism was through a weekly boxing class, headed by Reverend Harold Ewbank, who taught a Sunday school at St. George's church, Brookmill. With the Reverend's encouragement and coaching Johnny soon won a school's title, and in a bid to advance his talent joined Harvey Flood's gym in Fitzwilliam Street, before moving to yet another trainer, Ben Stanton. He had his first recorded pro fight in February 1920, aged 15, and along the road to winning his first British title beat Elky Clark, Mick Hill, Harry 'Bugler' Lake, Billy Matthews, Harry Corbett and a young Jack Kid Berg. Three times he outpointed the reigning British featherweight champion Johnny Curley of Lambeth in non-title fights, before Curley finally consented to give him a title shot. 'What a record and reputation you had to have in those days to get a title fight,' recalled Gilbert Odd in an article on Cuthbert in 1977. Cuthbert had fought at least 90 pro fights by the time his big chance arrived at the age of 22. He defeated Curley over 20 hard-fought rounds, but lost the title to Harry Corbett in his first defence. Cuthbert and Corbett drew in a return championship match, then Cuthbert finally reclaimed the crown in a third title fight, at Olympia in May 1929. In all, the pair met eight times: Cuthbert winning four, Corbett winning two, with two drawn.

By the time he fought Pat, Cuthbert had beaten other top men such as Jack Hyams, Young Johnny Brown and the formidable French champion Gustav Humery. In Paris, eleven months earlier, he had drawn with the legendary Panama Al Brown – the verdict provoking loud boos from the French crowd, which considered it an injustice to the Englishman. In his first fight after winning his world bantamweight crown, Teddy Baldock took on Cuthbert in a six-round catchweights match at Olympia. It was believed Baldock's superior speed and reach would overwhelm the slower, shorter Cuthbert, but the resultant fight was surprising. In a *Boxing News* series on his life, Baldock later admitted the decision – which was a draw – should have gone to the Sheffielder. In late 1929 Cuthbert was at his peak and undoubtedly the best opponent Pat had faced.

Arranged by the veteran fight official Mr J. T. Hulls under the auspices of the members-only 'Stadium Club', the match would take place at the Holborn Stadium, which stood at 85 High Holborn and whose intimate auditorium held just 1,500 fight fans. Under the presidency of Lord Desborough, the Holborn Stadium had once hosted high-profile fights – such as Joe Beckett versus Bombardier Billy Wells, and Beckett versus Carpentier, when the Englishman was counted out before many ticket-holders reached their seats – but more recently pro boxing had been off the Club menu. But the Stadium Club's members were eager to see fight shows again, and by popular demand six subscription fight nights were arranged for the second Wednesday of each month. The first, headlined by Nipper Pat Daly and Johnny Cuthbert, was set for 9 October.

The Stadium Club – replete with billiard gallery, card room, ballroom, plus a restaurant serving first-class food and wine – was much like the National Sporting Club in its ostentation; but unlike the NSC it allowed female guests, a fact Pat's mother, who wanted to watch him box, was glad to discover. But besides members' guests and boxers' family members, the general public were barred from the six exclusive shows. The closest they could get to the action was reading about it next day. Stadium Club members would pay £5 5s for a ringside seat at the six shows, and could bring guests for £1 5s each per night. Other seats were £3 3s for members, with guests costing £1 1s each per night – expensive prices for 1929.

On 26 September, Pat was booked to box an exhibition and give a demonstration of the Professor's system of training at the Drill Hall on Pound Lane in Willesden. He had only boxed twice that month so the Professor was endeavouring to keep him busy. Afterwards, he went into strict training for the Cuthbert fight.

As usual, Pat trained at the Empire School of Arms, where he could call on any number of able sparring partners. The Professor told Norman Hurst of *The Sporting Chronicle* that he had taught Pat a special means of defence against Cuthbert's curious side-on attack. Each day was comprised of intense conditioning and sparring, including ring sessions with the Professor himself, who *The Daily Express* noted 'despite his 65-years, skips about as nimbly as a man half his age'. A photo of Pat using a special training device in the front yard of his trainer's gym appeared in several national papers, plus on the front page of *The Evening News*. The device, called the Lenglen Shadow Ball, was an inflatable punch ball attached by elastic to a strap that fastened around the forehead. When punched, even lightly, the ball would bounce back at the face with astonishing quickness. It was said to enhance hand-speed and hand-to-eye coordination. An advert for the Lenglen Shadow Ball, sold for seven shillings by a company called H. Lenglen Ltd., appeared in several newspapers with a statement from the Professor attesting to its usefulness in training the famous Nipper. Whether Pat found the device of genuine benefit, or was simply contractually obliged to endorse it, is not known.

Cuthbert's preparations, meanwhile, were more low-key. He trained up in Sheffield at his own gym in a converted room at The Old Brown Cow in Radford Street: a pub he had bought for his parents from his ring earnings. A tiny place with just enough room for a 14-foot ring, it was perhaps the most modest gym a champion ever used; but it served as his training quarters throughout his long career. A wall had been demolished so pub customers could watch him work out. Hundreds would flock to see the champion skip, spar and shadow box, as they heartily quaffed pints of ale – he usually trained in the evenings, which meant the pub did a roaring trade. Cuthbert told reporters he expected a harder fight than when he'd met Harry Corbett for the British title in May, and was preparing accordingly. He hired Jim Learoyd (Leeds), Harry Robinson (Mexborough) and Johnny Summers (Leeds) as sparring partners. Summers, who had boxed Pat seven times, was no doubt recruited for his familiarity with the wonder boy's style.

On the afternoon of Wednesday 2 October – a week before the fight – Pat gave a public training exhibition at the Empire School of Arms, attended by a big crowd, which included the sporting and national press. He began with a display of skipping, which he followed by going to work on three types of punch ball, one after the other. A conventional platform ball was used for arm and wrist work, then a ground punch ball was pummelled, demonstrating his suppleness of body, before, finally, a wall ball was used. The combination of the three was said to sharpen hand-eye coordination, perfect judgement of distance, and call upon every muscle in his body. He then performed a series of exercises, threw a medicine ball with three other boxers, before donning the gloves with four sparring partners: Charlie Mack, Jim Carr, Arthur Everitt and Dave McCleave.* To keep him employed at maximum speed his partner was changed each minute, and he thus took on all four men during every round they sparred. The best exchanges were

---

* According to Pat's eldest son, John Daley, Dave McCleave was the only boxer Pat ever paid to spar with him. McCleave was extremely skilful and gave Pat a very close fight over three rounds. 'But Dave wasn't as robust,' recalled John, 'and he didn't have dad's stamina.' McCleave had a glittering amateur career and won an ABA schoolboy title, three senior ABA titles, a European title, an Empire (now Commonwealth) Games gold medal, and represented Great Britain at the 1932 Olympics (losing by a controversial quarterfinal decision to the eventual welterweight gold medallist). As a pro he won the British and Southern Area welterweight titles and the Southern Area middleweight title. In the 1950s Pat occasionally took John and some other schoolboy boxers to McCleave's pub-cum-boxing gym, The Union Tavern, on Camberwell New Road, for sparring.

seen when he took on Charlie Mack and Dave McCleave, both of whom were fast enough to keep him at full stretch. After the hour-long exhibition Pat gave a brief speech saying he'd watched Cuthbert box Harry Corbett at Olympia back in May, and was confident he could beat him. 'Daly showed great speed and at the finish his wind was as good as when he started,' observed the *Daily Mirror*. 'I have watched some hundreds of boxers in their training,' remarked A. J. Daniels of the *Sporting Life*, 'but never once one whose work afforded greater interest and enjoyment than Pat Daly... much of it is devoted to callisthenics and physical exercises, which demand instant response of the mental and physical faculties to the word of command from his mentor. It is all too long and varied to describe here in detail. I can only say that it is unique in my experience.'

The next night Pat was headlining a special Anglo-French bill staged at the Ilford Skating Rink. The promoter was the leading referee Moss Deyong and the matchmaker the famous Ted Kid Lewis. In his *Daily Express* column, Trevor C. Wignall criticised the timing of the match: 'Hard work and plenty of it may suit Daly, as Newton pointed out to me in a letter some days ago, but less than a week is not a sufficiently long time for him to get ready for the most important fight of his career.'

His opponent, a powerfully built southpaw called Arques Treves, certainly looked like he might take Pat the full 15-round distance. From the opening seconds Pat attacked the Frenchman with his long straight left, and immediately found the target. Treves tried to counter but fell short and was clipped to the head by a snappy right. They went close, where Pat tattooed his rival with both hands, beating him to the punch every time. A quick left hook to the jaw put Treves down for the count of eight. He got up, rushed at Pat, but was easily held off and punished by long-range shots. Before the round had ended he was down again – this time from a flashing right to the jaw. The minute's rest was insufficient for Treves to recover, and when he came out for the second, few were surprised by what followed. The Frenchman was peppered with lefts and rights to the head and gamely survived two more knockdowns, before a hard left hook to the jaw put him out for the full count. The performance had been clinical. They could have counted all night.

'I suppose the hero of all British boxing boys today will be Nipper Pat Daly,' wrote Clyde Foster in *The Evening Standard* that week. 'J. Ferrand, of Hackney Road, E., writes me to say that he is the proudest boy in London because after seeing Nipper Pat Daly beat the French boy, Arques Treves, at Ilford Skating Rink, he obtained the "Nipper's" autograph. In neat handwriting on a leaf from an exercise book young Ferrand says:

"After the fight I passed by Daly's dressing room and took the liberty of peeping in, and there I saw Professor Newton and Co. chatting merrily with young Daly. The "Nipper" spotted me, and I beckoned to him. He left the others and came over to see me, and I produced a photograph of him I had purchased a few months ago at Premierland, and asked him to autograph it for me. With a cheery "Righto, chum!" he went over to young Andy Newton and borrowed a fountain pen and ever so carefully inscribed the words "Yours sincerely, Nipper Pat Daly." He handed it back to me, and as we shook hands I wished him success with his bout with Johnny Cuthbert next Wednesday. When he is world's champion (and of that I'm certain) just think how proud I'll be to show my pals his photograph with his signature attached."'

★★★

The schoolboy was not alone in his conviction that Pat should beat Johnny Cuthbert – press opinion largely backed the Nipper to win as well. The same papers that prophesised his demise against Kirby, Biquet and Pattenden had learnt to put their faith in the youngster, however huge the task. Wrote *The Daily Chronicle*'s correspondent:

'If Daly should defeat Cuthbert he will do what, as far as memory serves, no other 16-year-old has ever done and give a beating to a champion... [But] most of us who have watched Daly so often are willing to believe him capable of anything. His versatility is astounding. Daly is possessed of pretty well every trick and feint that is known to boxing. I think Daly will get through this great trial with honours.'

The general mood of the press was summed up perfectly by fight pundit Fred Dartnell, who wrote under the pseudonym of 'Long Melford':

'With all due respect to Cuthbert, who is a very able champion, the chief glamour about this match centres on Daly... There is no boxer before the public at present who puts more vim and variety into his work than Daly. Although so young, he is a consummate artist with the gloves, and has an old head on his young shoulders. Daly believes in the Napoleonic policy of attack, and always attack. Even if he retreats he makes it an aggressive retreat... [Cuthbert] is not a dazzling performer like Daly. He is not a virtuoso of the gloves like Len Harvey or Baldock, but he is eminently a good workmanlike performer and a hard man to beat. If I were asked to indicate the supreme quality of Cuthbert I should say it is his stubborn, unyielding spirit and a knack of preventing an opponent from showing off his best paces. Cuthbert is not much on finesse, and he does not deal out the knock-out punches. To some people his style might seem cramped and lacking in enterprise, but those who saw him give Teddy Baldock something like a boxing lesson know better than that... I fancy Daly will win, but Cuthbert must not be underrated. The occasion is one of very great moment for him. He can hardly afford to be beaten by this youngster still in his teens. And even if he is not this evening I am still of the opinion that the featherweight belt will be worn later by the "Nipper".'

Despite this general expectance that the Nipper should triumph, there were some who remained uncertain. '[Cuthbert] can deal out heavy punishment,' wrote Billy Wells in the *Sporting Life*. 'Daly will be meeting a man who is set and who can last the distance. I only hope that if Daly does lose it will not mean a defeat that will hurt him for the future.' In a piece in *The Sporting Chronicle* headed 'Danger of Daly', James Butler elected to focus on Pat's handling rather than the fight itself:

'...one must admit that the boy is almost a genius with his boxing knowledge. Whether he is being overworked is a matter of opinion. I doubt if there is another first-class boxer who has had so many bouts this year as young Daly... Andrew Newton, who is Daly's mentor and manager, has continually assured me that his protégé's strength and stamina is not, and will not be impaired by his busy career. I hope for the sake of boxing and Daly himself that Newton's belief is right.'

Butler's point about Pat's over-activity was certainly well founded. In the last 12 months Johnny Cuthbert had boxed just eight contests, while in the same period Pat had fought 34 times; his only defeat, incidentally, had been the one-round knockout at the hands of Douglas Parker.

On the morning of the fight Pat was still vigorously training; a reporter from *The Evening Standard* was there to write about it:

'Nipper Pat Daly, London's bright boy boxer, who is taking on tonight the fight of his young life, was a lad of few words but many clothes as he put the finishing touches to his training today... Daly, before devoting a brisk half an hour to the gadgets which adorn his trainer's gymnasium, put on a bathing costume, thick woollen fleshings above and below, boxing boots, and an old Army jerkin. Then he entered the ring and the muscle-loosening began. He aimed blows at the jaw of his trainer, Professor A. Newton, stopping miraculously half an inch short of knocking him out. Danced, skipped, and clinched with another boxing lad. Pummelled punching balls of various heights and sizes, including one on the floor and another – a light one – clutched in the teeth by means of a length of elastic.'

'I'm feeling fine,' he told the reporter, 'and I hope I'm going to win.' But behind the scenes, as his many layers of clothes had hinted, things were far from fine. His preparation had been tougher than ever. 'I was not able to eat breakfast for two weeks before the fight,' he would remember. 'And I had very little to eat for any other meal, because everything I ate doubled in weight as soon as I digested it.' Six days before the bout, when he boxed Arques Treves at Ilford, he had weighed 9 stone 4 lb. He was able to comfortably sustain this weight, but to boil down any further, he recalled, 'was sheer murder'. Under Newton's instruction he trained wearing five sweaters and a sheepskin jacket. He would sweat off a couple of pounds, go home to lunch, drink half a cup of tea and eat a piece of dry toast, then return to the gym several ounces heavier than when he'd started. On the morning of the fight he was a pound over the 9 stone 1 lb contracted weight. Several hours training brought him dead on the weight, but the Professor feared his scales might be slightly out, and so sent Pat for a session at the local Turkish Baths. He returned and did some more training but still his weight remained unchanged. It seemed physically impossible for the lad to lose any more bodyweight and time, at any rate, had now run out. With trepidation they went to the official weigh-in at 2pm, but discovered that Newton's scales had been accurate after all. Pat was inside the limit and very relieved, but now he felt a complete wreck. Weak and white as a sheet, he went home to rest before leaving for Holborn.

Weight trouble alone would be sufficient cause for worry for any boxer entering the fight of his life, but Pat had other problems too. When he'd been told some weeks ago the purse he would receive for fighting Cuthbert, although it was the largest of his career, he still felt something was amiss. He'd seen the purses earned by big-name fighters when they topped high-profile bills and realised his was considerably lower. Despite Cuthbert holding the British title, Pat was the 'big draw' and knew it. 'I'd like to see the contract, Andy,' he told the Professor's son. 'What you talking about, you wanna see the contract?' he snapped back. 'You're getting too big for your bloody boots, boy.' But Pat would not be brushed off. 'I'm the one doing the fighting, Andy, and yes, I wanna see the contract.' Eventually Andy agreed he could see it, but first he needed to dig it out. Days went by, and then whole weeks, but Pat still had no sight of it. He repeatedly asked for the contract, but Andy was repeatedly forgetful. 'Oh blast! Could've sworn it was in me pocket,' he'd say, and in the dressing room before the fight it had still not materialised. 'If you don't show me the contract, there'll be no fight,' Pat bluffed. 'I won't go out there.' Andy, however, wasn't easily kidded. 'I ain't got it Pat, you'll have it later. And besides, I know you won't let all those people down. They've paid an arm-an'-a-leg to see you fight.' (Moreover, Andy himself had bet a large sum on Pat to win. 'On the day of the contest you could only get even money on Cuthbert's chances. At this price I backed Daly for £300,' he would write in 1940.) Pat, the Professor and Andy argued heatedly, but after a while the boy fell silent. Andy was right; contract or not, he would not disappoint the fans.

***

There was not a spare seat in the Holborn Stadium that evening. Dinner was served in the restaurant at 6:30pm, after which the Club's members sauntered out into the auditorium. Nearly 1,600 people, with their eyes glued to a brightly lit square, sat and waited, the expectation palpable. At 8pm the boxing began and they saw Charley Wheeler of Bermondsey outpoint George White of Peckham over six rounds. They then watched Pat's stable-mate Charlie Mack outbox George Thompson of Newport to secure a 10-round decision, and in a spectacular heavyweight clash witnessed Bermondsey's Alf Noble knock out Charlie Hickman of Birmingham inside a round. Up next was the fight they had paid to see: a top o' the bill 12 three-minute round affair. Most of the assembly were rooting for the 16-year-old, hoping and half-expecting he would upset the champion and cause yet another sensation.

As Pat approached the ring the contractual debacle was left in the dressing room, and even the debilitating weight-making was forgotten. Seated near ringside were his proud parents and all around him an expectant army of supporters. Six years of dedication had led him to this one night. Victory meant big money and a shot at super-stardom. Defeat was unthinkable. The pressure piled on Pat's young shoulders was immense, but if he harboured doubts his calm expression did not show it. He was about to do what he did best; what he was born for. The roped-off square more familiar, more natural, than any place he would ever know.

As Pat and Cuthbert stood together their difference in make-up, as Ben Bennison of *The Daily Telegraph* observed, was striking:

> 'It was a remarkable affair, if only because two considerable opposites were at war – Cuthbert, a square-cut fellow, big-eyed, teeth clenched tight, a man of no nonsense and a severe workman, was opposed to a tall, rangy lad, unconcerned, self-contained to an extent astonishing... the one with a stubbly chin, the other baby-faced – disparities were so marked as to make for the ridiculous.'

Audience members who studied their programmes would have noticed Pat stood 5 feet 8 inches tall, while the broad-shouldered Cuthbert was 5 feet 3½ inches and two inches shorter in reach than the 16-year-old. The boxers were called to the ropes by the referee Eugene Corri, who sat atop a raised ringside chair, to receive some final instructions before returning to their corners. At the chime of the bell they met in the centre of the ring, and for the first time exchanged leather.

Pat immediately found his rhythm, firing lefts into the champion's face, which repeatedly pierced his guard. 'Daly's footwork was as fast as any seen in the ring,' remarked Geoffrey Simpson of *The Daily Mail*, 'and his long left came out to Cuthbert's face as a shot from a gun. The pace of it was extraordinary. Cuthbert could not have survived long against such treatment had there been a man's power behind the punches.' Cuthbert repeatedly tried to counter with his right, but his blows whistled harmlessly above Pat's head or over his shoulder, as he skilfully slipped or ducked. Cuthbert charged forwards and bustled Pat into the ropes, spraying the youngster with a fusillade of blows. But Pat blocked or slipped the majority and resumed his own onslaught with straight lefts and occasional but expertly timed rights.

Cuthbert seemed determined to change matters at the start of round two. He rushed from his corner ferociously, evidently intent on taking the youngster out of his stride, but his efforts again proved futile. 'The boy came right out for the second,' wrote *Boxing*, 'shooting in left after left to the face, ripping home the right, and earning loud applause for his skill, speed and singular powers of anticipation.' The action was swift and ceaseless. Pat outreached Cuthbert at range, then in close caught most of the champion's shots on his arms and elbows. After some clever feinting Cuthbert shot out a right cross that might have ended the bout, but Pat avoided it by an inch and countered with a lightning left that caught Cuthbert flush on the nose. The champion lost the round, said *The Times*, 'through being baffled for the most part by his opponent's defence and capacity for turning every opening to account.'

The pace grew faster in the third. Cuthbert was fighting fiercely and making the body his main target. But Pat's defence showed no signs of wavering, and he continued his bombardment of quick, accurate lefts that rarely missed. At one point six lefts and a right struck Cuthbert's head without reply. The champion seemed puzzled and for once uncertain of how to handle his opponent.

Early on in the fourth it appeared Cuthbert might turn the tables. He managed to drag Pat into a close-range battle, where he was having the better of the exchanges. But suddenly Pat whipped the crowd into a frenzy when he eschewed all caution to stand and trade with the champion. Pat's faster hands beat the Sheffielder to the punch, his eye-catching barrage drew gasps of awe from spectators, but he couldn't match Cuthbert for power and so the blows did little damage. At one stage Pat feinted with his left and landed a splendidly timed right, a punch that might have troubled the champion had it not landed a little too high. It was a far closer round than the previous three, but Pat, most newspapers felt, just nicked it.

Cuthbert cut a blistering pace from the start of the next round and forced Pat to box uncharacteristically on the defensive. But Pat intercepted most of the shots with his gloves and arms, and repeatedly made the champion miss with clever footwork and fast head movement. After weathering the storm, the boy fought back fiercely to gain a slight lead in the round. As he walked to his corner several reporters observed a stream of blood trickling from Pat's right ear.

In the sixth Cuthbert again strove to make up the points deficit, but this time he was completely outboxed. As Cuthbert came forward, Pat used his left to halt his attacks; he would then advance on Cuthbert using the left again to mount his own assault. Early on he visibly shook Cuthbert with a perfectly timed right, and landed several more, besides countless left leads, as the round progressed. The crowd were on their feet applauding. 'Go home, Cuthbert, he's got you licked,' someone shouted. It was Pat's round by a mile.

The seventh was a similar story. Cuthbert put up a sterling battle, but Pat was more than equal to it. Several times he connected with unanswered rallies of lefts and rights that left Cuthbert utterly bewildered. The Sheffield man's chances were fading fast and he knew it. It was equally evident, however, that Pat lacked the power to seriously hurt him, and this gave the champion some hope. There were five more three-minute rounds and he intended to make amends.

Cuthbert charged from his corner at top speed at the eighth bell and was upon his boyish rival from the first moment. With brutal efficiency he forced Pat back towards the ropes, showering blows on his head and body with all his might. 'I could see the look of alarm in Daly's eyes as Cuthbert belaboured the breath out of the boy's body,' wrote Clyde Foster for *The Evening Standard*. Gasping from the body shots, Pat got away to the centre of the ring, from where, rather than retreating, he decided to fight back. A hectic exchange followed and after slipping a vicious left swing Pat suddenly stepped backwards and, inexplicably, turned his head towards the crowd. 'We do not understand why the Nipper sent his attention wandering like this,' puzzled *Boxing* afterwards. Andy Newton, writing a decade later, claimed 'a woman's voice made Daly turn his head'. In the instant he turned his head he also carelessly dropped his hands, whereupon Cuthbert, seizing the opening, ripped a lightning right-hand – a cross between a hook and an uppercut – onto Pat's unguarded chin. The boy was knocked to the floor and as he fell his head flew back and struck the boards with a sickening thud.

Distant, like the tide coming in on some far off shore, he could hear the crowd's roar. There was an urgent need to get to his feet, but at first he did not know why. Then he became aware of the referee's counting, and he knew that he *must* get up. 'Three... four... five... six...' He tried desperately to rise at 'seven' but collapsed again. At 'nine' he had struggled to one knee, but as 'ten' was called he pitched face forwards and collapsed in a heap. 'As the fallen boy-idol struggled in vain to regain his feet during the count a young girl near me turned her head away and burst into tears,' wrote *The Evening Standard*'s Clyde Foster. The Professor and Andy Newton lifted him to his corner and had to steady him as he left the ring. 'The knockout, indeed, was so complete,' wrote Trevor C. Wignall of *The Daily Express*, 'that Daly was still only semi-conscious when he was assisted to his dressing room. It was probably this fact that caused an excited woman to shout, "He is too young for this sort of fighting. Why let him do it?"'

Also watching Pat's exit, Clyde Foster observed:

> 'When Mr. Corri spoke a few sympathetic words to the "Nipper" as he descended the steps from the ring his legs tottered under him... I asked the referee what he said to the boxers when he called them up to the ropes to administer a few words of counsel before the fight. "Only this," said Corri. "Both you fellows know the game. Now play it – and they did. I cautioned Daly once for holding Cuthbert with his left hand and pulling his head forward. He did not repeat it. Once Cuthbert hit Daly with his elbow but I felt it was accidental. I never refereed a cleaner fight".'

The mood in the auditorium had changed suddenly from one of excitement and anticipation to one of sadness and pity. Cuthbert looked relieved that the fight was over, but otherwise remained composed, showing little sign of jubilation. 'Johnny Cuthbert had my sympathy,' wrote Clyde Foster, 'on the score that to have been beaten by even the cleverest boy boxer in the world – a distinction that is conceded to Daly – would have done much harm to his reputation, and to win could not greatly add to his fame.'

The atmosphere in Pat's dressing room was one of gloom and recrimination. Pat sat slumped in a chair, nursing a pounding headache – the result of cracking his head on the canvas. Barely a word was spoken by anyone in the room. There was a polite knock at the door. 'Come in,' called the Professor, and in walked a small, smartly dressed man, whom all of them recognised. 'Hello Jimmy. What can we do for you?' the Professor said. 'Hello Professor,' the small man replied in a Welsh lilt. 'I just wanted to say what a great boy you have there.' He turned to Pat. 'I know it feels like the end of the world now, son. But you'll be back.' 'If he'd have paid more attention to Cuthbert's right hand,' the Professor interrupted before turning an accusing eye on Pat. 'The fight was yours,' he shot out. 'The boy should be rested,' the man said quietly but firmly. 'Don't rush him, Professor. Given time he'll be champion of the world.' 'I think we've done all right so far without your advice. You should mind your own bloody business,' the Professor growled. The small man shook his head. 'Have it your way,' he said. 'But I couldn't just walk out of here without saying something.' Jimmy Wilde, the 'Mighty Atom', left closing the door quietly behind him.

20

Down, but Not Out

The next day Pat arrived at Newton's gym early, keen to do some light training and prove that the knockout hadn't upset him. Later that morning he purchased several newspapers, which he pored through eagerly to discover how the match had been reported. He may have been worried that losing to Cuthbert had discredited him; but if he was, any such fears were soon allayed:

> 'Never have I seen a more gallant fight than that put up by Pat Daly, a 16½ year-old Welshman, against Johnny Cuthbert... Daly was knocked out by a right-hand punch to the chin in the eighth round, but not before he had given the champion one of the hardest fights of his life.' Geoffrey Simpson, *The Daily Mail*

> 'Daly boxed cleverly, and for seven rounds succeeded in puzzling the champion as he has not often been puzzled.' *The Daily Mirror*

> 'The finish of the fight was as unexpected as anything that has happened in professional pugilism for many years. When the eighth round opened Daly was so well ahead on points that victory seemed to be assured for him.' Trevor C. Wignall, *Daily Express*

> 'One mistake – and a knockout. That is the summary of Nipper Pat Daly's defeat by Johnny Cuthbert... The winner, who is the featherweight champion – and a worthy one – was puzzled beyond words for seven rounds. He did not know how to get at this remarkable London boy... He had hit Cuthbert with so many different kinds of punches that the featherweight champion scarcely knew what to do... Daly went down like a little hero.' *The Daily Chronicle*

> 'It was man against boy; the man triumphed; age and experience, not superior boxing skill, carried the day... Daly had proved to be the better boxer... he might have passed for a hard-bitten campaigner so cleverly had he ridden blows and so quietly had he turned defence into attack... He kept his hands high; his quick eye and keen sense of anticipation

nullified the effects of the bludgeon which Cuthbert carried. His ear had been cut and blood trickled from the wound; but he held out no signs of distress... Daly is of the stuff of which champions are made; but he should bide awhile. Immensely clever he is: his relish for fighting is obvious: it is only necessary to see him in the ring to know he is a fighter by instinct... He stands correctly, so that he may punch from any angle. He thinks quickly, he has a rare sense of distance, his heart is gloriously big.' Ben Bennison, *The Daily Telegraph*

Amidst the lavish praise, however, were several stark warnings concerning the lad's future:

'If the backers of Nipper Pat Daly wish to see their protégé attain the highest honours to be gained in the boxing game, they must make up their minds to nurse him.' A. J. Daniels, *Sporting Life*

'We were as proud of the Marylebone boy as we were sorry for him. To all concerned there was a great lesson that a boy boxer can be overtaxed. Pat Daly must receive a little more consideration in future lest lasting injury be done to him alike in body and spirit. He is well worth all the care that can be taken of him, for we have not looked on his like before as a young boxer.' Clyde Foster, *The Evening Standard*

'My own opinion is dead against young fellows being allowed to engage in such contests until they reach maturity. Johnny Hill [who had recently died aged 23] boxed too much; so has Baldock. Now this boy, who looks like being a world-beater, is working too hard also. His fight last night was too stiff a proposition. I don't think it is good for the boy, and it is not advantageous to the country, because it stops championships from coming here.' Mr C. H. 'Pickles' Douglas (leading referee), quoted in *The Evening Standard**

And perhaps the most damning judgment of all came from the sport's leading pundit:

'The whole thing was a tragedy for this child of boxing. I retain my opinion that he has been worked too hard, that his jaw has been made

---

*   'Pickles' Douglas was a brother of J.W.H.T. Douglas, 1905 ABA middleweight champion, 1908 Olympic middleweight boxing champion, and captain of the England cricket team that won the 1911-12 'Ashes' in Australia.

glassy and vulnerable to one accurate smack, and that a very promising career has – temporarily, it is to be hoped – been blighted... He should now be given a long rest, and be allowed to grow in a normal way. If this is not done his life as a fighter will end long before he is twenty.' Trevor C. Wignall, *Daily Express*

Even Bombardier Billy Wells, hitherto a staunch supporter of the two Newtons, had changed his tack, saying in his *Topical Times* column that they should take a leaf from America and limit the lad to six-round fights. 'I am not one of those who advocate that Professor Newton's prodigy should be given a rest. Nor do I advise that he should never be put up against the top-notchers,' wrote Wells. 'I am merely concerned with the length of his fights.' *The Evening Standard* noted that the bout's scheduled distance – 12 three-minute rounds – broke BBB of C rules, which limited fighters younger than 18 to 30-minutes' actual boxing per fight. It criticised the Board – which must have known of the match – for having raised no objection.

The criticism was widespread and collectively damning, but Professor Newton took no notice. He had already booked his colt for a two-month series of fights, which he had no intention of cancelling. If the press remarks troubled him, it did not show. He had coached for longer than many of his critics had lived, and he was not prepared to let anyone tell him how to manage his fighter. 'Burned out,' he told *Boxing*. 'Wait for another few years and then see whether any intelligent boy can get "burned out", so long as I train and manage him. Some boys may have got "burned out", but if they were, it was only because their trainers did not know their business.' The sport's trade paper, he was probably pleased to discover, for the most part still supported him:

'There has been a moral to it all; but we do not agree that the Nipper should take a lay-off. It has been suggested that he has a glass jaw, but he took many heavy punches, and stood up to them. He was caught off balance, and the back of his head had a bad crack on the floor. He is still an immature boy, and he was fighting a man whom we recognise as a real champion. The Nipper has lost nothing in fame or reputation. The worst – and, as we are now able to see, the best – which has happened to him is that he will not now be booked for contests with potential world beaters for four figure purses, at least not for a year or so. He can still be a top-liner, so long as it is possible to find opponents who can give him a fight on anything like even terms, and these will not be found readily... he has shown that he is the most brilliant boxer of the day, and has supplied the one and only Professor with a wonderful advertisement.'

It seems the contract dispute that had raged in the dressing room had now been forgotten, or at least that Pat had decided – despite not seeing the paperwork – to let the matter rest.

On 13 October he travelled to West Bromwich to watch Bert Kirby (whom he'd beaten 10 months previously) face Manchester's Jackie Brown for the vacant British flyweight title. The title had become vacant after Johnny Hill's sudden death from pneumonia two weeks previously. Jack Hood (reigning British welterweight champion), Johnny Cuthbert and Pat were introduced from the ring, with Pat, according to *Boxing*, receiving a special ovation from the crowd. When asked about the Cuthbert fight, Pat naturally said he felt disappointed, but at no stage had the champion seriously hurt him. The ear injury was negligible and had been caused by the laces on Cuthbert's glove. He rolled up his shirtsleeves to reveal bruises on his arms from blocking Cuthbert's blows, but the reporter observed that his face was unmarked. The bump on the boards did cause a swelling at the back of his head, and if it weren't for that bump he felt he would have won. He said he would like a return with Cuthbert but for the championship, and would fund a £100 side-stake from his own pocket. There would be no return fight, however, and he must have realised he would now never make the 9-stone championship limit.

Exactly two weeks after the Cuthbert bout, Pat was back in the ring for a fight in his own district, at Paddington Baths on Queen's Road, W2. The bill was part of a new venture by local fruiterer Fred Austin (who would later play a part in Pat's career), and Alec Lambert, who as a fighter met Ted Kid Lewis for the British featherweight title and as a trainer at one time or other would handle Nel Tarleton, Seaman Tommy Watson, Jack Bloomfield, Benny Lynch and Harry Corbett. Lambert's current young protégé was Jack Millard, whom Pat had been matched with at the top of the bill. Lambert ran a gymnasium at Bell Street in Marylebone, so an element of local rivalry was no doubt in evidence. In the audience that night was Lord Knebworth, a conservative politician and pilot, while the referee was Alec Lambert's old adversary Ted Kid

Lewis. Millard was a promising young fighter who had lost just five of 34 pro contests and hadn't been beaten for two and a half years. He had age, height, weight and reach advantages, but as *Boxing* noted they proved insufficient:

> 'Along came the flashing left hand and the rapid footwork that have taken Daly to his now eminent position. Try as he would Millard found it a sheer impossibility to evade the onslaught of leads and hooks, and he gradually faded away, until at the end of the eighth round – at which stage referee Kid Lewis stopped the bout.'

But during the early rounds Millard had put up a game display. *The Evening News* considered Pat's performance 'was not over convincing'. Millard had made him miss at times, and once or twice had caught Pat with rights to the chin. It was less than they expected from the impeccable Nipper; some of his usual shine was missing. Professor Newton had representatives in every bout that evening. In a six-round preliminary one of his charges, Arthur Everitt, lost to an unknown novice called Dave Crowley. Crowley, who was three years older than Pat, would go on to win the British lightweight title and box Mike Belloise for the world featherweight crown at Madison Square Garden. By then Pat would have long retired.

The Nipper's next engagement was not staged in a ring but on a pitch. On 28 October, he played in the annual celebrity 'boxers versus jockeys' football match at West Ham United's ground, in aid of the Excelsior Philanthropic Society – all proceeds going to London hospitals. The jockeys had the famous Harry Wragg* on their side, while Pat's team-mates included Teddy Baldock, Kid Pattenden, Ernie Jarvis and Johnny Cuthbert himself. Silent-film and early talkie cockney character actor Alf Goddard also played on the boxers' team. The match was kicked off by the Earl of Westmorland and 'Mighty Atom' Jimmy Wilde served as one of the linesmen. After 90 light-hearted minutes, the jockeys finished 3–2 winners, proving that slick footwork in the ring does not necessarily carry onto the football pitch.

---

* The jockey Harry Wragg (1902-1985) won 13 Classic races and was champion in 1941. He was later a leading trainer, saddling five Classic winners.

Three days after the match, and eight days on from his fight with Millard, Pat was back in action at the Ilford Skating Rink, where the show sold out as soon as he was announced as the headliner. His opponent, Jim Ashley of Stepney, had lost just three of 35 recorded fights. If official records had existed, Ashley's would have shown that almost half his wins had arrived inside the distance. Punching fiercely with both hands from the first bell, Ashley forced Pat to box on the retreat. The Nipper endeavoured to 'box clever' but simply could not find his rhythm. The crowd reached fever pitch in round two as the Stepney man continued to bewilder his young rival. And in the third Pat was caught by a heavy bombardment of body blows, before a hard right hook hit his jaw and put him down. He scrambled to his feet at the count of 'nine' but his head had yet to clear. Wisely, referee Moss Deyong gazed hard into his eyes and then waved the fight off. (Following his unexpectedly short fight, Ashley, who worked as a fish porter at Billingsgate market, was said to have gone to work at 2am.)

Fans and pundits alike were stunned by the defeat. Pat had faced big punchers before – men of a better class than Ashley – and readily outboxed them. For him to struggle as he had was puzzling. 'It would seem to be impossible to discover any excuse for this,' remarked *Boxing*. Bombardier Billy Wells in his *Topical Times* column opined that the manner of the knockout suggested Pat's 'condition' had 'gone off considerably'. 'I certainly think Daly should go easy for a few months,' wrote Wells. 'Six rounds, as I have already said, ought to be the limit of his fights.' 'Daly really wants a rest,' wrote *Reynolds's Illustrated News*. Pat would later consider that he had been carrying a slight concussion since the Cuthbert fight; but even if he had, there was no chance of him resting. He was already booked for four more 15-rounders, all within the next three and a half weeks.

His next was at the National Sporting Club, or rather what remained of the once pre-eminent club. The NSC had finally been forced to vacate its famous Covent Garden premises. The freehold, which had been bought in 1922, was sold, under mounting financial pressure, in October 1929 to a firm of fruit merchants, who would use the building as a head office and warehouse for many years. Lionel Bettinson (son of 'Peggy' Bettinson), who had inherited his father's assets, had taken charge of the NSC and vowed to restore its former glory – a feat he would never achieve. In January 1930, the NSC would relocate to 21 Soho Square, but in the meantime it was temporarily based at the suitably grand Holborn Stadium, site of the Daly–Cuthbert fight. Pat had not boxed for the Club since he fought Giovanni Sili 18 months earlier, and this was also his first time topping an NSC bill. Among those present that night was Earl Beatty, a Royal Navy admiral and a Freeman of Huddersfield. The bill was an annual charity event, organised by Moss Deyong for the Lion Hospital Aid Society, which that year raised £300. Pat's opponent was 21-year-old Harry 'Kid' Berry of Bethnal Green, a former junior and senior Federation champion who would later become one of the East End's leading trainers. Among those he coached were the infamous Kray twins, Ron and Reg, who were boyhood friends of his son 'Checker' Berry.* On Harry's death in 1989, the Kray twins sent wreaths to the man they still respectfully called 'Mr Berry'. After a closely fought first half, Pat dominated the latter stages and finished the fight a clear points winner.

He was in Nottingham for another match five days later, and when he stepped off the train the evening before the fight, he was greeted by a large crowd of admirers. 'It would be difficult to name a more popular boxer, at least as far as Nottingham and district is concerned, than Nipper Pat Daly,' wrote the *Nottingham Evening Post*. His opponent was the tough and rugged Midlands featherweight champion, 28-year-old Ted 'Biff' Cullen of Mansfield – a man who, according to manager George Biddles, had a peculiar ring ritual. 'He always had taken into the ring with him a half bottle of whisky,' recalled Biddles, 'no, not to drink. Whenever Ted Biff told me, and it was usually halfway through the contest, I had to rub the whisky into his legs and thighs. Of course, whisky in those days was around 10 shillings a bottle... Ted Biff never made a champion inside the roped square, but he was a real champion on the outside. The Japanese murdered him in a POW camp during the Second World War and I am certain he went down fighting.'

---

* Another of Harry's sons, Ted Berry, amassed an unbeaten pro record of 19 wins in the 1940s, but eye trouble forced him to retire from boxing. In January 1964, while walking alone along an East End street, Ted became the victim of a drive-by shooting. Both of his legs were seriously injured and his right leg had to be amputated.

Cullen had trained especially for the contest with Pat and believed, along with many locals, that he had the punch and strength to cause an upset. 'If the Nottingham Victoria Baths had been twice the size, the building would not have accommodated all the people who clamoured for admission last night,' reported *The Nottingham Guardian*. A newspaper photo shows a gaunt-looking Pat weighing in, while the shorter, powerfully built Cullen looks on. Pat had a torrid time in the opening minute as Cullen repeatedly charged at him, ripping ferocious shots into the youngster's body. Most of these were blocked by arms and elbows, before Pat got to work shooting long-range lefts and rights into Cullen's face. These had the Midlander in a bad way by the end of the round. Pat continually troubled him in the second, snapping his head back repeatedly with left after left. But Pat's long legs, coupled with a height advantage of several inches, made his 'belt-line' considerably higher than Cullen's natural 'punch-line' and he was left grimacing as he was struck below the belt. By the third it was one-way traffic. Pat repeatedly drove Cullen to the ropes with barrages of lefts and rights. During one flurry Cullen slipped to the canvas, and as he did, his head collided with Pat's groin. Cullen flew through the ropes, while Pat dropped to the canvas in agony, although he quickly regained his feet. The moment Cullen re-entered the ring he charged Pat across it, knocking him through the ropes to the right of his own corner. Luckily, a second saved Pat from a nasty fall, and helped him back into the ring, whereupon the pair fought furiously until the bell. Pat opened the fourth in brilliant fashion, shaking Cullen with a left and a right to the head that sent him halfway through the ropes. Cullen never fully recovered, and as Pat bombarded him with blows, he desperately slung his right fist at the boy's groin, once more sending him to the canvas where he writhed with pain. This time the blow appeared intentional, and Cullen was immediately disqualified.

With only six days to recover, Pat was back in action at Collins's Music Hall to take on Johnny Edmunds of Treharris, a former bantamweight champion of Wales. The Welshman put his weight advantage to full use, bustling-in in aggressive style and swinging punches. His swings, however, were neatly countered. 'Pat's left hand was a very prominent feature,' wrote *Boxing*, 'it kept shooting out with fine force and precision to the head, and the Welsh lad was compelled to force to close quarters to do anything in the way of effective work.' Edmunds's plan of attack was to swing heavily at Pat's head, then rush in close to avoid his stabbing lefts to the face. But Edmunds's punches were poorly timed, and in the second round this proved costly. 'Daly waited for one of these swings, got under it, and then whipped a beautiful short left clean to the point, which brought the Welsh lad forward flat on his face for the full count,' said *Boxing*. 'It was a beautifully planted punch which did not go more than six inches,' wrote *The Evening News*. 'There are occasions when Nipper Pat Daly can make an opponent – and a good one at that – look very cheap.'

Shortly after the contest something unexpected happened. Despite his mantra that rest creates ring-rust, the Professor announced through *Boxing* that he would give Pat a short rest. He would have no further fights until February, and in the meantime would box a series of exhibitions. Was there something the Prof had noticed in Pat's performances, in either the gym or the ring, which gave him cause for concern? Had he decided the boy was in danger of burn-out after all? Whatever the reason, Pat had one more commitment to keep before his rest period could begin. It was a 15-rounder at Premierland against Peckham's Jim Briley, who was a decent second-class fighter but hardly in the same league as Pat. It was a fight in which the Professor's protégé was expected to sparkle. 'The Marylebone lad, with advantages in height, reach and weight, travelled much too fast for Briley, who was well beaten on points,' said *The Evening News*. But the newspaper also criticised his display: 'Daly appears to have deteriorated, and if he is to meet with success when opposing class lads of his own weight he must show far better form than he did in this bout.' 'Is Daly on the slide?' pondered *Boxing*.

After an evidently lacklustre performance, Pat began his two-month sojourn of training and exhibitions. He had certainly earned it; 1929 had been the busiest year of his career. He had had 33 fights in 11 months, which comprised 29 wins, one draw, and three defeats (all inside the distance). Nobody had outpointed him and the draw was hotly disputed by the press. At the art of boxing, he still appeared unbeatable, but there seemed a vulnerability and signs of fatigue that he had never shown before, like tiny cracks appearing on a finely polished surface.

***

Pat returned to the ring slightly sooner than expected. On 19 January 1930 he faced fellow west-Londoner Jack Wright of Paddington over 15 rounds at Kilburn's Vale Hall. Wright had lost only one of 28 traceable fights, but he had never boxed at Pat's level. 'The rest that Daly has had apparently has done him good,' reported *Boxing*, 'as he came out to meet Wright like a fighting machine, adopting a non-stop method and keeping busy with both hands working all the time.' Wright fought back gamely but was hopelessly outclassed. The fight finished suddenly, in the sixth, when the Paddington man struck a low blow and was disqualified.

Nottingham's Victoria Baths eight days later was the setting for Pat's next bout. The opponent was his stable-mate Charlie McCleave, whom he had boxed in some of his earliest contests back in 1925, conceding height, weight and reach. By early 1930, Pat had grown considerably and was now the same height and weight as McCleave. Charlie, who had adopted the pseudonym 'Charlie Mack', had recently boxed exhibitions with Pat in Watford and Nottingham. The pair had put on a fine display on both occasions, and a 'local sportsman' had declared he would back Mack in a real match with Daly for £50 a side. Nottingham promoter Mr Lazzarini offered to stage the match and put up a purse of £200, which Newton and Newton promptly accepted. When two fighters from the same stable met in a real match (which seldom happens today), the result was usually either a glorified exhibition or a serious battle for supremacy. This one, as Pat would recall, was closer to the latter:

> 'Charlie Mack and Nipper Pat Daly fought each other nine times, of which I won seven and two were drawn. We were both on every occasion all out to win, and our management could not go wrong – they drew money from both contestants. We were not big punchers but we were both scientific, and both knew the game, so the paying customers were satisfied with our efforts to give them what they wanted. Charlie and I have met at Fulham Baths, Peckham Rink, Manor Hall Hackney, Nottingham Baths, Vale Hall Kilburn, among other venues. Charlie was managed by Newton Jnr., and I was managed by Newton Senior. Newton Jnr. badly wanted Charlie to have a decision over me as it would have increased his earning capacity, but the best he could do was two draws at two of his own promotions.'

Mack had done a week's training in Nottingham with Andy Newton at the Nottingham Sports Club gym at the Notts County football ground. Pat, meanwhile, remained in London nursing a cold, which had refused to shift, and according to *Boxing* he entered the fight 'not appearing to be in the best of health'. True to form the exchanges were fast and frenetic. Pat dominated the early part of the bout, but during the last few rounds Mack did most of the forcing. At the end of 15 two-minute rounds the referee declared a draw. It transpired that Pat had hurt an ankle while training for the bout, and it had been damaged further amid the fighting. He was to have met a Frenchman named Raymond Treves at Alexandra Palace five days later, but the injury forced him to withdraw. Charlie Mack replaced him but lost to the Frenchman.

On 21 February – four days after his seventeenth birthday – Pat headed to the West Country to take on 20-year-old local hero Jack Sheppard, who, fighting mostly in his home town of Plymouth (then a hotbed of boxing), had lost just eight of 60 traceable contests, which included wins over Harry 'Bugler' Lake, Kid Kelly of Plymouth and Kid Brooks of Aldgate. Pat mentioned the bout, plus a return-fight they had, in his memoirs:

'At the Civic Hall, Exeter after 14½ rounds had been fought the referee stopped my contest with Jack Sheppard, lightweight champion of the West of England, but Sheppard protested so vigorously, together with the audience, who wanted local boy Sheppard to go all the way, the referee obliged and ordered us to continue fighting. Not being sadistically inclined, I did not throw another punch but I fell into a clinch and stayed there for the few seconds that remained. I think the referee was wrong as he did not know how I would react, and both of Jack Sheppard's eyes were badly cut. The paper next morning said 'Daly wins two verdicts'. Jack Sheppard's backers and followers said in the papers next day that they wanted a return fight, which my manager's son agreed to, same terms, 15 rounds, weigh-in 9 stone 6 lb at 2pm for a side-stake of £200. The return bout took place exactly four weeks after the first bout, the only difference was the referee stopped the bout three rounds earlier in my favour. There was no suggestion that we have another bout.'

In between the two Sheppard matches Pat squeezed in two more fights. On 2 March he had a return with Charlie Mack at 9 stone 6 lb at the Vale Hall in Kilburn, and this time the result was clear-cut. 'Daly dominated the fight all the way through,' said *The Evening News* and won 'easily on points'. Then a week later he fought a return with Jim Briley of Peckham, who substituted for Willy Michel of Belgium. Pat's form had been bad in their first encounter, shortly before his two-month exhibition tour. On that occasion he was criticised for not finishing Briley inside the distance; this time he left no provision for such criticism. Putting height, reach and weight advantages to full use, Pat punched Briley at will, flooring him several times before the referee wisely stopped the fight in the sixth.

On 18 March, *The Daily Express* ran a piece headlined 'England's future champions' in which it profiled the great young talents in various disciplines most likely to win worldwide acclaim. The newspaper's picks were: R. W. V. Robins (cricket), Miss Betty Nuthall (lawn tennis), H. W. Austin (lawn tennis), Rex Hartley (golf), Miss Joan Manning-Saunders (painting) and Nipper Pat Daly (boxing).* Although Pat had been out of the limelight of late, he was clearly still seen as Britain's brightest boxing hope:

> 'Boxing, the firmament in which we have been accustomed too long to the glitter of foreign stars, holds a wonderful future for "Nipper" Pat Daly, who is probably a world champion in the making. He looks frail, but he is tough, and his victory over Petit Biquet when he was sixteen was the gem of the evening last March at the Albert Hall. Then he was knocked out by Johnny Cuthbert, the featherweight champion, after a magnificent showing last October. He should take things very easily for some time. Johnny Hill and Baldock both boxed too much.'

---

* Most, but not all, of *The Daily Express'* choices achieved world fame. Walter Robins played first-class cricket for over 25 years, played for England 19 times, and was England captain in 1937. Betty Nuthall was world ranked from 1927 to 1933, won the US Championships in 1930 and eight Grand Slam doubles titles. Bunny Austin was the last Englishman to reach the Wimbledon Men's singles final (in 1938 – he was also a finalist in 1932). He was a key member of the team that won the Davis Cup three times from 1933-5. Rex Hartley played for Britain in the Walker Cup against the USA in 1930 and 1932. Joan Manning-Sanders, the daughter of author and poet Ruth Manning-Sanders, found minor fame as a teenage artist in the 1920s.

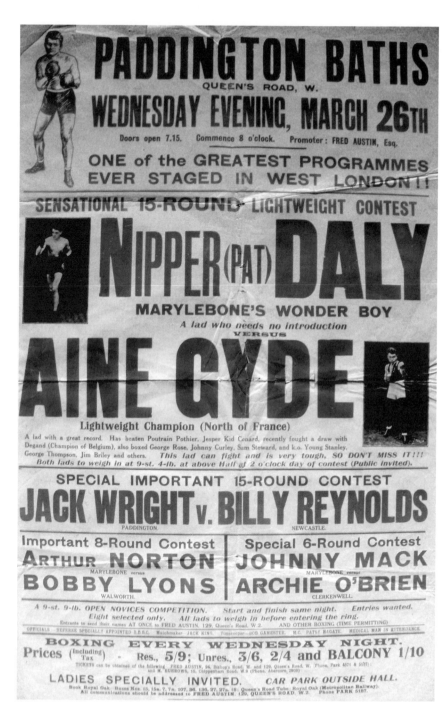

A poster advertising Pat's fight with Aine Gyde.

Pat's next two bouts were at Paddington Baths. On 26 March he took on tough 25-year-old Frenchman Aine Gyde (a brother of future European flyweight champion Praxille Gyde), who had given Johnny Cuthbert and Johnny Curley hard fights. 'It is the custom of some first-class attractions to take good care that their reputations are not exposed to risk of any sort, but this charge can never be levelled at Daly,' opined *Boxing*. Pat came in half a pound inside the stipulated 9 stone 6 lb weight, but Gyde was 1½ lb over. Pat waved the forfeit, however, and the fight proceeded as planned. The Frenchman was comprehensively outboxed, although he did prove possessed of a powerful punch, which floored his young opponent in the seventh. Come the final bell, though, Pat was streets ahead on points. Six days later he boxed Len George of Custom House – who substituted for Fred Green of Blackfriars (a man Pat would box later) – as part of a charity show for St. Mary's Hospital, Paddington. The bill comprised a series of 12-rounders, but Pat's fight was cut to eight rounds due to the late hour. He floored Len George several times but the Custom House man hung on gamely to lose by a wide points margin.

Two days later, Pat was at the Holborn Stadium to box on another charity bill, this time organised by Jack Bloomfield to help raise part of the £3,500 needed to build a new boxing hall at the Dockland Settlement at Canning Town, which offered welfare and recreation to the youth of the local slums. It was a cause close to the hearts of fighters and fans, as the Settlement gave many pros their start in the game. Sir Reginald Kennedy-Cox, founder of the Docklands Settlements (of which there were several), introduced the famous variety artists Norah Blaney and Gwen Farrar, who hosted a £1 per ticket draw to win a bag filled with 100 gold sovereigns. The draw and an auction held by Moss Deyong raised £600, but the proceedings took longer than expected, and Pat's bout had to be cut from 10 to eight rounds. His opponent, Henri Baudeart, official champion of the French marines, was well beaten on points.

Around this time, Pat went down to the Star and Garter Hotel, a Windsor pub with a boxing gymnasium, where many leading fighters trained for their big fights. Pat was there to help Al Foreman of Bow prepare for his forthcoming British lightweight title clash with Fred Webster. Foreman, who also boxed as Bert Harris, had begun his career in London, but in 1923 decided to try his luck in Canada and the USA. He spent seven years out there, amassed a fine record and reputation, which included a record for the world's fastest knockout: 11.5 seconds (including the count), when he chopped down Ruby Levine in Montreal on 25 April 1928. Foreman returned home in early 1930, knocked out several of Britain's leading lightweights, then negotiated a shot at Webster's title.

The Bow man was taken aback by the youngster he had picked for a sparring partner, in particular by Pat's dazzling straight left. In all his time boxing, he said, no one else had hit him so often. The sparring work evidently paid off; on 21 May Foreman made short work of Webster with a dramatic one-round KO, and simultaneously pocketed a great deal of cash. He had not only won his British title fight, but promoted it as well. He had hired out Premierland for the occasion, and a full house ensured that the gate receipts were sizeable.

After his wonderful showing in sparring with Foreman, Pat felt sure he was back near his best. Negotiations were underway for a fight with the gifted George Rose of Bristol, who was part of Fred Dyer's stable, but meanwhile Newton matched him with a highly promising, up-and-coming 21-year-old. It was a tough assignment, but just the sort of scalp Pat needed to stake his place among the country's best lightweights, which as a newcomer to the weight-class he was required to do. The name of his opponent was 'Seaman' Tommy Watson.

21

The Fighting Sailor

The Royal Navy has a fine tradition of turning out quality boxers. As early as 1906, Seaman Arthur Hayes of Hoxton challenged Johnny Summers for the British featherweight crown but lost over 20 rounds. He tried again in 1910, but on that occasion the reigning champion, 'Peerless' Jim Driscoll, stopped him in six. He'd had the misfortune to go in with two all-time greats of the British ring; but 12 years later another Navy fighter, a Scot named Seaman Nobby Hall, had better luck in outpointing Ernie Rice to become British and European lightweight champion in 1922. The following year he saw off challenger and fellow Scot, Hamilton Johnny Brown, but in his second defence lost both titles in frustrating fashion, when he was ruled out for a low blow against Harry Mason. There were scores more Navy and ex-Navy men who earned high honours in the paid ranks of the pre-war ring, but their names, like those of Hall and Hayes, are now all but forgotten. Best of them all was a man from Newcastle named Seaman Tommy Watson.

Sixth of nine siblings, Thomas Samuel Watson was born on 2 June 1908 and grew up in the poor district of Byker in the East End of Newcastle, an area lined with row upon row of run-down Victorian terraces. To supplement the family income, he sold newspapers from the age of eight from a pitch at the top of Byker Bank. 'I found out early in my career as a newsboy,' recalled Tommy, 'that it was a hard school and if you weren't able to take care of yourself the other lads would soon get you down. There were plenty of arguments, usually ending with a walk up a quiet lane, sleeves rolled up, papers on the ground, and then a stand-up fight.' Being a small lad, there were many early back-lane scraps for Watson, but before long he was the accepted 'King of the newsboys'; the other lads, like many men in the years to come, had learnt not to tussle with Tommy.

He first hit the headlines at the age of 13 when a pal fell into the River Tyne and Watson, with no thought for his own safety, dived in and rescued him. To acknowledge his bravery the Lord Mayor of Newcastle presented him with the Royal Humane Society's Certificate for Bravery, in front of his whole school. At 14 he left school to become an errand boy at a glass works, before spending a stint as a riveter's heater at a Tyneside shipyard. At age 15, while working at the shipyard, he joined a boxing gym on Stephen Street, just off Byker Bank, and paid 1s 6d a week to train there under the tutelage of a local pro called Jim Falcus. Aged 16 he joined the Royal Navy, where his gift for the noble art was quickly spotted and developed. He trained diligently, won three boys' championships within a year, then at 17 made his pro debut while on home leave in Newcastle. He won the fight and another the next week, before returning to base and being sent off to sea. He had to wait 17 months to resume his ring career, but when he did there was no stopping him. After a transfer to a barracks at Chatham in Kent, he fought regularly in bouts staged at the barracks or at Rochester Casino, and occasionally travelled to London for fights. By early 1928 he had notched up a long unbeaten record, but he wasn't too proud to admit he still had a lot to learn.

Realising he had a future in boxing, and wanting to learn from one of the best, he travelled to the Bell Street, Marylebone gym of Alec Lambert, whom he asked to train and manage him. And after seeing the sailor in action, Lambert agreed. The dour, poker-faced Geordie was a man of few words, but a whirlwind in the ring and a glutton for hard work. He had bags of natural talent and an ideal cool-headed temperament for boxing. He won the Imperial Services lightweight championship in 1928, and was lightweight champion of the Royal Navy and Marines from 1928 until 1930, when he bought his Navy discharge to concentrate on his ring career. By the time he faced Pat two years after joining Lambert, he had fought at least 56 pro fights, of which he had won 52, drawn two and lost two. Nipper Pat Daly was easily the biggest name he had faced at this juncture. It was a fight that he realised could make or break his career. He had a wife and two small children to feed, and would train for this match like never before.

In alarming echoes of the Cuthbert clash, Pat had weight trouble in the run-up to the fight. The contracted poundage was 9 stone 6 lb, and although he had made that weight for several consecutive months, his growing physique made it an increasingly difficult task. Four days before the fight he was three pounds too heavy with no fat to spare. On the morning of the contest the excess remained, but at the weigh-in, having once more trained and starved, he scraped inside 9 stone 6 lb. Professor Newton had seen Watson in action around the London rings and advised his colt to be careful. 'Take it easy, Pat. Box him and you can't lose. But don't take any gambles.'

Much of north-west London's fight fraternity had seen Watson in action as well. In recent months he had boxed in Kilburn, Paddington and Shepherd's Bush, and had seen off local favourites such as Tommy Little of Notting Hill, Jack Wright of Paddington, and Slosh Saunders of Marylebone. There were no doubts in the minds of those excited fans that they were going to witness some first-class action.

It was Easter Sunday and, Kilburn being an Irish area, many had snuck out of Mass early to secure their seats. They were the men who inhabited the gallery; sat at ringside would be well-heeled men and women from Mayfair, many of whom had been drawn to the sport by the boy prodigy. Before the doors had even opened they were clamouring for admittance and queuing far back along Kilburn High Road. The promoter, Fred Austin, gazing out through his office window, recognised in their eager faces a long line of pound notes. There would be no spare seats in the Vale Hall that afternoon.

Inside the hall, at the clang of the first bell, a cheer shot up as local boy Pat leapt from his stool and got straight to work. The Marylebone youth planned to boss the fight from the outset but Watson it seems had the same idea. A series of blazing exchanges followed and whipped the crowd into a frenzy. Watson appeared to hurt Pat with savage body shots early on, but the Nipper fought back in his usual style to win a hard-fought first round.

The second started sensationally as Watson charged straight at Pat with both hands peppering the body. He pinned the boy against the ropes, saw a brief opening and seized it. A short, sharp right caught Pat clean on the chin. His head spun, his legs sagged and his hands involuntarily fell to his waist. Watson put over another lightening right. Everything went black, the boy's body ached as he hit the canvas and the referee began to count. At eight he rose to his feet and groggily staggered across the ring. Watson gave chase, and with his arms still hanging limply, Pat was wide open for another crashing right to the jaw. He was floored for another nine seconds, but managed to drag himself up before the count of 10. Then, much to Watson's annoyance, the bell sounded.

Back in his corner Newton threw water over Pat for all he was worth. 'Box him. Box him,' the old man screamed. 'Don't go in and mix it with him – that's asking for trouble.' Pat took his mentor's advice, but was so badly shaken by the blows from the previous round, that he spent the next two trying to avoid being knocked out. The third, fourth, and fifth went to Watson, but the Geordie was tiring, having used lots of energy trying to finish the boy off. Sitting on his stool between rounds, Pat caught sight of his parents' worried faces and heard his father shout, 'Come on, Pat – show 'em what you're made of. You can win it, son.' Spurred on by his father's words, and summoning his reserves of strength and self-belief, Pat charged out for the sixth. Before Watson could throw a punch he was bombarded with fierce straight lefts. He tried to fight back but was out-speeded and outboxed, and Pat took the round by a wide margin.

When he returned to his corner this time the Professor was full of encouragement. 'Good work, boy. Keep that up and we'll win the fight.' In just two minutes the action had taken a u-turn, and the noise inside the hall was deafening. 'The crowd were amazed to see Daly make a big recovery in the seventh and eighth,' remarked *Boxing*. 'He was boxing like his old self – full of confidence.' Pat got on top in the eighth with flurries of rapid lefts and rights, and Watson had to soak up plenty of heavy punishment. But Pat was caught by a right himself, and it shook him up. The Seaman put up a ferocious battle all the way; the pace was unrelenting, the intensity overwhelming, and the fans loved every second of it. The sixth, seventh, eighth and ninth were unmistakably won by Pat. But the next round saw another twist in the drama.

'Pat was clearly feeling the effects of the fight,' observed *Boxing*, 'and when Watson hooked him with the right in the tenth, and followed up with uppercuts and rights to the head, he was all in. Although dazed, he continued to fight back, and on one occasion, when in a corner, he surprised Watson by fighting his way out.' Pat had never fully recovered from the knockdowns earlier in the fight, and his brave efforts to regain ground, along with the Seaman's unremitting assault, had taken a great deal out of him. By the end of the round Pat was practically out on his feet. As the bell chimed, according to *The Evening News*, he 'hung on the ropes to steady himself'.

Still feeling unsteady he stepped from his stool for what was to be the most tragic round of his career. Watson now sensed the end was close.

The tall, skinny figure, that had absorbed and repelled so much punishment, clearly could do so no more. Realising this, Watson charged in for the kill. A lightening left-hook struck Pat's jaw and smashed him to the floor. He got to his feet at nine, but only to be felled immediately by a swift right hand. He scrambled up at six and, fighting purely on instinct, staggered backwards around the ring. Watson flew after him and within seconds put him down again. With his last reserves of strength Pat struggled to his feet and tried desperately to raise his hands. But they seemed to be bound by lead weights, and he could not lift them higher than his waist. He was helpless now and Watson was punching him at will. Another right to the chin floored the boy for the fourth time in the round. Watson, it seemed, would have to nail Pat to the floor to stop him from rising. 'I have some dim recollection of trying to get up,' he later remembered, 'but when I did nothing hit me. The fight had been stopped.'

During the final knockdowns ringsiders were rudely jostled by a man manically clambering over their heads. It was Pat's father, who in a blind panic had tried to reach his corner. He said afterwards that he was going to throw in the towel.

'The way that Daly took punishment only to recover and fight back like a tiger stamps him as one of the gamest battlers of the day,' declared *Boxing*. 'Had he quitted in the second nobody would have grumbled, but he was out to beat Watson and fought on gamely against big odds.' Pat could no more have given up than stopped breathing, and his braveness had cost him dearly. What was needed was some compassion from his corner or from the referee. Friends told him afterwards that when the end came there were women crying at ringside.

Among the crowd that afternoon was John Black, a 10-year-old fan and amateur boxer watching the fight with his father. Now 90, John later worked alongside Pat at the Handley Page aircraft factory and remembers the Watson fight well:

'Nipper came out boxing beautifully – he was marvellous, quick as lightning. And I said to my father "Isn't he good?" "Yes," my Dad said, "but that boy won't have the stamina of that Seaman Watson – Watson's a stronger, older man." And it turned out just as he said... My father called out "Stop the fight" long before it ended, as soon as he saw how hurt he was. "You're gonna ruin that boy. Stop it!" he said. I remember it vividly. I remember the complaints that went round the hall as well. My father said to me, "It's not fair. That boy's got a great future but that Professor Newton's gonna ruin him." And he turned round to Professor Newton, my father did, and said, "Why are you putting that boy against an experienced man like that already?" He should have never fought grown men and Seaman Watson – I can see him now – was a real cagey, tough fighter...

My memory of that fight at the Vale Hall left a great impression on me. I was only 10 but I knew enough. Right from the time I was four or five my dad, who boxed with Bombardier Billy Wells in the Army, put the boxing gloves on me practically every time I came home from school. But that fight played on me and that's what stopped me ever boxing again. I thought, "They won't do to me what they did to Nipper." And I told my father, "I'm not boxing any more, dad – ever." And I never did.'

The hard-earned victory over Pat convinced many of the critics that Watson was a coming champion. They were right. Within 19 months he defeated Nel Tarleton for the British featherweight crown, and in January 1933 outpointed Fidel LaBarba to earn a shot at the world featherweight title. In his world championship challenge he took on the famous Cuban, Kid Chocolate, at Madison Square Garden in New York. He lost on points and never got another shot. But he did become British lightweight champion, and in a glorious 10-year career, spanning at least 123 fights, he suffered only nine defeats. Seaman Watson was probably the greatest fighter that the North East ever produced.

22

End of the Road

The next morning Pat awoke in a daze. His body ached from head to toe, and his face, arms and torso were covered with bruises. This, in itself, was not unusual after such a hard fight; but there was something that troubled him more. His head spun with a nauseating dizziness, an intense ache, and a disorientation that he'd never known before. No fight had ever left him feeling this wretched.

With some effort he hauled himself out of bed. But as he stood, he wobbled, his legs gave way, and he collapsed in a heap. In a state of bewilderment he returned to his bed, where he remained for the rest of the day. His mother checked on him regularly, and his father, after returning from work, looked in on him and asked what was wrong. He'd be all right, he answered; all he needed was a good night's rest. But the next day he felt no better. The dizziness persisted, his head still pounded, and his mother's attempts to get him out of bed resulted in him taking a few steps and falling over.

The days passed and he did not improve. Whenever he stood he felt unsteady, and when he walked he tottered from side to side or fell down. Only days ago he'd been about the swiftest, most graceful thing on two legs, but now, quite inexplicably, he couldn't walk in a straight line. A doctor was called and quickly diagnosed the problem. The final rain of blows from Watson had given him a concussion: a disturbance to the nerve cells of the brain caused by a blow or collision, when it bounces against the bone of the skull. Parts of the brain's functions are temporarily disrupted, and symptoms ranging from headaches, nausea and dizziness, to vision disturbance, memory loss and indeed walking difficulty and loss of balance, can be the result. The only remedy is rest.

On 29 April, nine days after the Watson fight, Pat was to have boxed at Waverley Market in Edinburgh on a benefit show for former British featherweight champion Tancy Lee. His opponent would have been Peter Donaldson of Leith, and the scheduled distance 12 three-minute rounds.

Needless to say, he didn't keep the engagement, and was replaced by fellow Londoner Harry Corbett, who defeated Donaldson on points.

According to *Boxing* there were renewed claims that Pat had been 'burnt out' by too many and too tough contests. As before, an indignant Professor hit back through the trade paper's columns, and also offered a curious excuse for the defeat:

> 'It is all rot... The marvellous manner in which he recovered from the punch on the jaw in the second round, and the trouble in which he had Watson subsequently, prove that he has all the energy and fighting spirit, as well as the reserves of stamina necessary. The whole trouble arose when I left him to himself during the interval between the weighing-in and the fight itself. In order to satisfy Pat and his people, I had him thoroughly overhauled medically the next day. He will be put through an intensive course of training, and I propose to send him against Watson again in the near future. The public will then be able to judge for themselves whether Pat is going back or going to fulfil the whole of his early promise to the letter.'

Pat felt too ashamed to leave the house during daylight hours. The gaze of the locals – some of whom hero-worshipped him, all of whom knew him – would be too much to bear. He couldn't let them see him like this. So instead, he went out after dark, and with his father's help he practiced walking along the quieter backstreets behind the Edgware Road. It was a depressing, extremely frustrating time, but after five weeks his balance was much improved, and with Newton's encouragement he returned to the gym.

On 26 May, just days after resuming training, Pat was billed to box Donald Jones of Penycraig over 15 rounds. At the last minute, however, a medical professional intervened:

> 'It came as a distinct disappointment to the large crowd present at Alcazar, Edmonton, last night, to learn that Nipper Pat Daly, of Marylebone, was under strict doctor's orders not to box, a medical examination showing that he was still suffering from the effects of some concussion sustained in a recent contest.' *Boxing*, 28 May 1930

The crowd had to settle for a substitute in Haydn Williams, another Newton fighter, who beat Jones on points. Coincidentally, towards the bottom of the page appeared the following note about the future of another Newtonian boxer:

> 'Andy [Newton] informs us of regrettable news of Ranger Harkin, who in his contest with Dick Burt, at Edmonton last week, sustained concussion, which, although considered slight at the time, has caused his doctor to order him out of the game for good. Harkin has, therefore, returned to Ireland to resume his ordinary occupation, and we trust that he will make a good recovery.'

The doctor's pronouncement underscores the seriousness of concussion for boxers, and suggests that the dangers, if not fully understood, were at least partly known in the '20s. It is understood today that returning to the ring too soon following a concussion is dangerous. A second concussion received before the sufferer has recovered from the first can cause permanent brain damage or even death. Modern research suggests that athletes with repeated concussions are more likely to suffer lasting cognitive damage. Insufficient rest between fights can lead to an ongoing concussion, which will often only become apparent when the symptoms become serious. Pat believed he had suffered a smaller concussion when he fought Cuthbert, which could explain why his symptoms this time were so severe. Was he suffering ongoing concussion between the two fights?

On 5 June he returned to the ring. The opponent should have been Selwyn Davies of Caerau, but a week before the fight another Welshman, 22-year-old Nobby Baker of Trealaw, was drafted in when Davies withdrew. Baker's contract for the match, penned and typewritten on Premierland-headed paper, some eight decades later is remarkably well preserved and in the safe hands of his granddaughter, who kindly provided a copy. It offers some idea of the draconian terms a stand-in fighter like Baker would be forced to accept in those days. Win, lose or draw, he was paid a flat fee of £12 10s. He would be disqualified if the referee felt he was 'not trying or guilty of a deliberate foul', and if disqualified, or in the event of a 'No Contest' (the disqualification of both fighters), he would not be paid. He was not permitted to box publicly for 14 days before the fight without the consent of the Premierland management. He would deposit a sum with them to guarantee his appearance and contracted weight; should he fail to appear for the fight he would be at their disposal for another contest within 21 days. He would grant the management the option of using him in a further two contests within six weeks of the first, and he would not box elsewhere until the contract was fulfilled. 'Should he break his contracts in any way,' stated the final condition, 'he agrees to pay the "Premierland" management £25 damages.'

Clearly the hall's owners Berliner and Lyttlestone made their contracts watertight. But Baker, who earned around £3 a week as a miner at a Welsh colliery, would years later remember that he and his fellow part-time fighters in those desperate days were only too grateful for the extra cash: 'Money was so short in the '20s and '30s. We fought for whatever money they offered. If we were lucky we got our rail fare.' Mining and fighting had always gone hand-in-hand for Baker. He was already an amateur boxer when he first went down the pit at 13. Within three years he turned professional, and like many fighters of the era he learnt his trade on the booths:

> 'I used to fight in the booths and to do six or eight rounds was training for me. The first thing you did in such fights was hit the holy hell out of the other man. I fought against one fellow who turned his fist with his thumb out when he hit you in the body, pinching your skin. There was dirty stuff, but it was a case of "you do it to me and I will do it to you". The ref never saw it.'

By the time he fought Pat, Baker had notched up 86 recorded pro fights. In the course of his career he'd have at least 252 bouts, which included three unsuccessful tilts at the Welsh title. It was only after a 1946 mining accident, which damaged his spine and severely impaired his movement, that he reluctantly hung up his gloves aged 39. He was a short, stocky, all-action puncher but some way short of top class. A typical game but limited substitute, who should cause Pat no problems. The weight was 9 stone 7 lb and the scheduled distance was 15 two-minute rounds. The event, as *Boxing* reported, proved astounding:

> 'Daly was a head taller, and about a foot longer in reach. He made good use of these assets for a couple of rounds, but there was something about his work that was the opposite of convincing. He was easily baffled and made to look awkward by a boxer who would not have been placed in the same street with the Nipper a month or two ago. Time after time Baker got home with swinging rights to the head which, although not heavy, seemed to make a big impression on Daly.

Pat tried many of his pet short punches to the face with each hand, but he was always in a position to be punched when he came away. This is something new in Daly's boxing make-up... when a punch on the chin dropped him for eight in the eleventh round, there was no mistaking the obvious fact that the blow would not even have disturbed the Daly of 12 months ago.'

He arose from the knockdown and boxed well, but he was floored again in the twelfth. Within his memoirs, Pat recalled the finish, which occurred in the thirteenth:

'I think I was leading on points narrowly up to the thirteenth round when Baker caught me with a wild swing, which previously I would have avoided, and I went down. I got up and was put down for two more counts and referee Jack Hart stopped the fight. I protested as I felt all right. The punch hadn't hurt me and I could not understand why I was knocked down, but Mr Hart with all his experience knew better. I'm glad now that he did stop it. That fight might have killed me! I realised afterwards that I'd had concussion ever since the Cuthbert fight.'

Stunned by what he had witnessed, *Boxing*'s reporter issued a warning to Pat and his mentors:

'There were obvious signs about this defeat of the Nipper which appeared to bear out rumours that young Pat has of late taken too much out of himself. Neither of the Newtons appeared at all surprised at the collapse of young Daly. Had the blows he had taken been of heavy calibre there might have been some excuse for Pat wincing or staggering as he did, but from the start of the bout Daly appeared far from well, and certainly not at ease... Daly must look carefully after himself. The pitcher can be carried to the well once too often.'

Jack Hart's swift action had saved Pat from further damage, but the fight still took its toll and he fell ill once again. He was beginning to wonder whether the damage he had suffered was irreversible, and if he'd ever recapture his former brilliance. Weeks ago he'd still seemed destined to be champion of the world, but now, at 17, he suddenly felt like he was on boxing's scrap heap. But surely that was absurd. The 'scrap heap' was for old washed-up fighters who had gone on too long, and the old fighter was the only one who didn't know it. You couldn't be washed up at 17! But no matter how much he rationalised, he could not escape the growing conviction that he was indeed a spent force. Inevitably, he descended into deep depression.

In a desperate frame of mind, he wandered alone along the Grand Union Canal: a picturesque waterway that links London to the Midlands, part of which runs through Paddington. A trawl through the local west London press of 1930 reveals it as a common site for suicides and accidental drowning. It was here, gazing hopelessly into the dark, murky waters that he seized upon an idea. He related the experience to his son John many years later, as John recalled:

'He was on the Grand Union Canal, and he seriously contemplated suicide. He was finished. He couldn't walk. He was stumbling all over the place. Everything seemed lost, you know, finished. He had no future. He'd lost his health. He'd lost his chance of doing what he wanted to do, which was be champion of the world, and he was only 17. He said, "I felt so low". And he thought of throwing himself in the Grand Union Canal. He considered it very seriously. But anyway, he didn't, and instead he made a sort of compromise with life.'

The decision he made next would have been unthinkable only weeks ago. He told the two Newtons that he was through with fighting for them. He would rest for two years, eat and drink what he liked, and allow his body to heal and grow to its natural size and weight. Then, with a fully formed physique and bones fully set, if he felt ready, he would return to the ring. The Professor and son tried hard to talk him round, but to their dismay they found his mind was made up. At the time they were preoccupied with an even more serious matter. Andy Newton, who had his left eye removed earlier that year, was about to undergo a series of operations to save the vision of his right eye. These would ultimately fail and by September he was completely blind. How vehemently they pursued Pat after he announced his decision is not known, but the fact is he never boxed for them again.

It must have frustrated Pat immensely to stay on the sidelines of the sport he loved, but that's precisely where we find him three months later. Fred Austin, buoyed by the success of his shows at Paddington Baths, had taken over promotions at the Vale Hall, Kilburn, and extended its seating capacity. His opening show was topped by Billy James of Birmingham and Andy Devine (formerly known as 'Young Siki'). Devine was an early opponent of Pat's, who *Boxing* noted on this occasion was guilty of hitting with the open glove:

> 'We remarked on the faulty hitting of Devine to our near neighbour, Nipper Pat Daly, who was an interested spectator, and ventured the opinion that "Young Siki", who scored a sensational K.O. over Daly at Premierland, was punching to more effect in those days. Nipper Pat smiled in acquiescence. From a mere stripling then, Daly has grown into a fine up-standing youth – certainly more than a lightweight, and his three months' rest has certainly done him good.' *Boxing*, 10 September 1930

That same week there were rumours afoot that Pat was to make a ring-return, not under the Professor, but for somebody else. Newton, as ever, was quick to quash the gossip through *Boxing*:

> 'There have been rumours suggesting that Nipper Pat Daly will make an early return to the ring, but we can say definitely that the "one and only Professor" has no knowledge of this... It is evident that the Nipper will have to be tested in one or two "try-outs" before he can re-enter the game seriously, and as his contract with the Professor has still several more years to run, Pat can only get busy again under his old banner.'

In truth, Pat was itching to get back in the ring, but he still had concerns about his health. When an offer arrived from the high-flying, silver-tongued American Jeff Dickson, however, it did not take long to talk him round.

Pat's boxing licence.

23

The Comeback

'...his dream must have seemed so close that he could hardly fail to grasp it. He did not know that it was already behind him.'

The Great Gatsby, F. Scott Fitzgerald

Young, debonair, a risk-taker with a brilliant business brain; Jefferson Davis Dickson Jr. was a man destined to succeed at whatever he turned his hand to. Born in Natchez, Mississippi on 30 March 1896, his first real job was as a newsreel cameraman in America's burgeoning cinema business. At the outbreak of the First World War he had the audacious idea of travelling to Europe to capture the conflict on film. To help his scheme along, he secured the backing of the US Government, who sent him across the Atlantic on an official mission. To get closer to the action he registered at the American Consulate as a US Army soldier, but was wounded at the Battle of Saint-Mihiel, after placing his camera on a hill rather too close to the fighting.

When the war ended he remained in Paris as part of the US signal Corps, and for a fee shot staged footage of American Soldiers, who'd actually seen no action, engaged in mock battles against actors in rented German uniforms. He even had trenches specially dug for the films, and they brought him a healthy profit. After demobilisation he toured Europe filming novelties such as lions in Abyssinia, before drifting back to Paris, where he decided to try his hand at sweet manufacture. To leapfrog the competition Dickson packaged his sweets in an original and enticing manner. His 'Pouchette Surprise' comprised a box of sweets with a surprise gift (a cheap necklace, silk stockings, a whistle, a doll, etc.) and were sold at theatres across Paris. They proved a roaring success until the French government shut him down on the grounds that he was running a lottery.

While living the high-life in Paris, on his nights off Dickson fed his passion for pugilism. The two main boxing halls in the French capital at the time were the Cirque de Paris and the Salle Wagram, and Dickson was a regular patron at both.* Business was on the slide at the Salle Wagram, and after bailing out its promoter with a series of loans, Dickson was sold the ailing fight hall for the cut price of 5,000 francs. Although only a side-project at first, he soon saw enormous potential in his new venture.

The fights he had witnessed across the world had given him a broad insight into the business. He avoided the mistakes and deficiencies of other promoters, and his natural gifts for organisation and promotion delivered rapid results. Dickson was soon staging boxing shows at the Cirque de Paris as well as the Salle Wagram, and not long afterwards took over Paris' largest indoor arena, the Vélodrome d'Hiver. Before long he was putting on shows before enormous crowds across Europe: Berlin, Brussels, Rome and Barcelona were all host to extravagant Dickson promotions. He had the connections and oratorical gift to draw the top Americans across the pond, and the nerve and financial muscle to stage lavish, big-budget shows that no one else dared to. What had started as a sideline had quickly grown into a vast sporting empire. When he wasn't promoting boxing Dickson staged wrestling, cycling, circuses, indoor bullfighting and, on one occasion – at his most adventurous – a mock lion-hunt involving 100 ex-circus lions he had bought at auction. He was fittingly dubbed 'the Tex Rickard of Europe', after the man who brought boxing its first million-dollar gate. Anything that offered spectacle and colour was prime Dickson territory.

He opened a London office in 1929, and after a running battle with the Board of Control – which attempted to keep him out of British boxing by repeatedly refusing him a licence – he took over the Royal Albert Hall tenure of the late Harry Jacobs. He sold out the Albert Hall at his first attempt, and drew gasps of astonishment from London spectators by featuring the freakishly gigantic future world heavyweight champion, but

---

*   Another regular patron of the Parisian boxing halls was the writer Ernest Hemingway, who lived in the city during the 1920s. In the Preface to *A Moveable Feast* he refers to 'the great twenty-round fights at the Cirque d'Hiver'. He also mentions watching six-day bicycle races at the Vélodrome d'Hiver later in the book. 'A Strange Fight Club', which appears in the 2010 'Restored Edition' of *A Moveable Feast*, is about Canadian heavyweight champion Larry Gains, who Hemingway watched train in Paris. It also briefly mentions Britsh middle and light-heavyweight champion Frank Moody, who the writer calls 'quite a good fighter'.

then unknown, Primo Carnera in an eight-rounder. He was instrumental, in fact, in building the 'Ambling Alp' into an international star.

At that precise time Dickson had also come very close to staging a super-fight between Pat and the legendary American Fidel La Barba; but it had fallen through after Pat's defeat to Cuthbert. The enigmatic boy wonder had long appealed to the showman in Dickson – there were limitless possibilities in a boy who could beat grown men – but the tight rein of his two handlers had hitherto placed him off limits. A year later some were claiming that Pat had been 'burnt out', but with the boy now apparently a free agent, and with little to lose, Dickson made an approach. If the burn-out rumours were untrue then, properly handled, he could soon be in the possession of the sport's most lucrative fighter.

Pat was offered a slot on Dickson's next Albert Hall bill. There would be no rushing or over-matching him this time, he assured the lad, and to facilitate a careful return his first fight would be an easy six-rounder. (Dickson's claim of wanting to take good care of the youngster may have been genuine. He was, at any rate, probably the only promoter at the time who took out insurances on boxers, so they or their families would be compensated in the event of death or injury.) After some consideration, Pat accepted. He was desperately missing the thrill of the ring, and such an offer from such a renowned figure was not to be baulked at. Dickson, he realised, had the cash and the connections to take him all the way to the top. For Dickson, it was a chance to test whether Pat still had his old magic.

News of the Nipper's comeback soon swept the sporting press. He was to oppose Tom Banks of Birmingham in the chief six-rounder, which was billed on posters as 'The Nipper's New Start'. Naturally, the Professor and Andy soon caught wind of the match, and promptly fired off cease and desist letters to Pat and Dickson, as well as issuing warnings through *Boxing*:

'…the "one and only" begs to remind all and sundry, his contract with Daly will not expire for some few years yet, and that he cannot be booked without the Professor's approval.' *Boxing*, 8 October 1930

'…"the one and only Professor" wishes to inform all and sundry that he and he alone has any authority to make matches for Nipper Pat Daly, and further, that he is far from agreeable that Daly should meet Tom Banks at the Albert Hall on Oct. 28th.' *Boxing*, 22 October 1930

The Professor warned Pat and Dickson that unless the boy was taken off the bill he would start court proceedings against them both. Dickson told Pat not to worry, and for the first time made the youngster aware of a scam that had taken place right under his nose. Several promoters had told him that Andy Newton had demanded 'off the record' payments whenever Pat appeared on a bill. These, of course, were concealed from the youngster, and he never received his contractual cut. 'If that comes out in court,' insisted Dickson, 'and there are witnesses who will back me up – those two won't have a leg to stand on.'

The precise details of the hearing, and the evidence put forward by each side, all these years later, is unknown. But the outcome made the front page of the next day's sporting press:

> 'Mr Gilbert Paull, instructed by Mr Freke Palmer, solicitor, applied to Mr Justice Branson in the King's Bench Division on behalf of Mr Andrew Newton for an injunction to restrain Nipper Pat Daly and Mr Jeff Dickson from proceeding with a contract under which Daly is to box at the Albert Hall to-night. Daly is matched with Tom Banks (Birmingham) over six rounds at Mr Dickson's big show to-night. Mr O'Connor, on behalf of the defendants, contended that plaintiff was not entitled to the relief asked for. His lordship refused to grant application.' *The Sporting Life*, 28 October 1930

The judge – who, incidentally, was the paternal grandfather of billionaire entrepreneur Sir Richard Branson – declared the contract Newton held Pat under, which he had signed in his early teens, to be legally untenable. 'The judge said the contract was worthless,' remembers Pat's widow, Mary, 'and he threw the case out of court.' Pat was then free to fight for whomever he pleased, and his former managers, forthwith, had no legal claim on him. And so, after a futile eleventh-hour hijack attempt, the match that night proceeded as planned.

That month Pat paid £5 for his first and only BBB of C boxer's licence, which bore the number '2108'. (The Board still had difficulty convincing fighters to purchase its yearly licences – some still considered them a 'fly-by-night' organisation and were loathe to part with their money.) Pat's registered weight on the licence was 9 stone 6 lb, although fight reports suggest he weighed considerably more. The manager's section he left blank.

On the top of the bill that evening former British middleweight champion Jack Hood was up against top American contender Dave Shade, who Dickson had brought over especially. The second-tier event saw Dick Corbett take on top North East bantam Benny Sharkey, who had recently beaten Teddy Baldock. Corbett, who Pat of course had defeated the previous year, outpointed Sharkey, and six fights later would be British bantamweight champion. Pat's opponent, Tom Banks of Birmingham, had only once fought outside the Midlands, and had won just 14 of 26 recorded fights, which had all been against modest opposition. He had never opposed anyone even approaching Pat's class and held a fraction of his experience. Banks was someone Pat should have shone against; someone he should have beaten with little effort. But the outcome, as *Boxing* observed, was astonishing:

'The most startling revelation of all was the decline of the erstwhile Nipper Pat Daly. This former "wonder boy" can no longer lay claim to the label of "Nipper". We did not learn his present poundage, but he looked to be almost, if not fully 10 stone, and it is by no means impossible that he was out of condition. This fact, if it was the case, would not, however, fully account for a falling off in form, which was the most remarkable we have seen in so short a time and in one who held out so great a promise... there was an inaccuracy in his leading and a distinct lack of snap in his punch... The erstwhile brilliant "Nipper" was unable to produce the ring generalship he had previously shown and we were left to wonder where, also how, his former "boxing brains" had departed from him.'

According to *The Sporting Life* 'Daly, although not now a "wonder boy", [made] it a near thing.' While *The Daily Herald* said he 'fought back gamely only to lose by a small margin of points'. In his career up to this point, in no fewer than 109 fights, some against the best men in Europe, he had lost only twice on points; and both times the newspapers felt he'd been the victim of a bad refereeing decision. At the art of boxing, until now, he had seemed unbeatable. So to suddenly lose by even a fraction on points, to a fighter so far beneath his class, was utterly mystifying. Sat ringside was the reigning world junior-welterweight champion Jack Kid Berg, who had recently returned from America. Appalled by what he had seen, he spoke to a reporter, who summed up his comments in a piece headed 'The Little boxing tragedy – slave-drivers who try to fool nature':

> 'At the last Albert Hall show, when Dave Shade and Jack Hood met, I saw Nipper Pat Daly in the ring and was appalled by the tragedy of it. If ever there was a boy cut out of brown paper to be champion of the world it was this one. Yet before he had reached the age of 17 he had engaged in over 200 fights. Sheer exhaustion compelled him to leave the ring for a few months. Today, though he has tried to resume his ring career, he looks an overgrown youth with neither nerve nor stamina... In the States the law will not allow boys to be treated thus, so fewer promising lads are lost to the game through mismanagement and overwork.'

The defeat was a great shock to Pat, who had not felt right from the opening round. He tried to stay optimistic, however, and decided that if he continued to rest and recuperate he might still rekindle the old magic. He directly told Dickson of his plan and the astute American, having been equally astonished by the atrocious performance, made no attempt to talk him round.* Could the Nipper's former brilliance ever be restored? Another promoter seemed to think so, and he successfully talked Pat into another early comeback:

> 'After I had rested for a week, I was contacted by Fred Austin, promoter at Paddington Baths. He wanted me to box for him as I was a local boy. I refused and I told him that I intended to rest for two years and when I made my comeback I would be stronger and bigger, and if I showed my early form, with the extra strength and added punching ability, I would still be middleweight champion of the world. In the end he persuaded me to box at Paddington Baths. I did

---

* Dickson remained Europe's number-one promoter throughout the 1930s, and for his success was awarded the French Legion of Honour. In 1931 he replaced the Paris Vélodrome d'Hiver with a new venue, the Palais des Sports, which he modelled on New York's Madison Square Garden. When America entered World War Two, Dickson was drafted into the US Air Force and stationed in England as an intelligence officer. He was attached to a flying bombardier squadron and embarked on several missions. In 1943, during a mission over Germany, the plane he was in was shot down. Witnesses saw five parachutes leave the aircraft and open but Captain Jeff Dickson was never seen again. He was inducted into the International Boxing Hall of Fame in 2000.

not have any rest and went into training in the front room at his home. Tommy Little of Notting Hill was my chief and only sparring partner. Tommy later became famous as a referee, also Billy Matthews, former European feather champion, was in charge of the training.'

Despite their humble training quarters, Austin had hired a good calibre of sparring partner in Tommy Little, who was a decent professional in his own right. Perhaps the most memorable night of Little's boxing career arrived at Wembley Stadium 33 years in the future, when he refereed the 1963 Cassius Clay–Henry Cooper match, in which the timely intervention of the bell and the swift but controversial actions of cornerman Angelo Dundee (who it seems used illegal smelling salts to revive his fighter and complained of a split in his glove to buy time), saved the soon to be renamed Muhammad Ali from probable defeat. Pat's new trainer, Billy Matthews, was notable, aside from his ring achievements, as a brother of the famous actress Jessie Matthews.

'My first fight at Paddington Baths was with Fred Green of Blackfriars, who was supposed to be "an old mug",' remembered Pat. 'The fight was 12 rounds and went to a draw after we had both visited the canvas several times.' Green's record reveals that he was actually a very good fighter, but even so, it was a match Pat should have comfortably won. After a comparatively dismal display he again considered retiring. But he was already committed to another contest, at the Vale Hall the next Sunday afternoon. And when he dominated and knocked out Jimmy Laws of Deptford in three rounds, again his view altered, and he decided to carry on with the game. Laws, however, was far below Pat's class, so the smoothness of his victory was misleading.

He had an unconvincing start in his next bout, against 23-year-old Dave Danahar of Bethnal Green (an uncle of the later famous welterweight Arthur Danahar), but in the ninth he finally gave the crowd what *The Evening News* called 'a bit of the old Daly', when he plastered Danahar with a furious barrage of blows, floored him twice, and forced him to retire. But despite this, the newspaper still concluded, 'His form up to this success was very patchy... it was not a convincing performance on the part of Daly.'

The following week, the Professor made it publically known that the partnership with his prize pupil was unequivocally over, at the same time taking a parting shot at the lad:

'The "one and only Professor" wishes it to be known that he has no longer any interest in Nipper Pat Daly, as also that he is preparing several other good boys whom he fully expects will eclipse the Nipper's now somewhat dulled brilliance.' *Boxing*, 17 December 1930

On the same page of the trade paper, in a move both predatory and tasteless, Andy Newton sought to capitalise on Pat's sudden decline by challenging him to matches (complete with wagers) against men he would undoubtedly have beaten before:

'Andy Newton, Junior, wishes to apprise Mr Fred Austin, of Paddington Baths, that he is willing to match three of his charges – Bob Cotton, Pat Bransfield, and Billy Cain against Nipper Pat Daly for consecutive weeks, and will wager £10 a side on each of these. Furthermore, he is willing to match Charlie Mack against "the Nipper" at 10 st. 7 lb ringside, and will wager 2–1 up to any amount Daly cares to stake that the Nipper will not stay the distance.'

Neither Pat nor Fred Austin dignified the 'challenge', or the Professor's remarks, with a response.

Pat's next bout was against Johnny Allen of Bermondsey who was 'outclassed and outboxed, and only had his great gameness to recommend him' (*Boxing*). Allen was floored and punched round the ring until the referee rightly applied the closure in the fourth. A glance at the Bermondsey man's record indicates that in a career comprising 21 fights, he lost 13 and only won eight – a far cry from the pedigree of the men Pat had previously faced. His next two opponents, André Beghin of Belgium and Albert Ryall of Ealing, were likewise outclassed. Ryall retired at the end of the fourth, and Beghin 'was simply made a punchball until the referee intervened in the fourth round.' (*Boxing*)

Pat's next opponent was a somewhat tougher proposition, but still somebody he should beat without difficulty. Tom Handley of Hoxton, *Boxing* noted, 'cannot boast the skill and ringcraft of the "Nipper" but is a very strong and tough fighter'. Pat was thrice floored at various times in the contest and dragged into a slugging match, before dropping Handley in the eighth and grinding out a narrow points win. Pat was the biggest name Handley would ever fight in an unremarkable career that comprised 37 wins, 41 losses and 8 draws.

There was something markedly wrong with Pat's performances. His speedy footwork had slowed, his lightning reflexes and coordination had diminished, and he could no longer sustain his boxing through the course of a long fight. After his match with Dave Danahar, C.E. Nash of the *Evening News* had written:

'Pat Daly, the once almost invincible featherweight, has dropped to a low level now that he is a welterweight... Danahar is just an ordinary boxer. He has won a good many fights, but when Daly was at his best a boy of Danahar's class would not have been considered good enough to test his merits. There is no disguising the fact that Daly is not the force he was. Admitted that he is still good, it looks as if he is paying the penalty of the hard work which was slipped into him when he was a youngster. The fire has partly burned out, and only smouldering embers remain. Whether they can be fanned into life again remains to be seen. Daly nowadays appears to suffer from an over anxiety to do well, and this, I think, affects his boxing to a certain extent. His great desire to do well, and this spirit, is commendable. But Daly was once looked upon as a likely world's champion, and the falling away is more noticeable in his case than it would be with a boy whose merits were not so highly extolled... it was not a convincing performance, but his victory contained a promise that he may one day again occupy the high position he once held in the boxing world.'

The day before a scheduled bout with Johnny Reed of Plumstead, Pat was laid up in bed with flu. He had plenty of time to reflect on his future and on the events of the past few months. He realised he was slipping, and he knew he could no longer perform the feats of boxing that had once been his trademark. As he recalled for *The People* newspaper in 1949, 'I told myself, "You've had it, Pat; you'll never be a world champion now".' He decided, there and then, he would fulfil his final engagement and then take a long rest. Harry Jenkins of Camden Town came in as a substitute for Johnny Reed. Pat boxed as well as could be expected under the handicap of flu, and Jenkins retired in the fourth with a profusely bleeding and broken nose.

'In all I had 10 fights for Mr Austin, I won nine of them and drew one. I was so disappointed at my performances and my lack of form, that I decided to adopt my former plan to rest for two years and grow into a man and then make my comeback. My form must have been so bad, that even Fred Austin agreed with it (my retiring, I mean).'

He never did make his comeback, and the match with Jenkins on 27 January 1931 – exactly three weeks before his eighteenth birthday – was his last. The curtain had fallen on a unique career. Never again would fight fans see Nipper Pat in the ring.

24

What Next?

'It is tragic to see a promising young boxer carry all before him, whilst still in his teens, and then sink into oblivion... If the American custom of short-distance fights had been adopted over here five years ago, we would have had a potential world champion in Nipper Pat Daly, at this very moment. No fighter of this or any other age captured public imagination as Daly... Wake up, you stewards, who endeavour to govern the boxing game. Take a closer interest in the game that you claim to represent and to uphold... One of these fine mornings I am looking forward to the news that the British Boxing Board of Control have set an age limit for the number of rounds a fighter can take part in. Then I will send them a bouquet for the first real thing they've done to improve British boxing!'

Jeff Barr, *Topical Times*, 24 September 1932

Suddenly the dream was over. The most significant part of Pat's young life had ingloriously ended for good. The roar of the crowd, the glow of the arc lights and the thrill of combat – which had been food and drink to him – were now just memories. The fights, the fame, the newspaper headlines and the championship belts he would have to leave for other men. There were countless 'what ifs' and 'if onlys', but he purged them from his mind for the sake of his sanity.

The ring had left its mark on him – scar tissue, flattened nose, cauliflower ear, and a lump on each wrist-joint from the impact of punches on his unset bones. In addition, according to his brother Ken, it left him 'weak in the legs'. But besides these things, he was physically fit and very strong, and still perfectly capable of manual work. He had earned a good deal of money in his former profession, and this no doubt gave him breathing space. But even so, he was well aware that with no regular income his savings would soon evaporate, so he decided to get a job as quickly as possible.

Where before he had earned into the hundreds for less than an hour doing what he loved, he was now resigned to a future of earning perhaps £3 per week for 40 hours' toil. There were 47 working years ahead of him, and without a trade to fall back on he was unsure how he would fill them. To compound matters, he couldn't have picked a worse time to be out of work.

British industry was already in a recession in the late 1920s, but the October 1929 Wall Street Crash tipped her economy over the edge. By the end of 1930 British unemployment had shot from one million to 2.5 million, or 20 per cent of the insured workforce. Crowds of desperate men were literally fighting for tickets simply to do a day's work, while hundreds of thousands went on hunger marches in the hope of spurring the government into action. National morale was at its worst since the Great War.

But in spite of the economic crisis, an item in *Boxing* suggests that within two months Pat had found work. Astonishingly, rather than showing his support, perhaps out of ignorance of the facts, the writer coldly derides Pat's decision to leave the ring, and at the same time praises the Professor – who had of course had close ties with the newspaper since its inception in 1909:

'In reply to certain tender inquiries, we are happy to be able to state that so far as we are aware, the once famous Nipper Pat Daly has not been forced to seek sustenance on the dole. Our latest information as to the once famous "Nipper" is that he is, or was, engaged in the employment of a firm of repute and of long establishment, where he should have a happy future, provided he sticks to his job with greater interest and earnestness than he displayed in the boxing game. Quite a number of people have written us, displaying a real interest in young Daly, and expressing surprise that so highly promising a lad should have dropped so suddenly out of a game in which he seemed destined to attain the highest honours. We have to confess that we ourselves have shared this surprise. The "Nipper" did very well financially, as we happen to know, and could have, if he had been economical, bought a house with his savings before he was 17. His performances supplied ample evidence as to the quality of the instruction and of the careful training he was put through... There can be no doubt whatsoever that he would have enjoyed the brightest possible future if he had but stuck to the course on which he was being steered, instead of seeking to journey along other channels which would seem to have led him, temporarily at least let us hope, into his present more or less obscurity.'

But few, it seems, were fooled by such rhetoric. Criticism that they had ruined the sport's greatest prospect would plague the Professor and Andy for the rest of their days. *News Chronicle* and *Daily Mirror* reporter Gerard Walter, in his 1951 book *White Ties and Fisticuffs*, opined:

'The story of Nipper Pat Daly is perhaps the greatest tragedy the sport of boxing has to offer. This phenomenally clever little fighter would have been a world champion, almost without doubt, had he been handled in a proper manner.'

While renowned boxing writer O. F. Snelling, writing as late as 1985, reflected:

'Not only did they have a potential goldmine in this ferocious little battler, their ring experience should have told them that the boy was still growing and had not yet reached his full power. They were throwing the lad to the wolves... The boy was so potentially great, so keen and gifted, that with judicious handling it is no exaggeration to say that he might have boxed his way to a world championship had he been allowed to reach his full growth and strength. But he went up like a rocket, burst into sparks well before he had reached his peak, and sank into darkness – a great memory now, but that is all.' *Boxing News*, 20 September 1985

Considering the facts, it is hard not to agree with Snelling that by overworking Pat the Newtons had ultimately shot themselves in the foot. The long-term rewards of managing a world-class fighter in the big international fights that seemed destined to come, would have far outstripped the few hundred pounds they made from him in the short term. Perhaps they believed the boy's constitution was so exceptional that the exertion wouldn't affect him, or possibly their rationale never rose beyond the next payday. The following extract from a letter boxing manager and journalist Charlie Rose wrote to Andy Newton in May 1949 lends weight to this last theory:

'To speak frankly Andy, you know, better than most, that had Daly been boxing during the time the BBBC has been operating he would not have been permitted to box more than six two-minute rounds... I have to tell you that both [John] Murray and myself often suggested to your Dad that a policy of hastening more slowly with Pat would pay bigger dividends in the end. However, as his reply was always the same, "I need the money to carry on", we had, perforce, to drop the matter.'

At any rate, there can be no real excuse for the manner in which Pat was handled; and it appears that ordinary fight fans realised this as much as the sportswriters. An appeal for information printed in *Boxing News* in 2007 brought forth this response from Peter Judge of Bournemouth, whose father regularly watched fights in the 1920s:

'My dad, who was from Stepney, several times mentioned Nipper. Unfortunately he referred to the fact he was a terrible example of mismanagement, how a very talented and highly promising young boxer had been rushed into 15 round bouts at very frequent intervals against seasoned and experienced opponents. The result was that he was burnt out at a very young age.'

A similar spectator's view was held by Ned Quill – an elder brother of Pat's opponent, Johnny Quill. Ned's son, Eddie, now in his late 70s, recalls:

'My father used to talk about Nipper Pat Daly and what a brilliant fighter he was. I mean he was a name that was ingrained in my memory as a young kid, and I used to say to people, "Nipper Pat Daly, he was brilliant, he was a boy wonder". That's the opinion I got from my father; that he was something special, but unfortunately he wasn't looked after well enough. He started too early and he was given too many hard fights too soon, and they just burnt him out.'

That phrase, 'burnt out', is used repeatedly in reference to Pat, and seems an apt description of the effect of too many fights. Another man who recognised the 'burning out' of young British fighters was Mr H. Cristall of Ontario, Canada, a long-time admirer of Pat who had contributed towards the gold watch he received to mark his fifteenth birthday back in 1928. In a letter to *Boxing* in July 1932, the Canadian remarked:

'I have been told by one of the best American authorities of boxing – i.e., Mr. Nat Fleischer [founder and Editor of *The Ring* magazine], that England always has had the best and most promising young boys in the sport of any nation in the world, and the trouble is that they are used and burnt up before they have a chance to attain championship form... A couple of years ago I wrote both to the BBB of C officials and the then Editor of "Boxing" giving my views upon this matter and at the same time predicting what would happen to Pat Daly (Marylebone), who at sixteen years of age was England's best hope to bring the sport back to its original standing in that country. My assertions were ridiculed and the letters were consigned to the waste-paper basket, but I think you will agree that my words came true.'

In December 1934, nearly four years after Pat had left the ring, the Professor was still responding to criticism. His defence (as printed in *Boxing*, 26 December 1934) was highly irrational; apparently seeking to justify overworking the lad on the grounds that he had earned good money and was afterwards well enough to at least hold down a job:

Sir – As I was responsible for teaching, training, and bringing out Nipper Pat Daly, I will be greatly obliged if you will spare me the space in order to deny the many foolish rumours concerning this "Poor Pat Daley".

I am pleased to say that he is now a fine specimen of manhood (he weighs about 12 stone), and has a responsible position at United Dairies. He had never done a day's work until I had put him into the way of earning good money. I had Daly straight from school, and kept him whilst I was teaching him to box.

Perhaps it will be news to some people to learn that in the last eleven months he was with me he earned £1,500. I did not make the matches when he was beaten by third-class men, neither did I train him for these fights, although it seems I am (dis)credited with them.

I wish Daly and all my old pupils and sporting friends a Prosperous New Year.

Yours,
A. J. Newton.
Marylebone Road.

After Pat departed, the two Newtons tried desperately to fill the void he left behind. Every new prospect was billed as 'the next Nipper' or 'Marylebone's new wonder boy', but each of them fell streets short of the original. And for all his bravado, the Professor surely realised that a fighter like Pat arrives only once in a lifetime, and that his chance of worldwide fame had been and gone. As the great American trainer Ray Arcel once said, 'You're only as good as the fighter you work with. I don't care how much you know, if your fighter can't fight, you're just another bum in the park.'

And in spite of the Professor's undoubted excellence as a trainer, Pat found fundamental flaws in his methods:

> 'The Prof, despite all his criticisms of his rival trainers – [of] who he used to say "They do not know their right hand from their left" – he (the Prof) was good, but he did not seem to know how to teach the correct way for a boxer to use his feet. He used to teach his pupils, including me, to bring both feet together while advancing and retreating. Admittedly you may move a little faster, but if you get caught with a punch with the two feet together you are in trouble, as you have only one foot to stand on you must hit the canvas when hit or even pushed. I was floored three times in the second round, and three times in the thirteenth round, when I fought Seaman Watson at the Vale Hall, Kilburn in April 1930... I was never allowed to wash my mouth or gargle between rounds until the rest between the seventh and eighth round. The Prof would never tell me the reason. I can only assume that being an ex-amateur he would not know what it was like between rounds one and 15.'

Bill Chevalley made his name as the trainer behind the hard-hitting middleweight Mark Rowe, who with Bill's tutelage became British champion in 1970. Chevalley, who was raised in Islington, had around 160 amateur fights, and began sparring in pro gyms in the late 1930s. It was at this time, as a schoolboy amateur, that he encountered the Professor. 'He would have no time for the likes of me – I mean, I was young then, and he wouldn't even talk to you... He was an arrogant man. Very arrogant. He thought he was a God and that boxing wouldn't survive him.'

But the Professor wasn't a God and boxing, it turned out, would continue without him. He never found another Nipper Pat Daly but continued to teach boxing until his death on 27 March 1940, aged 75. Upon his father's passing, Andy Newton, although totally blind, took over the gym and trained amateur boxers there. To augment his income, he performed a unique club-swinging, sparring and ball-punching act on professional shows, which included turning his back to the ball and hitting it with his elbows. 'He could hit a speedball better than a man with two eyes,' recalls Bill Chevalley, who sparred at Andy's gymnasium several times.* Andy was forced to vacate the Marylebone Road gym by the landlord in 1959, and within two years the building – once a home to Victorian 'shoe blacks', the site of a battle between Pedlar Palmer and George Dixon, where Jack Johnson had once sparred, and where Nipper Pat learnt his trade – was sold and torn down.

Under the government's slum clearance operation, sometime in 1931, Pat and his family were forced to leave their Hatton Street home, as the houses were being demolished. They settled slightly northwest of Marylebone, at 59 Wakeman Road, Kensal Rise – the deposit for the house being funded by Pat's ring earnings. These, no doubt, were beginning to shrink, for by December that year he was again unemployed. This time the trade paper (which had recently acquired a new Editor, Sydney Rushton) was sympathetic to his plight:

'Nipper is now without a job and anxiously seeking employment of some description. He appeals, through his father, to sportsmen who may have enjoyed his ring performances to assist him in his search. Pat will take on any kind of work that might come his way, but is particularly anxious to secure an appointment as a gymnasium instructor. Daly is a beautiful boxer on strictly orthodox lines, and I can

---

* Andy did not blame boxing for his blindness but attributed it to two incidents from earlier in his life. He recalled that as a schoolboy studying science, a laboratory explosion left him sightless for three months. Then in 1918, during an Army 'gas training' exercise, he failed to get his gas mask on in time and was again blinded for three months. He claimed that he only passed the Army's eyesight test by memorising the optical test card beforehand. He said he lost the sight in his left eye during his contest with Len Harvey in 1926, and most of the vision in his right during his second fight with Marcel Thil in 1928. He had his left eye removed in 1930, and his right in 1931 – both being replaced by prosthetic eyeballs. He died in 1980, aged 79.

imagine nobody more fitted to impart knowledge to anyone anxious to learn the art.' *Boxing*, 16 December 1931

It seems Pat's appeal to the boxing fraternity had the desired effect. Our next snapshot of him comes a month later from a piece in *The Daily Mirror* (22 January 1932) entitled 'Nipper again':

'A boxer who was a prodigy at 15 and who "faded out" at 16 has won a chance of staging a comeback. He is Nipper Pat Daly, who, in 1928, when he was only 15, looked like a world-beater. Daly was permitted to have far too many fights at frequent intervals for one of his years, and after defeat by the featherweight champion when he was little more than 16 his decline set in rapidly. Now he is working as a labourer on the Earl's Court site where a new home for the National Sporting Club is being built. Mr. Lionel Bettinson, the manager of the club, explained yesterday that Daly wrote to him asking for a job. "I was so impressed by the look of him that we talked about a return to the ring," said Mr Bettinson, "and Daly will box on the opening night of the new premises. "Meanwhile his manual work will serve to keep him in good trim." Will Daly fulfil the promise of four or five years ago and become a champion? He is more likely to do so now that he has been allowed to mature on normal lines.'

He was not quite 19, but Pat's physique had developed markedly during his one-year rest. He now stood 5 feet 10½ inches tall, and his once fragile-looking frame was well layered with muscle. Another newspaper cutting from Pat's scrapbook is headlined 'Pat Daly to Return to the Ring. Former Boy Wonder Now a Middle-weight':

'When he makes his reappearance on the opening night of the new National Sporting Club he will be 11 st. 6 lb. – a middleweight. Mr. Lionel Bettinson, manager of the NSC, has agreed to look after the future of Daly, who is delighted at the prospect of a return to boxing. "When I left the ring a year ago, I thought I was finished," he said. "But I had determined to have two years' rest and then try again. Now I mean to make good".'

Pat's eldest son John would recall, 'The only British middleweight of the '30s he thought would have given him any trouble was Jock McAvoy. Not that he didn't think he could beat McAvoy, but because of McAvoy's dangerous punch.' In June 1932 *Boxing*'s columnist pondered, 'Will Nipper Pat Daly be seen in the ring next season? Pat has kept himself in light training... When I saw Daly he had not fixed anything definite, but he is not by any means finished with the game.'

The comeback, however, never happened. Pat's precise reason for changing his plans is unknown, but it is fair to surmise that when he resumed serious training he quickly realised the old Nipper had gone for good.

But although he did not engage in actual fights, Pat remained involved in the sport he loved. 'He used to go back to Marylebone to train, because everybody knew him there,' remembers Mary Daley, Pat's widow. 'There were a couple of gyms he went to: Alec Lambert's was one; I forget the other... he never went back to the Newtons, though.' And so he would visit different gyms, seek out new sparring partners, and further refine his boxing technique. Anything extra he could pick up was studiously absorbed and added to his repertoire.

On one occasion Pat found himself in the same gym as the latest British heavyweight prospect, the 6'4" 15-stone glamour boy Jack Doyle, nicknamed 'the Gorgeous Gael'. He offered his services as a sparring partner to Doyle, but was surprised by the response. With an embarrassed look the big man's trainer took him to one side and murmured into his ear, 'Sorry Nipper, I'm having trouble making him look good as it is; the last thing I'm gonna do is put *you* in with him.' Pat would encounter Doyle on at least one more occasion, two decades later and in rather different circumstances.

Although no longer his main source of income, boxing was still the fulcrum of Pat's young adult life. Though he would never take part in another pro bout, he did box some exhibitions, and a note in his memoirs suggests he probably had the odd booth fight too:

'One memory I would like to mention before I finish was when I challenged George Christian, the coloured heavyweight, who once fought the world heavyweight champion to a points decision. We had a three-round bout at Jimmy Butler's boxing booth at a fair in King Edward's Park, Willesden, where I was a local boy. It turned out to be a good bout, both knowing the game.'

There's no record of George Christian taking a world heavyweight champion the distance, but he did lose to future world champion Jack Dempsey via the KO route, and his résumé of opponents is nonetheless impressive. He had knocked out Arthur Pelkey, drawn twice with Willie Meehan, and been in with the likes of Joe Jeanette, Panama Joe Gans and Kid Norfolk. At any rate, Pat's visits to gymnasiums and booths were no longer part of any career aspirations. His focus, in fact, had shifted from himself to his younger brother.

Bobby Daley, quite naturally, had been encouraged to take up boxing by his elder brother. After several training sessions with Pat it was obvious that Bob had a natural gift for the sport. Pat's new-found mission was to mould his brother into the champion he himself should have been. And with Pat's nurturing he went from success to success as a schoolboy amateur. The following report gives some idea of his potential:

'The Daly who defeated Fletcher, of St. Helier, in the 7 stone class, is a brother of the once famous "Nipper" Pat Daly, who was making himself famous a few years ago as a professional. Boxing is evidently born in young Daly, and although it is giving him high praise, I think he is every bit as promising as his elder brother was at the same age. Daly had a very fine contest with Fletcher, and it was one of the best bouts of the evening. There was no fighting, but a bout of real scientific boxing, with good straight left hand leads. What agreeably surprised me was the clever footwork the lads showed. This is practically a lost art these days, but both Daly and Fletcher are really good at this branch of the game... It was hard luck for Fletcher that he had met such a good boy as Daly... Daly had little difficulty in beating Duckett, of Fulham, in the final. I quite expect to see Daly win the 7 stone championship, and unless there is a youngster really hot at the weight in the provinces he will very likely bring off the double.' *Boxing*, 14 November 1934

But Pat was an utter perfectionist and he was adamant that his brother should learn the finer points of the game and master them all just as he had. Bob, however, did not share his enthusiasm, nor his desire to have everything 'just so'. 'He was schoolboy champ,' remembered youngest brother Ken. 'But Bob wanted to do it when he felt like it. In fact, he wasn't that interested in boxing. He didn't like training. He wouldn't be disciplined. He actually did it just to humour Pat at the beginning. And as I say, when he got tired of it, that was the end of that. But if he'd stuck at it he *would* have been great.'

Apart from coaching Bob and keeping himself in shape, the first half of the '30s offered Pat the social life he had missed out on as a teenager. 'He didn't have any hobbies as such, only boxing,' remembered Ken. 'But he had quite a social life. There was a different girlfriend regularly appearing at the house – he was quite a flirt in his day. He liked to go to dances. As I say, he went out a lot with [his cousin] Davey John, they went out socialising. Even after he'd given up boxing, he was still well known.'

Another cousin, Harry Sivers, had a habit of talking himself into trouble and calling on Pat to bail him out. He ran a kiosk, selling sweets, cigarettes and other confectionaries, opposite The Falcon pub in west Kilburn. Pat hadn't seen him for a while when he turned up at the house and asked for help. He had fallen foul of some local hoodlums, who had threatened to smash up his kiosk. Obligingly Pat paid a visit to a drinking club the men frequented; but when he found them there was no confrontation. 'Sorry, Nipper,' said the ringleader. 'We didn't know he was your cousin. We'll leave him alone.' And Sivers and his kiosk were left untouched.

To make ends meet, Pat found a job as a groom at the United Dairies headquarters at Haycroft Farm in Kensal Rise. One of his duties was cleaning the stables; and as Ken recalled he would return home smelling of horse manure. This proved a great source of mirth for Bob, who would yell, 'He's back again – I can smell him!' or some other light-hearted remark. One particular horse at the stable was notoriously bad-tempered, and one day it made the mistake of biting Pat's hand. In a reflex action he punched the nag, knocking it fully off its hooves, and the animal never bit him again. His reaction may sound excessive but it certainly wasn't vindictive. When Pat saw another worker being spiteful to the horses he told the man in no uncertain terms that, if he knew what was good for him, he would treat them with dignity. The man never mistreated the horses again, or at least not in view of Pat.

Needless to say, this type of work was a far cry from the ring glamour Pat had been used to. But all the same, it brought in regular, honest money; and in the days of the Great Depression he had to be grateful for that. When an offer arrived to do something new and glamorous, however, he did not need asking twice. He was to make a return to the ring – only this time he wouldn't be boxing, but wrestling!

25

Marriage, War and Wrestling

'What are the great names that I shall throw in the faces of the youngsters of twenty-five years hence? I shall be proud to tell my great-grandchildren that I saw Al Brown when he was at his best... I have seen Len Harvey when he was first-rate, and I think he will be worthy of mention, and I am glad not to have missed Nipper Pat Daly and Teddy Baldock when they were at their best.'

Boxing columnist Ted Scales, 8 May 1935

British professional wrestling started out as a music hall novelty at the turn of the twentieth century. But in the hands of entrepreneur and theatrical manager Charles B. Cochran, it quickly rose to become a big-scale attraction with its own star performers, who drew fans at venues such as the Royal Albert Hall and Olympia. But a lack of credible performers, and the dullness of many matches, saw it decline as fast as it had risen, before the outbreak of war, in 1914, halted it completely. After the war, popular wrestling failed to re-emerge. It had proven no match for the spectacle of boxing and remained out of favour throughout the '20s; seemingly condemned to history. But in late 1930, quite unexpectedly, it would burst back into life in an exciting new guise.

'All-in' wrestling was the name of the new craze. So called because it blended catch-as-catch-can, jujitsu, and traditional Graeco-Roman wrestling into one exciting style. And, for added thrills, it incorporated bare-knuckle fighting, with the proviso that blows to the head were delivered with the open palm. Whereas before a match could drag on for hours, it would now, under the direction of a wrestling board of control, take place over timed rounds, with a win achieved via two falls, two submissions or a knockout. But what most helped this new wave of wrestling to flourish was a theatrical aspect that had nothing to do with skill or technique. Torture was a compulsory part of all-in: twisting and breaking of fingers, eye gouging, and other brutal touches were heartily cheered and loudly deplored in equal measure. A feigned loss of temper, an agonised scream and similar dramatics kept the crowds on the edge of their seats. The majority of spectators, of course, realised that these matches were fake. Each action and exaggerated reaction had been thoroughly rehearsed beforehand, and the outcome already decided. But the crowds of men and women who flocked to watch did not mind.

Although rather predictable and clichéd to modern tastes, back then this new blend of operatic fighting seemed fresh and exciting. For one or more nights a week, and for just a few shillings a time, the gloom of widespread unemployment, poor pay, and woeful working conditions was temporarily lifted.

All-in wrestling spread like wildfire and was soon being staged all over Britain. Popular boxing halls such as Kilburn's Vale Hall, Nottingham's Victoria Baths, the Liverpool Stadium and the Blackfriars Ring started to cater for the new craze. Each staged regular wrestling nights, or shows that featured boxing and wrestling. The leading wrestlers, much like the leading boxers, soon became popular and glamorous figures.

Pat started wrestling in either 1935 or 1936. His by then muscular, 13-stone physique was a total contrast to the rake-like figure of his boxing days. And the famous baby-face had gone too. He had developed a squarer, more masculine countenance, which, if anything, made him look older than his years. With his hardened appearance, his cauliflower ear and flattened nose, he certainly had the look for all-in wrestling.

As with former British heavyweight champion, Reggie Meen, who began wrestling around the same time, Pat's entrance into the sport caused quite a stir. 'Nipper Pat Daly, once the most talked-of boxer in the world, is now an aspirant to wrestling fame,' announced *The Sporting Arena*. But Pat had no illusions as to the validity of his new profession. The heart and gameness he had found throughout the sport of boxing, was conspicuously absent from some of the wrestlers, despite their Adonis-like frames. 'Some of 'em wouldn't wrestle with you if you were too rough,' he later recalled with a chuckle. Brother Ken was equally dismissive when asked about it 70 years later:

> 'Well, it was more-or-less a bit of a joke. No one was very interested, only him. And he only enjoyed it 'cause I think he got a kick out of it; you know, telling us all about the fiddles in wrestling, all that type of thing. It wasn't really serious.'

Even so, according to Ken, Pat earned enough from wrestling to make it his sole source of income. Surviving handbills show that he wrestled in Walsall more than once, while his mainstay, no doubt, was the many small-halls around London. But a cutting from Pat's scrapbook suggests that, initially at least, the more lucrative engagements evaded him:

'Nipper Pat Daly, not so many years ago one of the most popular boxers of his day, and one who never failed to put up a game display, has for some months past been seen in wrestling rings. He has practiced at this sport and claims a complete knowledge of the mat game, but he protested to the "Sports Gazette", promoters will not give him a "break". "Why can't I get a job at, say, Lane's Club or at the Kilburn Vale Hall?" he asks, "I know I can give the patrons a fine show. I know all the holds, all the ruses and I have the strength and stamina, but I can't get an engagement. I've been wrestling at some of the smaller halls, but I want to prove my worth at the more important venues. I've tried very hard to get a chance to wrestle there, but I'm just ignored and I hope that through the medium of the "Sports Gazette" the public will demand that I receive a "break". We do not know the circumstances why the important promotions fail to engage Nipper Pat Daly, but we are convinced he is a genuine fighter who deserves the "break" he asks for.'

Sometime in 1936 it seems Pat got his 'break', as he was finally on the bill at the prominent Lane's Club. The venue, which stood on King Street, off Baker Street in Marylebone, was run by Harold Lane, a large, amiable bohemian who had grown up in show business. This garish members-only establishment boasted a dance floor, its own bars and restaurants, and of course a hall where all-in wrestling was regularly held. Lane liked to give his club an image of prosperity and exclusivity. However, like the wrestling itself, this was all for show. The membership fee was just five shillings, and the initiation process as simple as paying the said fee. In *White Ties and Fisticuffs*, Gerard Walter, who was a member and a friend of Harold Lane's, recalled:

'Many of the types of persons who went to dance and watch the wrestling at Lane's can be seen any afternoon in Oxford Street selling nylons on the kerbside. I expect that is what most of them did in their business hours, but when they came to King Street they wore their best padded-shoulder suits of mauve and blue and purple, their hair was oiled and glistening like glass domes, and their narrow pointed shoes twinkled as they walked through the doors and up the steps with their lady friends on their arms. The low membership fee ensured two things, that the place would be packed every night there was a show, and that the people would not be too discriminating in their taste for entertainment... The thing was a colossal piece of showmanship, designed for entertainment of the onlookers. Lane was perfectly open about it. "My dear boy," he used to say to me, "I know that the whole affair is not real wrestling, but then they don't want the real stuff, these people who come here. They want a jolly good show, something to laugh at, something to give their girls a thrill. Well, my boy, I'm giving them what they want. Moreover, the crowd *knows* it's a fake." "And they like it?" I said. "Like it!" he cried. "Like it, you say? My dear boy, they wouldn't have it any other way"... The club membership list contained names of some very famous people who cared not two raps what took place in the square between the ropes so long as they were afforded a good laugh. Lane's was a part of London life, in exactly the same way as The Ring in Blackfriars.'

It was while wrestling at Lane's one evening that a pretty 19-year-old barmaid caught Pat's eye. Her name was Mary Newrick, and, had she not been employed there, the chances of them meeting would have been slim. Her family home was in the Elephant and Castle, so she had travelled across London to work at the club. The pair started dating, and before long introductions were made to both sets of parents. Mary's mother and father, on hearing her beloved was a former boxer, were slightly concerned. 'He's not rough, is he?' they asked her; but when they met the calm, polite, if slightly serious, young man – who, incidentally, did not drop his aitches – their fears were quickly allayed.

Pat and Mary were married at St George's Catholic Cathedral, Southwark on 10 July 1937. Pat, by then, was 24, and Mary four years younger. Their marriage certificate indicates that he was then working as a riveter at the Handley Page aircraft factory in Cricklewood, and it is likely his stint as a wrestler – which Ken said lasted about two years – was over. They honeymooned at Southend, and shortly afterwards, the Daley family and Mary spent a week holidaying on the Isle of

Wight, in a house rented from an acquaintance of Mary's mother's. Pat, for the first time, moved out of the family home and into a house with Mary at 68 Cricklewood Lane, close to the Handley Page factory. They would move twice more around Cricklewood during the next two years.

Mary was to discover that her husband was rather different from other young men. For one thing, he was held in a sort of reverence in boxing circles, and although she'd never followed the sport, she was assured by the various fight people she encountered that her husband had been something special. 'People used to shout to him when we walked down the Edgware Road; and it was always "Nipper" they called him – never Pat,' Mary recalls.

She felt proud, safe, and slightly awed in the company of this confident, yet self-contained young man. He seemed unusually mature, both in appearance and demeanour. It was as though, despite being only 24, he had already experienced all the highs and lows that life could throw at him.

In the autumn of 1937, at a charity boxing show, she got her first real glimpse of Pat in the ring. They had only arrived as spectators, but noticing Pat and British heavyweight champion Tommy Farr in the crowd, the organisers asked if they would box each other in an exhibition. 'I'd be glad to,' said Pat, but Farr, having recently returned from a gruelling world heavyweight clash with Joe Louis, had to decline. 'His face was a terrible state,' remembers Mary. And so another pro was found to take his place. After a quick change of clothes, Pat and his opponent entered the ring. At one point during the bout he was momentarily crowded into a corner, but a lightning-fast move drew gasps and applause from the audience. 'Pat was in the corner, and I don't know how he got out the corner. Marvellous it was to watch it,' recalls Mary. 'He turned the bloke right round, so the bloke was in the corner and Pat was facing him. He was *very clever*... I was sitting behind Jimmy Wilde, and he was telling this bloke he was sitting with all about Pat. "He should have been champion of the world," he said. Jimmy Wilde said that. "He should have been champion of the world." You don't see that clever stuff now – getting out of a corner like that.'

Despite her slender frame, Mary was a strong, resilient young woman, which was just as well, as a more sensitive type might have found life with

Pat rather trying at times. She quickly became aware that he would suffer rudeness from no one, and any slight on him would provoke a response. On a trip to the 'pictures' Pat's seat was repeatedly kicked by a young lad behind him. He turned around several times to admonish the boy, but despite his rebukes the seat-kicking continued. When the film ended, Pat complained to the two men who were with the boy that they should keep him under better control. 'Why don't you fuck off,' came the reply, and a brief scuffle ensued. Moments later, the two men were running out of the cinema, with Pat in hot pursuit and a bewildered Mary in tow. 'Just leave it Pat – it's not worth it,' she yelled after him, but despite her appeal the chase continued and only ended when both men clambered on to a passing tram.

But despite Pat's inclination to react when challenged, it seems the ring had taught him how to handle situations where self-control must prevail. One such event arose when Pat and Mary boarded a bus. As Pat handed their fares to the conductor the man mockingly inspected his money – slowly rubbing and then biting each of the coins – as if to imply that his cash could somehow be counterfeit. Uneasily, Mary watched her husband, wondering how he would react. But, to her surprise, he said nothing and his deadpan expression did not change. He had no doubt realised that (for reasons unknown) the man was trying to provoke him, and furthermore that an ex-boxer embroiled in a brawl with an on-duty bus conductor would be given little chance in court. He collected their tickets with no sign of vexation and did not utter a word.

Pat settled into work at the Handley Page aircraft factory, where he worked on an assembly line riveting wings and other aircraft parts. He refers to this period briefly in his memoirs:

> 'During the last war, 1939-45, I was working at a garage turned into an airplane spare parts factory, and during one lunch hour was in the pub opposite the factory in which I worked. Some of the lads in our works persuaded me to sing a song and, as there were several Welsh lads in the company, I got up and tried my best with "Saucepan Bach". A lady who happened to be in the pub asked one of my mates, "Why with the name Pat Daly, which is rank Irish, does he sing a Welsh song in Welsh?" One of my mates told her that I was born in Wales with an Irish father and a Welsh mother. "Ahh," she said, "No wonder the bugger can fight".'

Pat's day job may have been dull but in the evenings he once more did what he loved. He set up a gym in the main canteen on the Handley Page premises and taught workers, and anyone else who was interested, how to box. It was hardly a substitute for fighting in the ring, but at least he could impart some of his knowledge, and at a company employing over 3,000 staff he was never short of pupils. Pat put on several boxing displays at Handley Page, including an exhibition between him and Bob during the war. On one occasion the famous dance-band leader Geraldo and his band entertained the firm's employees from inside the ring. John Black, who as a boy watched Pat fight Seaman Watson at the Vale Hall, worked for the firm at that time:

'When I met Pat at Handley Page he was amazed that I'd seen him box – I was younger than him and he couldn't believe it. Then I said to him, "I saw you fight Seaman Watson. I even know who your manager was – Professor Newton." I liked Pat – he and I got on well. We went out a few times to The Crown in Cricklewood and a place in Neasden with another good friend, Fred Tyler, who was a southern area weight lifting champion, but Pat didn't drink much... I found him a very nice man. Very friendly, very calm. The only time I saw him lose his temper a bit was when the Handley Page boxing club fought the Hendon Police College in the ring at Handley Page – they had a tournament. He was telling them to box and not go rushing in, but they weren't listening to him and they were getting beaten. Most of them weren't that serious about boxing, they just did it for a bit of fun. But it was serious to him – boxing was his life.'

In 1938, Pat and Mary's first child, Jean, was born. (Two boys were to follow: Patrick John Daley, known as 'John', was born in 1940, and Terry Daley in 1944.) In 1939, Pat was contacted by a reporter from the sporting newspaper *The Topical Times*, who wanted to serialise the story of his ring career. After an interview with Pat, the man penned his story in the first person and it was published over several weeks. An announcement about the serial, complete with pictures of Pat – and one of Pat, Mary and Jean – adorned the paper's front page with the heading 'Nipper Pat Daly – Britain's most amazing boxer tells his own story.'

Less than three months after the final part of his career story was published, the second major conflict that Pat would live through began.

As the Second World War gathered momentum, gas masks, ration books and identity cards were issued to every British subject; road signs were removed to confuse the enemy in the event of an invasion, and large numbers of city children were evacuated to the countryside. Jean and John were sent to New Ridley in Northumberland.

As an employee at an aircraft factory, Pat was kept very busy. More than 7,300 aircraft were built nationally between January and August 1940, and used in the Battle of Britain. It seems Pat remained at Handley Page for most of the war, before changing jobs to work at a factory in Kilburn. He was not 'called up' to serve, as presumably his work was deemed essential to the war effort. In 1941, he got Ken his first job, working at the Handley Page jig and tools department at the age of 15. Ken, incidentally, was not one of Pat's gym patrons and had no interest in boxing. 'I didn't want a flat nose or cauliflower ear,' he later recalled with a chuckle.

Early on in the war, Pat and Mary moved into a room at Pat's parents' home at 59 Wakeman Road, Kensal Rise. It was here one evening that Pat's real feelings about his parents' culpability in his downfall suddenly surfaced. Outwardly, Pat would never blame his parents for failing to stop him being overworked, although he sometimes remarked to Mary, 'If I'd have had your mother, I'd have been champion of the world.' Late one evening he returned home from the pub extremely drunk (he was, according to son Terry, not a big drinker; so on the rare occasions when he did overindulge, he easily became intoxicated). He fell down in the hall with a crash, and Mary, and Pat's mother May, rushed out to see what was the matter. 'Leave him, May,' warned Mary. But May rushed over to help her son up. 'Are you hurt, my boy?' she asked with a note of concern. 'Get away from me,' he snapped back. 'You've done enough already. I'd have been a world champion if it wasn't for you.' It was probably the only time he ever uttered such a criticism, but deep down it seems he harboured some resentment over his parents' failure to prevent him being exploited.

Four and a half years of Luftwaffe bombings would alter the face of London forever. Churches, shops, hospitals, and schools were destroyed. Thousands of innocent people lost their lives, and hundreds of thousands lost their homes. Where once had stood a row of houses was now the odd smashed, stained wall bounded by rubble. The devastation would linger as visible scars on the landscape and mental scars on the people who lived through it.

Among the buildings destroyed in the war were some of the sites of Pat's ring encounters. The Alcazar in Edmonton – the Moorish-styled cinema that had doubled as north London's leading fight arena – took a direct hit in August 1940 and what remained of it had to be demolished. The Ring at Blackfriars was partially destroyed by a bomb in October 1940, then hit again and completely destroyed, in March 1941.* While the stately Holborn Stadium, where Pat had suffered his knockout defeat at the hands of Johnny Cuthbert, was itself permanently KO'd in February 1941, and the wreckage later hit by a second bomb. Plymouth's Promenade Pier, where Pat had boxed the local bantamweight hero Young McManus, was also destroyed by the Blitz in 1941, demonstrating that Hitler's attacks weren't just confined to London. The pier's wreckage was not cleared until 1953.

Extensive bombing of East London finished the job that had begun with the slum clearances of the 1930s – after rebuilding, most of the East End's old, worn-out streets were virtually unrecognisable. Although a reminder of East London's boxing history, the building that had once been Premierland, stood firm. The fate of the 'East End NSC' was decided by the Chancery Division in October 1930. Victor Berliner and Manny Lyttlestone, it was alleged, had breached the repairing covenants of their lease: the steel work was rusty, the roof leaked, the flooring was rotting, the brickwork needed pointing, and the heating had completely gone. Premierland's final show was staged on 30 October 1930. Thereafter, thanks to the court's ruling, the building was returned to its owners T. M. Fairclough and Sons. It served as a motor vehicle garage for many years, but ended its days as a disused warehouse. The twenty-first-century residents of Back Church Lane probably know nothing of the days when the street was packed with boxing fans three or four times a week; when the name Ted Kid Lewis, Jack Kid Berg, Teddy Baldock or indeed Nipper Pat Daly, would draw them there from across London.

★★★

---

* A large modern office block now occupies the spot where The Ring once stood. Across the road, however, still stands a public house where many 'Ring' patrons drunk before and after the shows. Today it is appropriately named after the venue, and its walls are covered with photographs of old-time boxers, many of whom fought at The Ring.

Pat lost some of his closest family and friends in the 1940s. His cousins Will and Leonard, along with their father Dennis, all died within weeks of each other between December 1943 and January 1944. Leonard of peritonitis, and Will after a series of strokes, while their brother Davey John died later of a kidney infection, and yet another cousin, Leslie, died at sea. Mac, one of Pat's close boyhood friends, was killed while serving in the RAF. We can imagine that losing so many people over such a short period would have affected him deeply.

★★★

After the war Pat, Mary and their three children for the first time moved south of the river to Hayles Street in Mary's home district, the Elephant and Castle, a keen boxing area where many locals remembered Pat's ring days. The family remained there for the rest of the '40s, before moving back to Kensal Rise, into a house on the same street as Pat's parents, at 82 Wakeman Road. Pat, as ever, stayed involved with boxing and served as trainer at the sports club of Smith & Sons, a large clock manufacturer based in Cricklewood. Among his pupils at Smith's was Ken Diston of Hendon, a top amateur who later turned professional.

What Pat really wanted, however, was a gym of his own. A base from where to develop a world champion; a place where keen young men could go to get the best of instruction. At the end of the 1940s, he found a location for this theatre of dreams.

BE TAUGHT

HOW TO BOX

By an acknowledged Expert

NIPPER
PAT DALY

" Wonder Boxer of his day "
(Vide Press)

Has a Modern Gymnasium
and School of Boxing and
Physical Culture at

**43-45, NEW NORTH ROAD
SHOREDITCH, N.I.**

(5 mins. from Old St. Tube Stn.)

A newspaper advert for Pat's gym.

26

A Gym and a Dance Hall

'They sweated the life out of Nipper Pat Daly when he was a kid – but they failed to quench his spirit. For last week Daly, the British lad who should have been world champion himself, opened his own gymnasium. And as he unlocked the door of the old concert hall in Shoreditch he said, "I couldn't win a title myself, but now I'm going to find a lad who will. And, believe me, he won't have to suffer as I did".'

The People, 15 May 1949

Pat's gymnasium, a former concert hall leased from a pub, stood at 45 New North Road in Shoreditch – next to the corner of New North Road and East Road; five minutes' walk from Old Street station. Shoreditch and nearby Islington were long-established boxing areas. Shoreditch Town Hall, Hoxton Baths and the Caledonian Road Baths were the popular local fight venues at that time.

While maintaining a day job, Pat spent every weeknight (except Friday), and every Saturday afternoon and Sunday morning at the gym. His pupils were mostly amateurs, but he did train and manage a few pros, including Swindon light-heavyweight Wally Curtis, Notting Hill lightweight Roy Paine (whom he had coached from boyhood) and Steve Brimah, a welterweight originally from Ghana.

In March 1950 *Boxing News* ran a feature on the gym, complete with photos. The writer was delighted by what he found:

'It is spacious, well-lit, clean and warm, and contains all the necessary apparatus and equipment, including a hot shower. Furthermore, it is run by Pat Daly... Boxing is ingrained in him; he was taught by one of the greatest fistic professors of all time, Andrew Newton, and despite the fact that it is nearly twenty years since he last fought, he has never lost touch with the game, and has been an instructor ever since.

Not all brilliant boxers make expert teachers, but Daly is the exception to the rule. We have personally seen him at work, and a more patient and untiring instructor it would be difficult to find. Daly, who is thirty-seven, has kept himself in fine physical trim, and he gets into the ring with his boys and puts them through their paces with ardent enthusiasm.

Daly's pupils range from nine-year-old nippers, schoolboys, to junior and senior amateurs. It is nothing to see two midgets being coached followed by two members of the local police station. All are put through the immaculate Daly system that corrects faults before they have a chance to become habits.'

Two decades before he steered Camberwell middleweight Mark Rowe to a British title, in the '40s and '50s Bill Chevalley earned money as a sparring partner for hire, counting world flyweight champion Terry Allen among his clients. During those days he inevitably became acquainted with Pat, and once spent a week sparring with Islington featherweight Jackie Lucraft at the New North Road gym.* After a chance encounter with Bill at a London Ex-Boxers' Association meeting, he shared the following recollections of Pat:

'He was a man who knew every facet of the fight game and a bloody good coach, you stand on me. I didn't mix with him overly outside boxing, but I met him obviously several times in different gyms, and he was just a nice person to know. I can still sort of see him, 'cause he was always a well-dressed man as well. He wasn't arrogant, but he couldn't suffer fools. He didn't stand any nonsense. If he liked you, he couldn't do enough for you, but if he didn't, you knew about it. When you've been a top fighter you get a lot of hangers on and people asking you silly questions; well he would answer 'em in such a way that they wouldn't ask 'em again... I think he had two or three gyms as far as I can recall, but the one that sticks in my mind was on the corner of New North Road. It was very clean, it was a well-kept gym. One of the real problems I think was the position of it, because it was just off a main road and you used to get the noise of the old rattling buses and God knows what.'

---

* Tragically, in May 1952, Lucraft, a window cleaner by trade, fell 30 feet whilst working and sustained internal injuries. He died in hospital five months later, aged just 28. According to *Boxing News*, he amassed a pro record of 46 fights, with 26 wins and 15 losses.

One of Pat's earliest pupils at the New North Road gym was a local boy called Terry Goldsmith, who back then was known as 'Goldie'. Today he lives and coaches boxers on the island of Grand Bahama in the Bahamas. He is happily married and has 14 grandchildren. Terry very kindly, and out of the blue, got in touch while this book was being written. He spoke at length, and with great affection, of his time under the tuition of the man he still calls 'Nipper':

'I was in trouble with the law for fighting, ended up in juvenile, and the court put me in the charge of my father and this police constable, who took me down to the Crown and Manor boys' club. But the Crown and Manor didn't have a boxing programme at that time, so they recommended Nipper, which was just round the corner. My dad took me down with this police officer, Constable Williams, and there was this bloke there, this boxer, this coach. He talked to my dad and charged my dad half a crown a week for four nights' training.

You went up some front stairs, along a hall and then down. It was like a church hall with a stage at the back. If you're facing the stage, Nipper used to change on the left hand side with a couple of men, and all the boys – there was about four or five of us used to go there – he put us on the other side to change into our clothes. I was the only one who used to come four times a week. The others used to come about two times a week. They were pretty poor at that time; it was just after the war.

Nipper was a taskmaster when it came to discipline and doing exactly what he said, but he always did it with patience, concern and kindness. We also had to have good school reports, or we caught hell from him. But honestly, great bloke; he had a heart of gold. But *he knew boxing*; you don't know how that man knew boxing!

No matter how good you were, or how old you were, you had to do footwork for 10 or 15 minutes every session. He said each foot should move about eight inches at a time. "Don't you know what eight inches looks like, Goldie?" You would hear him when you didn't think he was watching. Every session started that way, but he always told you why he made you do something and the reasoning behind it, and he'd also explain the consequences of not doing something correctly. He told us over and over again, "Footwork gets you where you need to go and gets you out of trouble. It's also the basis of your punching power." I did footwork until I dropped for almost three weeks when I first started – along with a straight left jab – over and over again, until I got it down to Nipper's satisfaction. Then he would teach me my first combination.

When Nipper taught any punch or combination of punches, you had to demonstrate that your head and/or body was protected. Your fist was always brought back to your chin each time to protect yourself. If you didn't, you'd feel his left flick out and catch you lightly on the nose. "Elbows in, boy, elbows in. Guard your body with your elbows. You hear me, Goldie?' If you didn't, he would catch you with a body shot. He would often stop you sparring, with him or with another lad, and ask you questions, like, "Goldie, you threw that left hook. Why?" Or, "Goldie, why do we always follow up a right cross with a punch from the left hand?" Nipper was always on your case, but always with patience and good humour. I can remember his words, his encouragement and his patience with us, no matter how many times we got it wrong.

He always made training sessions as real as possible, and he used one technique that we used to love to hate. In those days they didn't have the coach's pads that they put on their hands now. All he had was a 16 oz glove, and he used to cup it into his shoulder with his thumb under the armpit, and you had to hit that. He would make you hit it, but he'd hit you back at the same time, and you had to parry at the same time, and that's where the counter-punching came from. Sometimes he'd make you hit his left-hand glove, but he would hold the right-hand glove like a truncheon. He'd hold it close to him, so you're concentrating on punching at his left hand, then all of a sudden he'd swing this right hand at you, with the glove on the end, and catch you up the side of the head with it. He said you had to feel the leather – if you didn't, you'd start flinching. He expected you to duck under it, block it, or slip it, and counter. Sometimes you'd see it coming, you'd go under it, come up, and counter with the left hook. You don't know how many people I put out like that!

He had sets of Indian clubs that we had to learn to use. It builds the shoulders and the forearms, he would tell us. You weren't allowed the Indian clubs on the gym floor, 'cause if you dropped them they would clatter. So you did your club swinging on the stage, which was carpeted. He also had two heavy medicine balls that we had to throw to a partner from an 'on guard' position. We caught it with our right and steadied it with our left, then 'punched' it back with our left again, but we only used one hand to throw it. Then we'd switch and throw it with our right. You'd bend and twist the hips and turn the thighs and the right foot and toe so that it went with greater force. In other words, you threw a left lead and a right cross and you just happened to have a medicine ball in the hand at the time. You had to be on balance at all times or the ball would knock you over.

His greatest quality was not just his advanced skills but that he really made you *think* in the ring. He taught us to always evaluate the weaknesses of the other boxer in the first round, and if you can stop him, stop him, but evaluate his weakness as he comes to you. As he comes to you he's bringing his weight forward, sidestep and counter, then it's your weight and his weight coming together, and it's twice as much power and weight. And he was teaching this back in the '40s. He was way, way ahead of his time. The man was so fast and light on his feet, he was incredible. God knows, with all that knowledge, why he never became world champion... What made him different from other trainers was that he taught boxing in its purest form. Everything had to be perfect.

I could write a book on what he taught me and what he started when he did. You see, he not only taught me to box but – in cooperation with my father – Nipper also moulded my character. I cannot over-emphasise the profound effect he had on my life with his training, and the morals that he talked to me about. "Don't steal, son. Don't get in trouble with the law any more." He kept me out of trouble and I've never been in trouble with the law since.

After Nipper moved on I won the London Federation Championships and three British National Amateur Navy Championship titles. The year Terry Spinks won the gold medal at the Olympics in Australia, I'd beaten him twice in local club matches. My dad said, "You beat him twice, how come that's not you with the gold medal?" But he entered the ABA championships, and in those days you had to win the ABAs to go. I had 127 fights and only got beat six times, and that's only because of Nipper...

He told me, when you're watching boxing don't look at the guy that lands the blow, look at the guy that's receiving the blow and ask, what is he doing wrong that makes it easy for the other guy to hit him? He would drum that into you and from that point on he made you look. I became an international referee with AIBA, the world governing body for amateur boxing, and when I used to train officials that's what I'd tell them to look for. When I trained trainers, it was exactly the same thing.

I was the National General Secretary of the British Schools ABA and a member of the ABA National Council. I travelled all over the world and married a Bahamian woman. I attended college and university and I became a teacher and youth worker. I introduced amateur boxing to the Bahamas and also formed the first three boxing clubs there. My little YMCA boxing club beat the Florida state team – the state team! All I did was use the exact same teaching techniques and the skills that Nipper taught me, combined with my own experience. I still use his coaching and teaching methods to this day and I even used his techniques in my classrooms.'

Terry Goldsmith was a small boy when Pat took him under his wing. But Stanley Ekins, another pupil, was just nine years Pat's junior. He had taken up boxing relatively late to get fit following a serious illness, and boxed as an amateur in the late '40s and early '50s. His son Brian lived in Hoxton, Shoreditch until the age of 10, and vaguely remembers meeting Pat while very young:

'As far as I know my dad was unbeaten until forced to retire with eye damage. I know that he fought many times at Shoreditch Town Hall and during his boxing career was always trained by Nipper Pat Daly, who he later also worked with for many years at the *Daily Mirror*. Their relationship was a lot closer than that of trainer and boxer and dad thought of Pat as a true friend.

One story that I got about Pat came direct from my dad, who I assume got it from Pat himself. He told me Pat decided to go by himself to see a film and while he was watching it a man in the row behind him kept kicking Pat's seat. After asking him to stop, more than once, a row developed and they decided to go outside and settle it. As soon as they got outside the other bloke made the mistake of taking a swing and Pat decked him and then went back and resumed his seat. He then got kicked in the back again, but there was no one sitting there. He watched what was going on and realised that the cinema wasn't exactly upmarket and every time someone walked down the aisle, over the loose floorboards, it made the row of chairs move.'

Given time, Pat might eventually have unearthed a champion, but his tenure at the Shoreditch gym was to be short lived. According to Mary, the pub the gym was leased from was frequented by villains, and the local council were eager to close it down. When a man was killed on the premises, the council seized its chance. The pub had its licence revoked and, as a consequence, the gym was closed too. Reluctantly, Pat returned the key to the owner. He donated all the gym equipment, including the ring, to a nearby Catholic church. He was disappointed that the priest – a man he knew – never bothered to thank him.

No sooner had the gym closed than Jimmy Power, an Irishman Pat had become acquainted with, proposed a new way of making money. Mary disliked Power from the moment she met him and warned her husband not to go into business with him. Pat, however, ignored the warning, insisting that the man was 'all right'. The exploitation Pat had suffered as a boy had left him rather suspicious of human nature and its machinations. He would always be doubtful of the intentions of others, but this was really only a shield to ensure that no one took advantage of him. Beneath it was hidden a certain naiveté which men like Power were apt to exploit. It seems in this case plenty of 'smooth talk', along with the promise of money, clouded his judgement. Brother Ken remembered Pat's ill-advised business venture all too well:

'He produced Jimmy Power as a friend – no, an acquaintance – he wasn't a friend. You know Pat had a gym, well, it was about that time that Power came on the scene, but I don't know how they met. They got together this idea of opening an Irish dance hall and they opened this place in Peckham... Pat put up the money and Power was supposed to put up the know-how. My other brother Bob and I got involved going over there, but we were going under protest really, just 'cause it was our brother and we wanted to help out. Didn't like the dance hall, didn't want anything to do with it really, but we just sort of got involved with it. We didn't like Power and we didn't have much to do with him... He was a bit of a dark horse. There were all sorts of rumours about him; about IRA and God knows what. He wasn't a very desirable person, anyway. He was a crook in other words.'

Irish migration into London peaked during the years after the Second World War. A labour shortage led several organisations, including London Transport and the National Health Service, to carry out recruitment drives in Southern and Northern Ireland. New Irish communities sprung up and the existing ones expanded. The ranks of London's construction and nursing industries swelled with new migrants. As the city's Irish community grew, naturally Irish culture became more integral to London life. Catholic churches were a hub of Irish social life, but so too were the many pubs and dance halls that sprung up across the city. Bands, singers and other musicians from Ireland toured the dance halls. (The well-known music hall singer Cavan O'Connor made a couple of guest appearances at Pat's club.) The Garryowen Club in Hammersmith, the Blarney Club on Tottenham Court Road, the Galtymore in Cricklewood and the Bamba Club in Kilburn were among the most popular dance halls. And, for a couple of years in the mid-'50s, Pat's club in Peckham was part of the new craze.

The dance halls offered London's Irish an unrivalled chance to meet people from back home, and many marriages were made from acquaintances formed at dance halls. But like most forms of night entertainment where socialising and alcohol mix, there was a darker side to dance hall culture, as Pat would soon discover.

Built in 1894, the Central Hall, which housed Pat's dance hall, is a building with an interesting past. It had originally served as the headquarters of the People's League, a charitable institution run by the celebrated Victorian author, spiritualist and social reformer Robert James Lees, who it is claimed through his mediumistic powers knew the identity of Jack the Ripper.* Afterwards the building was used by a Reverend G. Ernest Thorn for religious purposes, and then became a cinema. It stood at 43 Peckham High Street and during Pat's tenure was above the Express Dairy and opposite the Odeon Cinema. In about 1953, Pat and his family

---

* Robert James Lees is depicted in several works of fiction about Jack the Ripper, including the 1979 film *Murder by Decree*, in which Lees is played by Donald Sutherland, and the 1988 ITV mini-series *Jack the Ripper*, which starred Michael Caine.

moved from Kensal Rise to Peckham. They bought a new house at 52 Choumert Road, but soon afterwards sold it and moved into a flat above the dance hall. Pat opened the hall several nights a week, and his eldest children, Jean and John, delivered leaflets to the local Catholic churches to drum up business.

On his spare evenings Pat was employed by Peckham Council to teach boxing classes in the gym at Peckham Manor School, and among his pupils were several Irishmen who also frequented the dance hall. One of them, Johnny Curran, became a close friend of Pat's. Curran had boxed in the Irish Army and, though unschooled in the finer points of boxing, Pat was impressed by how tough and game he was. If he'd discovered him sooner, Pat would say, Curran could have gone a very long way as a pro. Pat gave him a job as a bouncer at the dance hall, and Ken would eventually marry Johnny's younger sister, Betty.

The dance hall sold tea and sandwiches (prepared by Mary), but did not sell alcohol, as the council would not grant it a licence. This, it transpired, was just as well, for many of the patrons had already had a 'skin-full' by the time they arrived. Fights were a frequent occurrence, and Pat and Johnny Curran, tasked with ejecting the perpetrators, inevitably became embroiled in regular violent confrontations.

On one occasion, without warning and for no apparent reason, a group of men set about Pat. 'There were three of them and he was on his own, so they must have thought they could take him,' recalls Mary. 'But Pat gave all three a good hiding. They ran out of the dance hall and he chased them up the street. He wasn't afraid of anyone or anything... I remember, another night, this obnoxious bloke down there. He was going up to everyone and challenging them. Anyway, he squared up to Pat. "You're nothing special. Who d'you think you are?" he said. So Pat hit him and knocked him out. I didn't even see it, the punch was that quick. One punch and the bloke was out cold, and his mates had to carry him out.'

Among the dance hall's patrons was a renowned local tough guy, known for his acrobatic ability (he could do back-flips) that he put to good use in street fights. One evening Pat spoke sternly to the man about his unruly behaviour in the club. 'If you were a bit younger,' the man said, 'I'd give you a bloody good hiding.' 'Don't worry about my age,' Pat answered. 'Let's go outside.' Pat's son, John, and Johnny Curran sat on the pavement and watched the duel. The younger man proved every bit as tough and brave as his reputation implied. He took a severe beating and kept coming back for more punishment, before finally conceding defeat. 'I remember hearing about it from John,' says youngest son Terry, 'but I didn't know who the bloke was. Some years later I was talking to someone in a pub who told me all about him. Apparently he was a very well-known hard man round south London's Irish community.'

Trouble occurred regularly at the dance hall, but things were to turn from bad to worse. Jimmy Power, the man who'd thought up the dance hall business, had not kept his side of the bargain. And worse still, it transpired that he was cheating Pat. 'It all went a bit sour and ended up with bad feelings all round,' recalled Ken. 'It appears that Power was doing a bit of fiddling on the quiet and not taking a lot of interest. He just liked prancing around as an MC and things like that, and pocketing a few when he could. And they fell out about it. Pat more-or-less showed him the door – he didn't want him there any more, but it was a partnership so they had to go to court.'

Pat's solicitor was David Napley (later Sir David Napley), who would become one of the most famous and influential solicitors in England. His clients would include the Liberal Party leader Jeremy Thorpe, Princess Michael of Kent and Jeremy Bamber, but in the mid-1950s he had yet to reach such heights. The case was a slow, drawn-out affair, but eventually the partnership between Pat and Power was dissolved.

After the split, there were several visits by groups of 'heavies' whom Power had sent to the dance hall to cause trouble. On one occasion a group of decidedly tough-looking men arrived at the club, and among them was one particularly large figure. John alerted his father to their presence and Pat responded by walking straight up to the large man, whom he clearly recognised, asking him bluntly, 'What are you doing here?' 'Nothing, Pat,' he answered. 'I'm just here to sing.' John soon discovered that this was Jack Doyle, the famous heavyweight hope of the 1930s, who had once been married to Hollywood starlet Movita Castaneda (later wife to Marlon Brando). 'Jack Doyle was on his uppers at that time,' recalled Ken. 'You know, living on his name only. I suppose Power sent him along as some sort of threat. But Doyle didn't do anything, he was all bullshit. He just sort of smarmed all over Pat, "all boxers together" type of thing. Jack Doyle was anybody's for a pint at that time.'

But not every confrontation instigated by Power ended quite so harmoniously. One particular evening when Johnny Curran had a night off, Pat and a 14 or 15-year-old John worked inside the club alone, while Ken and Mary worked the door downstairs. Suddenly, a large group of men surrounded Pat and proceeded to lay into him. He fought back bravely, but was overwhelmed by the sheer number of his assailants. 'Most people, under the circumstances, would have curled up into a ball,' remembered John. 'But my dad never stopped fighting back.' Some of the men also attacked John who, though only in his mid-teens, was a well-made lad and looked much older. Eventually Pat was bundled to the floor, whereupon several of the men repeatedly kicked him in the head. 'I was down on the door with Mary when the trouble broke out upstairs,' recalled Ken. 'We went up and someone grabbed my tie and started strangling me. Pat had a few rolling on the floor, bashing a couple and they bashed him, and we both got wallops and all the rest of it. Then the police arrived and that was all that happened. They were people who'd come there obviously to start trouble and it turned out Power had sent them.'

Pat's face was severely bruised, swollen and cut for several days following the fracas. But not long after, yet another dance hall incident gave him more cause for worry. He was talking to a group of men he knew about the trouble with Power, when one of them handed him an object wrapped in a cloth. 'This is what you want to protect yourself,' he said, and Pat unravelled the cloth to reveal a gun. He did not know whether the gun was real and certainly didn't suspect it could be loaded. Absentmindedly Pat squeezed the trigger; a gunshot rang out and the man dropped to the floor in agony. He had been shot in the stomach.

He was taken to hospital and the police were called. Pat was initially concerned both over the condition of the injured man and the potential repercussions of the incident – 'I've had the biggest shock of my life,' he told Ken the next day. But the wounded man recovered and, after the police had taken witness statements, Pat was exonerated from any wrongdoing. The owner of the handgun, however, was reprimanded for possessing an unlicensed weapon.

There was no more trouble from Power after the dance hall fracas, but Pat closed the business six months later and the family moved to Crofton Road in Camberwell. 'The dance hall aged him,' recalls Mary. It had proven a perpetual source of worry and trouble. Everyone involved with the place was glad when it had closed.

27

Yesterday's Heroes

'They were of a breed which no discouragement, no setbacks, could subdue. They knew that they literally had to fight their way to the top and they went into the game determined to do so. Some became champions, the majority, naturally, did not. But while they were active in the ring, champions or not, they, each and every one, were wholehearted, give-and-take fighting machines.'

Gerard Walter, White Ties and Fisticuffs, 1951

One Sunday afternoon in the late 1950s, Pat strolled into a pub on East Street, site of the historic East Lane market, situated off the Walworth Road. The market traders had finished for the day; their wares packed up and their barrows put away. Some were already home, but many lingered on in search of liquid refreshment.

Amid the throng of refreshment-seekers Pat's eyes were drawn to a stocky little man in his early 60s. From the corner of his toothless mouth drooped an old pipe, above which sat a broad boxers' nose, while a badly misshapen left ear bore testament to ring battles waged long ago.

This was Tommy Noble, the Bermondsey British champion who, as a handsome young man three or four decades earlier, had boxed everywhere from New Cross Baths to Madison Square Garden. He had fought world flyweight champion Jimmy Wilde twice in 1916, flooring the legendary Welshman and almost finishing him off, before being punched to defeat himself in the fifteenth round of their second encounter. Noble stopped future world featherweight champion Eugene Criqui in 1919, and during the '20s took the USA by storm, scooping an estimated £60,000 and winning a magnificent diamond-encrusted (unofficial) world title belt put up by the legendary promoter Tex Rickard.

But by the late 1950s former champion Noble cut a forlorn figure. The money had gone, his fame had faded and, worst of all, his mental faculties were departing. He was suffering from an ailment that was the scourge of old-time fighters, officially called dementia pugilistica but better known as punch drunkenness. When Pat first spotted Noble, he was the butt of the jokes of a group of market wide-boys, who had decided to make fun of the 'punchy old pug'. Pat's customarily calm expression changed at once to one of rage. Furiously, he crossed the pub, approached the group and told them in no uncertain terms to close their mouths. After glancing at the man before them, realising he meant business, they wisely did as instructed and slunk off.

Pat and Noble then struck up a conversation. 'You earned all that money, Tommy,' quipped Pat. 'You must have been flash!' 'No, no, no. I wasn't flash,' he answered. 'Mind you, I've married three actresses.' Noble's hard-earned ring money – no doubt with the help of others, not least his three wives – had fully evaporated; his work ethic, however, had not. Tommy rose early each morning and set off on his bicycle, which he rode rather unsteadily either to Leather Lane market in Holborn or East Lane market. From his market stall he sold 'Nobline', his own special blend of embrocation, which brought pain-relief to aches and sore muscles. Pat's son, Terry, used Noble's concoction as an amateur boxer. 'It looked like liquor from pie and mash,' he recalls. 'It was as good as anything you'd buy in the shops.'

In an April 1977 *Boxing News* article, Gilbert Odd recalled meeting Noble one day at Leather Lane market:

'I asked him about his diamond belt and to my great surprise he told me he still had it. "I won that in New York in 1920," he told me proudly. "And I wouldn't part with it for all the money in the world."

Very hesitantly, I asked if it would be possible to see it and was told that if I met him when he packed up at 5pm, we would go to his home when he would be pleased to show it to me. Home for Tommy in those days was a single room in Streatham, smelling very heavily of *Nobline*, which could not have pleased the neighbours. But that did not bother me as I could not wait to see the famous trophy.

He felt under his bed and groped around. Of course, that was the safest place for such a valuable treasure. Then Tommy withdrew his hand to triumphantly display a worn piece of leather. It was certainly shaped like a belt, wide at the front and narrowing towards the back. But that was all there was, being completely unadorned except for a number of holes that had at one time contained the inscribed plaque and all those diamonds – 36 of them. I did not like to ask any questions, but just stood and stared, before departing saddened and disillusioned.'

Noble's oils were popular, but his income barely kept him above the poverty line. At the time he met Pat, Noble lived out of a room at Parkview House in Newington Butts, a Rowton House workingman's hostel, or 'doss house' to use the parlance of the day. After meeting him in the pub, Pat made it his business to look out for Noble, regularly visiting him and helping out where he could. One year Pat discovered that he had nowhere to spend Christmas, so he invited him to stay and spend Christmas Day with his own family. By then Noble was suffering from extreme forgetfulness. As a show of gratitude he insisted on going out on his bike to buy Pat a bottle of wine, despite Pat's appeal not to: 'Really, we're fine. And anyway, Tommy, by the time you get back we'll all be in bed.'

Sadly, Noble's mind continued to deteriorate. For several years he had used a shed at the rear of a cycle shop on Camberwell Road to prepare his embrocation and the shop owner, Desmond Edwardes, made no charge for the use of the shed. In September 1964 Noble accused Edwardes and others of interfering with his oils and adding cleaning material to the mixture. 'I told him, no one has touched your machine. You've got the only key,' said Edwardes in court. 'I was squatting down mending a cycle when I felt a blow on the back of my neck. At first I thought it had been done with the back of his hand. I looked round and saw an axe glinting in the sunlight. I put my hand to my neck and felt blood.' In his defence, Noble told the court, 'His son called me a bastard and a ponce. He himself called me a bastard on the morning I hit him with the axe.' Clearly, by this time he was suffering severe delusions. On 13 August 1965, *Boxing News* reported, 'Nipper Pat Daly tells us that former bantam champ Tommy Noble is ill in Ward G3, Tooting Bec General Hospital, and would welcome letters from friends and colleagues.' Pat visited him regularly, but sadly Noble never recovered; he died at the hospital on 1 April 1966. And yet, in spite of his poor circumstances, he had refused his old age pension as a matter of pride as a former champion.

Much to Pat's surprise, in his will Noble left him his sparse savings, as well as the patent for his precious oils. With the money he bought the ex-champion a proper funeral and he was buried at Streatham Park

Cemetery. But, a while later, a niece knocked at the house demanding to know where Tommy's money had gone. 'It was spent on him,' Pat answered brusquely. 'I buried him.' The woman, who had shown little interest in her uncle while he was alive, could say little in way of reply.

Tommy Noble wasn't the only pre-war champion to end his days in sad circumstances. A 1965 BBC TV programme, *Man Alive*, traced all 10 surviving fly and bantam champions from World War One to the end of World War Two, and found that five were, or had been, in mental hospitals. Tommy Noble, '20s British bantamweight champion Harry 'Bugler' Lake and the legendary Jimmy Wilde were all by then in mental institutions.

The seemingly indestructible Alf 'Kid' Pattenden (who Pat sensationally defeated in July 1929), appeared on the TV programme but looked and sounded in a very bad way. It appears he had paid the price for too many tough fights. After a glorious but gruelling three and a half years as a pro, his form rapidly declined. He lost 17 of his last 24 bouts before realising that he was finished as a fighter. He could not time his blows with his accustomed accuracy, nor could he duck or sway away from punches as he once had. In his last fight he was led from the ring completely blind. He recovered his sight but his eyes suffered nerve damage. Once the most fearsome 'little man' in British boxing, the famous 'Kid' was a spent force at 24. Months after his retirement, in 1932 *The Daily Express* reported:

'Kid Pattenden, once the bantamweight champion of Great Britain is down and out. He is a physical wreck, at 24. His nerves are shattered, he is waiting for a vacant bed in the Prince of Wales Hospital in Tottenham... He suffers double vision. He cannot judge distance. He will step off a tramcar and allow for a nonexistent drop... He never wasted his money. He lost hundreds of pounds in a confectionary business, and more in a bookmaking investment.'

Pattenden's great rival, the '20s ring-idol Teddy Baldock, was also compelled to retire at 24, remarking to the press after his final fight, 'I was a ghost of what I was... my ailments [he had numerous operations on his damaged fists], together with the many 15-round fights I had when I was a growing boy must have taken a deal out of me... it hurts to be made to realise that I must now leave boxing to others.' Baldock earned an estimated £20,000 with his famous fists, won a world title and made many friends in high places; yet tragically his last days were spent living rough on the streets of London and in hostels for down-and-outs. He died penniless in an Essex infirmary in 1971.

If such a fate could befall those at the top of the game, what hope was there for the many fighters who made up the rest of the bill? Most who earned their living through boxing could expect a return to ordinary manual work as soon as their ring careers ended; while many had actually never left fulltime work. In the depressed late '20s and 1930s most preliminary boxers needed day jobs. They trained in the evenings and picked up fights where they could; all the while hoping that they would one day make it big and fight fulltime. But the majority never did, and when their ring careers ended, their young bodies worn out after hundreds of fights, some were no longer able to hold down regular jobs.

Kid Rich, the sawn-off East End Hercules who fought three rousing battles with Pat, had at least 160 contests, lost 102 of them, but always put up an heroic display. When Charlie Rose tracked him down for *Boxing News* in 1950 for a series called 'Where are they now?', to his dismay he found that, 'Today Kid Rich is suffering from ill-health, and finds it difficult to secure regular employment. He is cheerful in spite of his adversity, and is one of those who could do with a helping hand.'

Rich was a victim of his own bravery and of the age in which he fought. His diehard attitude was typical of the boxers of his day. Pat MacManus, son of Plymouth bantam Young McManus, recalls, 'They all fought very hard because they were all hungry fighters in them days. My dad would never lay down. He would fight till the last bloody breath in his body. And if he *could* get up, he *would* get up. Some of them's not made like that these days.'

The hungry fighters MacManus talks of were a product of tough times. Unemployment was rife in the '20s and '30s, pay and job prospects poor, and so many boxed professionally simply to support themselves and their families. But often the stark reality of pro boxing was different from what they had envisaged.

A preliminary fighter would arrive – often straight from a day's work – into an unclean, crowded and uncomfortable dressing room where he would wait to be called out for his fight. To earn enough some were forced to travel long hauls in third-class train carriages to unfamiliar cities and towns. After a bout they would head straight home in time for work the next day, snatching a few hours' sleep on the train if they could.

While top-liners had access to a trainer, a well-equipped gym and a choice of sparring partners, hundreds of preliminary lads had to train in dirty cellars, sheds or lofts, some learning purely from the men they boxed or by observing others. Come fight night little thought would be given to their safety or career hopes – managers and promoters would often match them with heavier, older and more experienced men.

The 1929 formation of the British Boxing Board of Control was a much-needed first step towards establishing a governing body, but it took years for the sport to be properly regulated. In 1934 a national boxers' union (the NUB) was founded to try to improve conditions for preliminary boxers and stamp out exploitation by managers and promoters. According to NUB literature, an average six or eight-round fighter received less than £1 per fight. From this meagre purse he would have to pay gym fees, travel expenses, manager's commission and gratuities to seconds. Some promoters deducted a fee under the heading of 'seconds money' before the boxer had even been paid. If the boxer protested, he would be told that he would get no further work at that hall. And so he relied on his share of the pennies and sixpences thrown in to the ring by spectators at the end of his bout. However, to secure these he would have to put on an entertaining show.

It's not surprising, given these small purses, that a culture of constant fighting existed throughout the period. Bill Chevalley recalls watching fights at the Chalton Ring, a 1930s venue that stood on Chalton Street in Somers Town:

> 'I can remember outside the Chalton Ring, as a kid, I used to stand there until someone I knew would take me in. I was watching pro fights when I was about eight, ten years of age. If the kid was hungry, they'd have a fight, and they'd have a nice quick win – or they banked on quick wins often – at say the Chalton Ring, and say the Cally Baths [Caledonian Road Baths, Islington]. As they come out the Ring they wouldn't even change, they'd just put an overcoat on and go down the Cally to see whether they could get a job down there. It was a different game altogether. There's a lot that could have been better, much better, than they were. It was only a question of money, really. Half the fighters, they had to fight three times a week just to take home enough money.'

Some of these fighters, like Pat, were mere boys. Fighting for money from the age of nine and being finished at 17, Pat was an extreme example of a widespread culture of burning out young fighters. It was not uncommon to see lads making their pro debuts at age 12, 13, 14 or 15. Some – such as Len Harvey, who began his career aged 12 – were relatively well handled and went on to reach their full potential, but many others did not. They were matched week after week in gruelling contests, often with little concern shown for disparities in age, weight or experience. A boxer's best years are usually his mid to late 20s. But, by the time these teenage fighters were in their mid-20s – like Pattenden and Baldock – most were past their peak, if not finished. It is no surprise, then, that despite having such a large crop of fighters, Britain produced so few world champions. Jack Kid Berg was well aware of this – and the danger of weight reduction while very young – when he commented to a British journalist in 1930:

> 'In the last three years, since first going to America, I have added three inches to my stature. Between the ages of 16 and 18 I was exactly the same size, constant "boiling down" to weight while in my teens had stunted my growth. In the States the law will not allow boys to be treated thus, so fewer promising lads are lost to mismanagement and overwork.'

How many champions were lost to mismanagement we will never know, but one teenage boxer lost more than his career at the Gem Stadium, Broad Weir, Bristol in 1934. Jimmy Cooper was a 14-year-old lad who worked in a timber yard and fought occasionally, for a few shillings a time, on a Monday night. Tragically, on 12 February that year, he collapsed and died during a contest. An inquest found that he had died from paralysis of the respiratory centre as a result of the fall. His opponent, 'Young Fear', was a young man of 22.

These hungry fighters, like Pat, were part of a unique period in British boxing history. If the number of practitioners, the amount and regularity of shows, along with the number of fans following a sport can be used as a yardstick, then paradoxically the late '20s and early '30s were British boxing's golden era. 'Personally, I'm inclined to look upon that era as the bad old days,' wrote O. F. Snelling for *Boxing News* in 1986, 'but with the best will in the world I can't deny that they were exciting, fascinating quite beyond description, and with a state of euphoria among fans and fighters alike which just doesn't exist in the game any more.'

Boxing historian Miles Templeton has recorded every contest ever reported by *Boxing* and *Boxing News*, and also holds results from provincial papers for contests that weren't. His statistics tell the tale of the rise and decline of boxing in Britain.

In the years leading up to World War One, an average of about 8,000 pro fights were staged annually in the UK. However, with boxers and promoters joining the war effort, there were only around 4,000 contests per year between 1915 and 1918. But the fight game soon recovered, and an average of 7,000 bouts took place each year between 1919 and 1925.

A new wave of glamour, spawned by the likes of Dempsey, Tunney, Greb and Walker, swept the sport in the 1920s and sparked an increased interest on this side of the Atlantic. As a result, between 1926 and 1930 there was a rapid increase in the number of fights staged, while rising unemployment and the onset of the Great Depression meant that more men than ever wanted – or needed – to box professionally.

Over 18,000 fights were staged in 1930 alone and between 1931 and 1933 (the sport's absolute peak) more than 20,000 fights took place every year. But in the mid to late 1930s economic improvements meant that fewer men needed to box to supplement their income, and the rise of all-in wrestling drew promoters and fans away from boxing. With this, the number of fights inevitably fell. But even so, boxing was still clearly in demand in 1938, with over 10,000 fights that year. The outbreak of World War Two, however, caused a dramatic decline.

Promoters and boxers were called up to serve in large numbers and the threat of bombing made gatherings for public events such as boxing shows dangerous. In cities and towns such as Leeds, Sheffield and Blackburn – which all held regular shows before the war – boxing stopped altogether. London contests became far less frequent, and shows were moved to the Home Counties where there was less threat of bombing. Around 2,000 fights were held annually during the war years, while a post-war recovery saw around 5,000 bouts take place each year in the late '40s and early '50s. But boxing would never rekindle its pre-war popularity.

Its fate was sealed by a 33.3 per cent live-entertainment tax, introduced in the 1952 budget, which affected all boxing shows. Small-time promoters with low profit margins could no longer earn an income from their shows and many went instantly out of business. Some found a way round it and staged so-called 'charity shows', where a small portion of the profits went to charity, thus exempting them from the new tax.

Entertainment tax lasted until 1956, but by then, in line with wage rises and improved living standards, public tastes were evolving. With more disposable income and ever more varied and more sophisticated forms of entertainment – cinema in widescreen and 3D, the growth of sports such as football, speedway, greyhound racing and athletics, and eventually TV – far fewer people wanted to watch live boxing. In the late 1950s only around 1,500 fights took place each year. By the 1960s that figure had fallen to just a few hundred and has remained almost unchanged ever since.

It is estimated that there were between 6,000 and 10,000 active professional boxers in Britain throughout the late '20s and early '30s. Nowadays – with improved standards of living and boxing far less widespread and no longer taught in schools – most athletically inclined young men take up other sports instead. Britain has only a few hundred pro boxers today – men who have the benefit of a fully functioning Board of Control, have far fewer fights, are better managed and far better paid. On the whole boxing is run safely and fairly. But sadly such enlightenment arrived too late for the heroes of the pre-war ring.

28

The Final Round

'I remember my youth and the feeling that will never come back any more
– the feeling that I could last for ever, outlast the sea, the earth, and all
men... the triumphant conviction of strength, the heat of life in the
handful of dust, the glow in the heart that with every year grows dim,
grows cold, grows small, and expires – and expires too soon, too soon –
before life itself.'

Youth, Joseph Conrad

After the dance hall business folded Pat worked alongside Johnny Curran
as a doorman at the Harp Club, a dance hall in New Cross. He did a
number of day jobs over the next few years, including parcel delivery for
the post office and a stint as a plumber's mate. In the 1960s he finally
settled into a cleaning job at the offices of the *Daily Mirror* – at the time
the most read newspaper in Britain – where he remained until he retired.
Whilst at the *Mirror* he became friendly with sports reporter Peter Wilson
– whose love of boxing stemmed from his frequent boyhood visits to
Premierland – as well as the *Mirror*'s famous agony aunt, Marjorie Proops.
Also whilst there, Pat was an active union member and played a part in
the implementation of full cards for 'jobbers'.*

In the 1960s cheaper airfares meant that more working-class Brits than
ever took their holidays abroad. Pat and Mary for the first time went
overseas together, visiting Switzerland, Yugoslavia, Germany and Spain.
While in Spain, having heard about the heroics of the matadors, Pat
attended a bullfight – although it appears that he had little idea of what
one entailed. Halfway through, he stormed out of the arena in disgust. 'It
isn't a fair fight,' he remarked when asked his reason for walking out.

The family moved to a flat at 13 Howard Court, Peckham Rye in the
early '60s, then to a large house at 40 Lanercost Road in Tulse Hill in

---

* Casual workers who were hitherto not given full union protection.

about 1969, before moving again a year later to 135 Broxholm Road in West Norwood. Mary, by her own admission, could never settle in one place and was the instigator of their frequent house moves. 'He was ever so good,' she recalls. 'If I told him I wanted to move, he never minded. He'd just say "all right then".'

In 1971 the London Ex-Boxers' Association (LEBA) – an organisation for former boxers – was founded and Pat became a member the following year. 'I didn't recognise him at first, but meeting him again certainly made my night,' remarked Pat's former stable-mate Charlie Thomas to *Boxing World*, in a piece headed, 'Nipper Pat Daly makes welcome re-appearance at LEBA function' (18 August 1972). Although not a regular attendee at LEBA's monthly meetings, Pat, usually accompanied by son Terry, would go occasionally during the next few years. He enjoyed catching up with his old opponents, most of whom now barely reached his shoulder and appeared several weight classes lighter. 'I couldn't believe he'd once boxed Johnny Cuthbert down at featherweight,' LEBA member Peter Kent recalls. 'He looked like a light-heavyweight.' On one occasion Johnny Cuthbert travelled down from Sheffield to catch up with his London opponents and Pat and Terry went along to meet him.

On 21 January 1977 respected fight scribe Ron Olver wrote in his *Boxing News* column:

'One of the joys of being a member of an Ex-Boxers' Association is the opportunity of meeting those "greats" whose names one has only read about, or may have seen only a couple of times in the ring. Such a man is Nipper Pat Daly, who attended a recent LEBA meeting, and whose story is that of success yet tragedy... in 1928 came my first glimpse of him, when my father started taking me to watch fights at Plymouth. There over 15 rounds and at 15 years old he outpointed Young McManus, a capable performer I saw finish his career in the local boxing booths... I got my second and last glimpse of the kid in action, when he outpointed Jack Sheppard over 15 rounds at Exeter. That was in February 1930... Former flyweight titleholder Jimmy Wilde was just one of those shrewd critics who told Pat he could become champion of the world. The tragedy is that he could have been, if only...'

It was quite a compliment from Olver, who had met everyone from Jack Dempsey and Joe Louis to Rocky Marciano, Sugar Ray Robinson and Muhammad Ali.

Sadly, by the 1970s Pat's health was deteriorating; though physically still very strong, his speech now carried a slight slur and his short-term memory was becoming poor. He had always been good at mental arithmetic and, when costing out household bills, Mary had always asked him to do the sums in his head. However, over the years his responses had slowed. Where once he had worked the figures out promptly, Mary now found that she could do the sums quicker herself.

'He was always trying to improve himself in certain ways,' recalls Terry. 'He went to evening school for German, woodwork and boot mending, and for many years he did yoga exercises from about three or four books that he'd bought. He only stopped doing the yoga in the latter part [of his life] when his brain wasn't functioning so well. I think, as well as keeping him supple, he thought it might keep his brain alert. He must have been aware that it was deteriorating.'

Perhaps prompted by the realisation that his mental faculties were declining, in 1981 Pat decided to tell his career story in book form. He contacted distinguished boxing writer Gilbert Odd (author of biographies on Bob Fitzsimmons and Len Harvey, plus a host of other books) and asked him to write it. Odd agreed and so Pat set about recording his recollections on notepaper, which he forwarded to Odd. A letter he wrote to Pat dated 22 October 1981 confirms that Odd had written a prologue, first chapter and foreword. Terry recalls driving Pat to meet the author at his home in Northiam, East Sussex, where they discussed the book; but the project was never completed.

By the 1980s London was a very different city from the one Pat had known for much of his life. Crime rates had risen sharply, society was changing and London's old-time community-spirit – to those who remembered it – seemed to be missing. Moreover, 'the old smoke' was no longer a safe environment for an ageing man, out of touch with modern culture and ideals, who, by his very nature, would let no slight go unanswered.

These dangers became starkly apparent one afternoon in a Tulse Hill pub. Pat was playing darts with a younger man with whom he had bet a small sum of money. After winning the game, Pat naturally asked his opponent to pay what he owed. 'Forget it, man,' came the reply. But Pat, who would have readily paid had he lost, would not let the matter rest. Their conversation became heated and suddenly the man produced a knife with which he threatened Pat. At this point the landlord asked Pat to leave and reluctantly he did. A few days later, he spotted the man leaving another pub which he himself was about to enter. He was given no time to reach for his knife on this occasion as Pat taught him a short sharp fistic lesson. Luckily, Pat was unscathed; but the incident served to highlight the dangers of living in London for a man of his uncompromising nature and old-fashioned values. It convinced Mary that they should move and in about 1982 they relocated to 31 Friar's Way in the seaside town of Hastings, where Terry and his family were already living. Far removed from the smog and the hustle and bustle of city life, it made an ideal retirement spot.

As the years passed Pat's memory continued to deteriorate and then a brain scan revealed that he had Alzheimer's disease. For the first time in his life he was in a fight that he could not win. During the next few years he attended a local daycentre, and made occasional trips to the pub for darts and a couple of pints of bitter. LEBA members Charlie Thomas, Ernie Laxton and Pat's former pupil Ken Diston paid him regular visits and chatting with them about boxing seemed to brighten his mood.

But Pat's continued deterioration and his unpredictable moods were an increasingly heavy burden on Mary. She went on holiday for a week for a well-earned break and sent Pat to stay at a care home while she was away. But a few days into Pat's stay, the care home manager phoned Terry to say that they were sending him home. He had punched and knocked over another patient and the staff there could not control him. Terry then had to stay with his father until his mother returned from her break.

Eventually, the burden of looking after Pat grew too great for Mary and, with great reluctance, she placed him in permanent nursing-home care at the nearby village of Crowhurst, where the family visited him regularly. During one visit, while sitting alone together in the home's quiet garden, Pat turned to Terry with a sudden warning. 'Be careful what you do, son, or you might end up in here,' he said solemnly. It was clear that in his confused state he thought he was being punished for some transgression. Although Pat's mental deterioration continued, he had retained much of his strength and physical capability. The nursing-home staff soon found that they could not control him and, although his was not a psychiatric condition, he was moved to a mental hospital near the village of Hellingly, which was more adept to handle unpredictable patients.

A former professional fighter with increasingly erratic behaviour presented a quandary to the care-staff and, to keep his mood swings under control, they sedated him. But with the heavy dosage of drugs Pat became very unsteady and prone to falling over and his waking hours were now spent sitting quietly in a chair.

In September 1988 he was admitted to St. Helen's Hospital in Hastings with a heart complaint. As his medication was modified he became more mobile and more responsive but it was apparent that his mind had deteriorated further. On 25 September, quite unexpectedly, his great heart gave way. One of boxing's brightest lights had finally faded out. The cause of death was thought to be deep vain thrombosis. He was 75 years old.

He was buried in Hastings and members of LEBA travelled down to pay their last respects at his funeral. He had failed to attain the wealth and championship honours his talented fists should have brought him; but at least, unlike some of his contemporaries, he had ended his days without financial worry and with family around him who cared.

After his boyhood dreams were snatched from under him, it seems Pat got on with life as best he could and for the most part stoically conceded that 'what's done is done'. 'It was a fantastic achievement really – the measure of the man,' remarked his son John shortly before his death in 2006. 'He got himself together, got married, had children and a fairly normal life. To come to terms with the emotional trauma of being exploited by everybody. And I mean everybody – especially his own parents. To overcome that sort of dilemma in the way he did, I think is a measure of the man's integrity and indomitable spirit. Yeah, I think he had an indomitable spirit.'

'He was quite unlike anyone else I've ever met,' remembers daughter-in-law Maureen. 'If you met him once, I don't think you'd forget him. He was a gentleman with old-fashioned good manners – he would open doors for ladies and he didn't like swearing. He wasn't an emotional man and he wasn't a friendly man, but at the same time he wasn't unfriendly either. He was secure in who he was and what he was and he didn't feel that he needed to step out of that to impress anybody. Whether he was dealing with a tramp or a king he would be the same person and would treat them the same way. He didn't smile easily but when he did he had a lovely smile that lit up his whole face.'

Pat was a man of few words and could hardly be described as a 'people person'. He would cut to the crux of any conversation without wasting words and did not often speak unless spoken to. He had a wonderfully dry sense of humour, took a dim view of human nature, and nothing much impressed him. He did not easily like or trust others, but ironically he did form very strong friendships with those whom he did like and trust. His taciturn manner and generally stony expression was off-putting to some but it seems that beneath it was a genuine, impeccably honest and kind-hearted man. 'He'd help anyone who he thought was weak or vulnerable in some way,' recalls Terry, 'it seemed to bring out a protective side in him. I think that's why he helped Tommy Noble – because he saw he was vulnerable... Once at the dance hall there was a bloke who'd had too much to drink and had actually messed himself. Instead of throwing him out, dad took him to the toilet and cleaned him up. I remember my mum saying, "I don't know how he could do that – wash him down!" But he didn't mind, he didn't care. Whereas most people wouldn't have done that, would they? Especially for someone they don't know. But that's the sort of bloke he was.'

'I loved to fight,' Pat told *The People* newspaper in May 1949. 'I used to say to myself, "If I can do this at 16, what shall I be able to do when I'm 26?" They never allowed me to grow up naturally. In those days I looked like a matchstick. If I had been allowed to grow naturally I think I might have ended up as a light-heavyweight.' In the 1980s he told Ron Olver that if he had his time over he would not even start serious boxing until he reached 18. He was never openly bitter about the way his career ended, but it seems he naturally harboured some misgivings and must have pondered many times the unanswerable question of how far he would have gone had he only been handled with care.

Nipper Pat Daly deserved to be remembered and there was a story to tell – a remarkable story. Perhaps the telling of it will stand as a tribute – not to the famous fighters who already have their epitaph in print – but to the long-forgotten men of that era who boxed for money and the prospect of glory, but for whatever reason did not make it.

Appendix 1:

Nipper Pat Daly's Fight Record 1923–31

Date	Opponent	Result	Location
1923			
?	George Brown (Marylebone)	W pts 4	Marylebone
?	John Brent	W pts 6	Euston
1924			
?	Young Smock	W pts 6	Peckham Winter Gardens
Aug 4	Ernest Morris (Saunderton Lee)	Drew 3	Prestwood
Oct 5	Johnny Summers (Leeds)	W pts 6	Manor Hall, Hackney
Oct 5	Johnny Summers (Leeds)	W pts 6	Peckham Winter Gardens
Oct 6	Johnny Summers (Leeds)	W pts 6	King's Hall, Sidcup
Nov 30	Young Brooks (West Ham)	W pts 6	Manor Hall, Hackney
1925			
?	Young Deary	W pts 6	Central Hall, Canning Town
Jul 11	Young King	W ko 1	Becontree
Jul 30	Billy Boulger (Canning Town)	L pts 6	Premierland, Whitechapel
Aug 3	Charlie McCleave (Marylebone)	W pts 6	Prestwood
Sep 3	Jim Hocking (Canning Town)	W pts 6	Premierland, Whitechapel
Oct 4	Johnny Summers (Leeds)	W pts 8	Manor Hall, Hackney
Nov 1	Charlie McCleave (Marylebone)	W pts 10	Peckham Winter Gardens
Nov 2	Charlie McCleave (Marylebone)	W pts 6	Ilford Skating Rink
Nov 4	Jim Hocking (Canning Town)	Drew 6	NSC, Covent Garden
Nov 18	Charlie McCleave (Marylebone)	W pts 6	Fulham Baths
Dec 17	Teddy Tompkins (Clapham)	W pts 6	Pimlico British Legion
1926			
?	Sid Raiteri	W pts 6	Peckham Winter Gardens
Jan 10	Johnny Quill (Stepney)	W pts 10	Premierland, Whitechapel
Jan 25	Teddy Tompkins (Clapham)	Drew 10	Pimlico British Legion
Feb 14	George Brown (Paddington)	W pts 6	Peckham Winter Gardens
Feb 15	Boy Deary (Custom House)	L dis 8	Premierland, Whitechapel
Apr 15	Moe Mizler (St. George's)	L rsf* 5	Premierland, Whitechapel
Nov 8	Johnny Summers (Leeds)	W pts 6	NSC, Covent Garden
Dec 2	George Brown (Paddington)	W pts 8	Belgravia

stopped due to a cut eye caused by a clash of heads

301

1927

Feb 2	Taff Sharpe (Tottenham)	W rtd 3	Belgravia
May 2	Taff Sharpe (Tottenham)	W ko 4	Alcazar, Edmonton
Jun 16	Kid Silver (St. George's)	W pts 10	Premierland, Whitechapel
Jul 3	Charlie Rowbotham (Birmingham)	W rsf 5	Premierland, Whitechapel
Jul 10	Tank Fowler (Birmingham)	W pts 10	Premierland, Whitechapel
Jul 21	Alf Gudge (St. George's)	W pts 10	Premierland, Whitechapel
Oct 3	Jack Ellis (St. George's)	Drew 15	Premierland, Whitechapel
Oct 17	Glover's Nipper (Barnsley)	W pts 15	Premierland, Whitechapel
Oct 31	Jack Ellis (St. George's)	W pts 15	Premierland, Whitechapel
Nov 10	Dick Inkles (Sheffield)	W pts 15	Premierland, Whitechapel
Nov 21	Tom Fitzsimmons (Leicester)	W pts 10	Victoria Baths, Nottingham
Nov 28	Alf Thornhill (Leeds)	W pts 15	Premierland, Whitechapel
Dec 19	Ginger Johnson (Edlington)	W pts 10	Peterborough Corn Exchange
Dec 29	Jimmy Thornton (Bethnal Green)	W dis 6	Premierland, Whitechapel

1928

Jan 2	Boy Sharpe (Nottingham)	W rsf 6	Victoria Baths, Nottingham
Jan 6	Johnny Summers (Leeds)	W pts 12	Marathon Stadium, Preston
Jan 16	Kid Rich (Aldgate)	W pts 12	Premierland, Whitechapel
Jan 29	Jack Bromley (Sheffield)	W pts 12	Premierland, Whitechapel
Feb 5	Kid Rich (Aldgate)	W pts 12	Premierland, Whitechapel
Feb 19	Harry Yates (Ashton)	W pts 10	Leeds NSC
Mar 5	Johnny Summers (Leeds)	W pts 15	Stockport Armoury
Mar 11	Mark Lesnick (Stepney)	NC 11	Premierland, Whitechapel
Mar 15	Lud Abella (Liverpool)	W pts 15	Liverpool Stadium
Mar 19	Tommy Brown (Salford)	W pts 12	Blackburn
Mar 28	Jimmy Lindsay (Fulham)	W pts 15	Fulham Baths
Apr 1	Lud Abella (Liverpool)	Drew 15	Premierland, Whitechapel
Apr 29	Young Siki (Liverpool)	L ret 4	Premierland, Whitechapel
May 18	Giovanni Sili (Italy)	W pts 10	NSC, Covent Garden
Jun 7	Kid Rich (Aldgate)	W pts 15	Premierland, Whitechapel
Jun 21	Dod Oldfield (Leeds)	L pts 15	Ilford Skating Rink
Sep 29	Ludwig Minow (Germany)	W pts 10	Dortmund, Germany
Oct 21	Billy Yates (Mexborough)	W rsf 7	Manor Hall, Hackney
Nov 4	Corporal Jack Connell (Aldershot)	W rsf 9	Premierland, Whitechapel
Nov 8	Frank Kestrell (Cardiff)	W rsf 12	The Ring, Blackfriars
Nov 26	Johnny Murton (Plymouth)	W dis 5	Alcazar, Edmonton
Dec 6	George Garrard (Acton)	W pts 8	Royal Albert Hall
Dec 11	Young McManus (Plymouth)	W pts 15	Plymouth Pier

| Dec 17 | Bert Kirby (Birmingham) | W pts 12 | Birmingham |
| Dec 22 | Tiny Smith (Sheffield) | W pts 15 | Sunderland Stadium |

1929

Jan 7	Willi Metzner (Germany)	W dis 2	Cologne, Germany
Jan 9	Arthur Boddington (Wellingborough)	W pts 10	NSC, Covent Garden
Jan 14	Jimmy Rowbotham (Birmingham)	W pts 15	Alcazar, Edmonton
Jan 26	Billy Smith (Sunderland)	W pts 15	Sunderland Stadium
Feb 17	Jimmy Rowbotham (Birmingham)	W pts 12	West Bromwich
Feb 24	Billy Boulger (Canning Town)	W pts 15	Premierland, Whitechapel
Mar 1	Archie Woodbine (Birmingham)	W ret 5	Portsmouth
Mar 9	Tommy Brown (Salford)	W ret 12	Sunderland Stadium
Mar 21	Petit Biquet (Belgium)	W pts 10	Royal Albert Hall
Apr 8	Arthur Adkins (Nottingham)	W pts 15	Victoria Baths, Nottingham
Apr 12	Packey McFarland (Dublin)	W pts 15	Portsmouth
May 2	Dick Corbett (Bethnal Green)	W pts 10	Royal Albert Hall
May 12	Kid Socks (Bethnal Green)	W pts 15	Premierland, Whitechapel
May 18	Joe Greenwood (Bolton)	W rsf 8	Sunderland Stadium
May 23	Jim Crawford (Wrexham)	W pts 15	Liverpool Stadium
Jun 8	Douglas Parker (Sunderland)	L ko 1	Sunderland Stadium
Jun 13	Jim Crawford (Wrexham)	Drew 15	Liverpool Stadium
Jun 21	Jack Garland (Belfast)	W pts 8	Clapton Stadium
Jul 7	Kid Pattenden (Bethnal Green)	W pts 15	Premierland, Whitechapel
Aug 5	Tommy Rose (Bolton)	W ko 3	Blackpool FC ground
Aug 11	Jack Garland (Belfast)	W pts 12	Premierland, Whitechapel
Aug 23	Karl Schulze (Germany)	W ko 5	Berlin, Germany
Sep 1	Con Lewis (Bethnal Green)	W ret 7	Vale Hall, Kilburn
Sep 8	Lew Pinkus (Mile End)	W pts 15	Collins's Music Hall, Islington
Sep 15	Billy Cain (Birmingham)	W ret 7	West Bromwich
Oct 3	Arques Treves (France)	W ko 2	Ilford Skating Rink
Oct 9	Johnny Cuthbert (Sheffield)	L ko8	Holborn Stadium
Oct 23	Jack Millard (Willesden)	W rsf 8	Paddington Baths
Oct 31	Jim Ashley (Stepney)	L rsf 3	Ilford Skating Rink
Nov 6	Kid Berry (Bethnal Green)	W pts 15	NSC, Holborn Stadium
Nov 11	Ted Cullen (Mansfield)	W dis 4	Victoria Baths, Nottingham
Nov 17	Johnny Edmunds (Treharris)	W ko 2	Collins's Music Hall, Islington
Nov 24	Jim Briley (Peckham)	W pts 15	Premierland, Whitechapel

1930

Jan 19	Jack Wright (Paddington)	W dis 6	Vale Hall, Kilburn
Jan 27	Charlie Mack (Marylebone)	Drew 15	Victoria Baths, Nottingham
Feb 21	Jack Sheppard (Plymouth)	W pts 15	Civic Hall, Exeter
Mar 2	Charlie Mack (Marylebone)	W pts 15	Vale Hall, Kilburn
Mar 9	Jim Briley (Peckham)	W rsf 6	Premierland, Whitechapel
Mar 21	Jack Sheppard (Plymouth)	W rsf 12	Civic Hall, Exeter
Mar 26	Aine Gyde (France)	W pts 15	Paddington Baths
Apr 1	Len George (Custom House)	W pts 8	Paddington Baths
Apr 3	Henri Baudeart (France)	W pts 8	Holborn Stadium
Apr 14	Charlie Mack (Marylebone)	ND 3	Basingstoke Pavilion
Apr 20	Seaman Watson (Newcastle)	L rsf 11	Vale Hall, Kilburn
Jun 5	Nobby Baker (Trealaw)	L rsf 13	Premierland, Whitechapel
Oct 28	Tom Banks (Birmingham)	L pts 6	Royal Albert Hall
Nov 18	Fred Green (Blackfriars)	Drew 12	Paddington Baths
Nov 23	Jimmy Laws (Deptford)	W ko 3	Vale Hall, Kilburn
Dec 2	Dave Danahar (Bethnal Green)	W ret 9	Paddington Baths
Dec 7	Johnny Allen (Bermondsey)	W rsf4	Vale Hall, Kilburn
Dec 23	Albert Ryall (Ealing)	W ret 4	Paddington Baths
Dec 28	André Beghin (Belgium)	W rsf 4	Vale Hall, Kilburn

1931

Jan 6	Tom Handley (Hoxton)	W pts 12	Paddington Baths
Jan 27	Harry Jenkins (Camden Town)	W ret 4	Paddington Baths

Contests: 120 (Won: 99 Lost: 11 Drew: 8 No contest: 1 No decision: 1)

Key:

W	=	won	dis	=	disqualification
pts	=	points	NC	=	no contest
ret	=	retired	rsf	=	referee stopped fight
L	=	lost	?	=	date unknown
ko	=	knockout	ND	=	no-decision bout

Career breakdown

Year	Age	Fights	W	D	L	NC	ND	Rounds
1923	9-10	2	2	–	–	–	–	10
1924	10-11	6	5	1	–	–	–	33
1925	11-12	11	9	1	1	–	–	67
1926	12-13	8	5	1	2	–	–	59
1927	13-14	14	13	1	–	–	–	143
1928	14-15	25	21	1	2	1	–	284
1929	15-16	33	29	1	3	–	–	319
1930	16-17	19	13	2	3	–	1	169
1931	17	2	2	–	–	–	–	16

Total rounds boxed in pro contests = 1,100*

---

* This figure includes rounds in which stoppages or knockouts occurred.

Appendix 2:

The Fighting Spirit Behind Pat Daly's Smile

By Clyde Foster

[From *The Evening Standard*, 12 August 1929]

I heard men say that a chance was missed yesterday of doubling the charge for admission to Premierland when Nipper Pat Daly fought and defeated on points Jack Garland in a contest that was characterised by gameness and skill on the part of both combatants. An official told me that hundreds were turned away. There was a long, deep queue in the street after the house was full. I arrived in reasonably good time, and had to elbow my way through a solid mass of standing spectators. That they allowed me to pass to the ringside was a tribute to their good nature, I was reminded of Eugene Corri's adventure when, arriving in similar circumstances to referee a match, he gave his name at the door and was told that there had been a dozen Corris seeking admission already.

It all afforded another proof of the drawing power of one really good contest. There was a general scurrying of men along the streets of the neighbourhood making hurriedly for the boxing Mecca of the East End. Women absented themselves yesterday with a few exceptions. Two had arrived early and secured seats in what was formerly the old cinema's radiation box whence an excellent view was had of the ring with a light thrown on it like a blaze of sunshine in a glade. Mr. Sam Russell, the well-known referee, sitting beside me in the enjoyment of a busman's holiday, called my attention to one woman mimicking the actions of the boxers with her arms so excitedly that I half feared she might emulate the waiter who knocked himself out while reading a graphic description of a famous fight.

It is astonishing where spectators will perch on such occasions. Some, for the first time, sat on the top of the cinema box – Premierland was formerly a picture palace – and a number of youths clambered on to the roof of a structure near the entrance, where they maintained a footing as if endowed with prehensile faculties in support of the Darwinian theory of man's descent from a Simian ancestry. The reward of their daring was a good view at a popular price in a perilous position. I have no knowledge of the purse shared by Nipper Pat Daly and Jack Garland, but whatever the figure, they earned it in their 12 rounds hard-fought contest. It was a fight between a man and a boy, but I doubt if pugilism in any country ever produced such a boy.

By consummate craft in guarding the vulnerable points of his face and body against Garland's blows, Daly passed triumphantly through the onslaught, and looked at the end astonishingly little the worse for the punishment he had taken. The almost cherubic face, with the pert little nose in the centre of it, wore much the same expression as when he first appeared, clean and trim, smiling in his corner with half-shut downcast eyes. There was a touch of truthfulness in one of many remarks I overheard: "Nipper could pass for a girl," said a man who had brought his own small boy with him. Young Daly certainly did not lack the look of shyness. Not once did he glance at the thousands of faces that were turned upon him.

The boy had no vanity. Fame was to him so far a mere bubble; fighting he frankly loved for fighting's sake. Too young yet at sixteen years and four months to think in banking accounts, this Jacky Coogan of pugilism just goes on boxing as other growing boys go to school or to business. His green shorts proclaimed the fighting Irish boy to whom blows, given or taken, were in the routine of his day's work. Yet no one in that gathering could have detected even a momentary look of ferocity on his face. It gave him no particular pleasure to wallop Garland – as he most unmercifully did towards the end of the seventh round, when men rose in hundreds and cheered the young Hibernian. Pat Daly was merely applying his art to the varying situations that arose, watching for openings and never failing to make use of them. "He can just do whatever he wants to do," said a critic talking to himself beside me. "What a boy!"

Said another, addressing the house: "They'll be wanting a sofa and a pillow for him soon," meaning Garland. But in this he was far wide of the mark. Pat Daly had to fight all the way for the verdict, and I make sure the card would show that Garland held his own till the tide turned with that terrific seventh round when Daly rained a succession of blows that fell so rapidly at all angles that they could not have been counted. But even then he wore a comparatively placid expression, except for the inconvenience caused by Garland's defensive returns landing in the neighbourhood of his little tilted nose.

He seemed to resent these facial visitations of his opponent's gloves as an impertinence, for this meek and mild-looking boy, with the downcast eyes and the small white teeth, not yet grown to maturity is an autocrat of his craft with a proud and almost patronising air towards opponents. Amazement sat on every face as men took account of Daly's age, his courage and his fistic skill. They wondered how far he might yet go and hoped that he would not be overtaxed, while yet so young, with disastrous consequences.

In his corner whispering words of wisdom and encouragement between rounds was his shrewd trainer and boxing foster-father: "Professor" Newton. By him, I think, the Nipper will be sagaciously developed till the time comes when his nipperhood is over and Pat Daly wins a sure place among the greatest boxers of the time.

Appendix 3:

Letters and Memoir Extracts

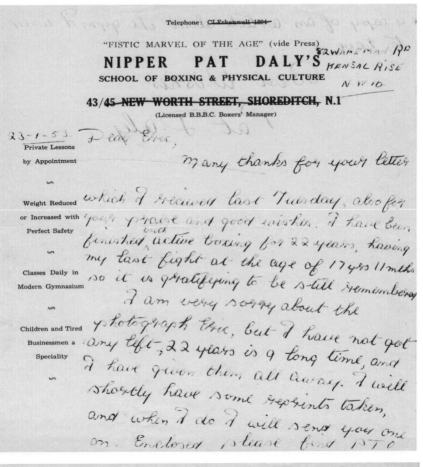

Letter from Pat to a fan (23 Jan 1953).

12-9-81

135 Broncholm Rd
West Norwood
S.E. 27.

Mr. Gilbert Odd
Little Court
Church Lane
Northeans

Dear Mr Odd,

Enclosed please find some notes on my carrier which I hope will help you. As different memories come into my mind I will forward them on to you. I hope you and the wife are feeling well as we are at present.

Yours Sincerely

Pat Daly.

Letter from Pat to Gilbert Odd (12 Sep 1981).

Appendix 3

GILBERT ODD : Little Court, Church Lane, Northiam.Rye.East Sussex TN31 6NA

October 22, 1981

Dear Pat,

     I am sending you a suggested Prologue to your proposed book, also the first chapter and my Foreword. These should be sufficient to approach a publisher with and I would like you to read them through carefully and make any amendments you think are necessary. These items will open the book and we can add that there will be up to twenty more chapters, plus your record (if they want it included) and that illustrations can be provided. There may be typing errors as I bashed it out after drafting by pen, but just ring these round to draw my attention to them and you have room between the lines for any corrections to the text. Any remarks you may have please put at the bottom of each page.

     When I get it back from you (registered or Recorded Delivery post), the whole thing will be retyped on good paper to impress a publisher, and I will draft a letter for you to send with it. We will then have to come to some financial arrangement.

     Sorry to have kept you waiting, but as you know I keep busy and have my garden to attend to before the winter sets in. Give me a ring - Northiam 2163 any evening if you wish.

Best wishes
Yours sincerely,

In your record. Willie Metzner.
Did this take place in Dortmund,
what was the actual result and
can you remember the date?
Also, was W.H.Ellis and Jack Ellis
the same person? Did you beat
Ginger Johnson at the Corn Exchange
in Peterborough on Dec.5 1929?
Who was Billy McCleave?

Letter from Gilbert Odd to Pat (22 Oct 1981).

24-10-81.

PHONE
670-6448.

135 BROXHOLM Rᵈ
WEST NORWOOD
S.E.27.

Mr. Gilbert Odd
Little Court
Church Lane
Northiam
Rye. East Sussex

Dear Mr Odd,

Thanks for your letter containing the suggested prologue, first chapter, and your Foreword. I am sending you some more of my memories as they come to mind, and will continue to do so. Enclosed please find the answers to your questions as accurately as I can answer them. How would I be able to get into the 'Guinness Book of records' as the youngest professional Pro fighter? it might sell a few extra books. I hope the wife is well, please give her my best Wishes

Yours Sincerely.

Pat Daly

Letter from Pat to Gilbert Odd (24 Oct 1981).

In 1924 Boxing was booming, there were boxing shows in almost every district, anywhere where there was room to put a boxing ring 10' square and have room for about 50 or less spectators was a potential Boxing Stadium, and with the lack of capital the purses were very small, 5/- shillings was the purse my manager used to recieve for a 6rd fight. One such hall in Pimlico I had several fights, also a hall at Camden Town and one at Euston. The Euston hall was run by Johnny Hughes ex Fly-weight champion of Gt Britain, before I went on Mr. Hughes asked me to take it easy with John Brent, my opponent, & to let the bout go the full distance 6rds as there had been several K.O's, and as it was then only 8-45p.m, the show started at 8p.m he did not have enough bouts to last until 10.p.m, the advertised finishing time. Mr Hughes said "You have got an easy job so you can take your time", I said "allright Mr Hughes it will go the full 6rds". I do not remember the first rd as the 'mug' had hit me on the chin and put me down, I was quite groggy for the whole of the 1st rd. As the gong went for the second rd I was unsteady, but I pulled myself together and outpointed him for the remaining 5 rds to win on points

Pat describes an early fight.

3

I had promised Mr Hughes to let it go the distance, so I kept my promise despite the fact that I wanted to kill my opponent. I was 10 yrs old.

Newton Jnr also used to promote shows at very small club at Pimlico and on his first bill had Charlie Mack and me on top. In those days Charlie was 6 yrs older, and 7 lbs heavier than me, we went 6 rds to a draw. We had 9 fights together Charlie & me, including 2 draws. Charlie was managed by Newton Jr while I was managed by Newton Sr.

I caught Charlie up & when I was 17 yrs we were the same height & weight 5ft - 6ins and we both weighed at 9st. 6 lb at our last match at the Vale Hall Kilburn which I won on points over 15 rds in January 1930. Newton Jnr badly wanted Charlie to have a desicion over me as it would have increased his earning capacity, but the best he could do was two draws at two of his own promotions.

Pat continues his early fight description and mentions his fights with Charlie Mack.

316

1st & 2nd
Garland fight

undefeated bantam-weight & A.B.A CHAMPION

I met Jack Garland at Clapton Stadium in June 1929 over 8 rds. It was a very big bill and several contests had to be shortened to allow the management to show all the contests advertized. Our contest was not altered so we met over 8 three minute rds as arranged. Garland had caused a sensation in winning an A.B.A bantam-weight title in 1928, beating among others Johnny Peters and when he turned Pro was undefeated beating some of the best bantams in the country. He was matched with me and we met at Clapton Stadium. Only one thing worried me, we had to weigh-in at 8st-9lb which would mean more starving & sweating for me to make it. He was very strong and was a heavy puncher as he twice shook me up in the first rd with right hand punches and he also had an accurate left lead which was nearly as fast a mine, but when it conected was it was heavier. After 8 closely contested rds the referee, who was Bombadeer Billy Wells a former Heavy-weight champion of Gt Brittain, gave the verdict to me. The verdict was very well recieved by the audience, but loud protests came from the opposing corner. Garland demanded a return fight, which the Prof agreed to, and the Premierland promoters offered a purse which was accepted by both sides. Garlands advisers insisted on the bout being 12 x 3 minute rds at & weigh-in at 9st at 11 A.M. At the weigh-in neither of us both never moved the beam at 9st. Jack & his manager were very pleased as they thought that at the new weight being 9 stone instead of 8st.9lb would be decidedly to his advantage

Pat describes his first and second contests with Jack Garland.

Garland 2nd fight

Garland was supremely confidant as the weight 9st suited him as he aged 20 yrs was still growing. The weight suited me as I was able to have a light breakfast, which normally I never had before a weight match.

"Premierland" was literally crowded to the roof the doors being shut at 3 p.m and nobody else was admitted, as to how the fight went I will quote from cuttings from my book. "Daly's convincing win over Garland, no doubt this time. Good as Garland undoubtably was, Daly won all the way Daly confirmed his superiority in no small measure and gave the game Garland a rare boxing lesson." There was much discussion about the verdict in our bout at Clapton Stadium but this time the verdict in my favour was undisputed. My manager must have missed his regular income, although our purses were getting larger I was not having as many fights so he booked me to box several exhibitions as well as all the bouts he could book up. Despite all the training & fighting I was doing, nature would not be denied, I was still growing and putting on weight. With every mouthful I ate was making me weigh heavier and I used to get very depressed, because as I was outgrowing the various weight limits it seemed that I would never stop growing, as soon as I would be elligable to fight for a title at one weight I would grow into the next weight, and so on. There were so many good fighters about in those days to contest the elligability of a new-comer into a new weight sphere, that it would take too long, and I would have to go into the next weight

Pat describes his second contest with Jack Garland.

Bibliography

Bell, Leslie, *Bella of Blackfriars*, (Odhams Press, 1961)

Broadribb, Ted, *Fighting Is My Life*, (Muller, 1951)

Burke, Thomas, *The Real East End*, (Constable, 1932)

Conrad, Joseph, *Youth, a narrative, and two other stories*, (Blackwood, 1902)

Constantine, Stephen, *Social Conditions in Britain 1918-1939*, (Methuen, 1983)

Corri, Eugene, *Gloves & the Man: The Romance of the Ring*, (Hutchinson, 1927)

Deghy, Guy, *Noble and Manly: The History of The National Sporting Club*, (Hutchinson, 1956)

Finn, Ralph L., *Grief Forgotten: The Tale of an East End Jewish Boyhood*, (Futura, 1985)

Fitzgerald, F. Scott, *The Great Gatsby*, (Bodley Head edition, 1958)

Fleming, Denis, *The Manchester Fighters*, (Richardson, 1986)

Foot, David (edited by), *Hungry Fighters of the West*, (Redcliffe, 1988)

Fraley, Oscar, *The Million Dollar Gate*, (Macmillan, 1966)

Golesworthy, Maurice, *Encyclopaedia of Boxing*, (Hale, 1988)

Graham, Stephen, *Twice Round the London Clock*, (Benn, 1933)

Hamnett, Nina, *Is She a Lady?*, (Wingate, 1955)

Harding, John, *Jack Kid Berg: The Whitechapel Windmill*, (Robson Books, 1987)

Harding, John, *Lonsdale's Belt: The Story of Boxing's Greatest Prize*, (Robson Books, 1994)

Hemingway, Ernest, *A Moveable Feast*, (Jonathan Cape, 1964 and 2010)

Herbert, Michael, *Never Counted Out! The Story of Len Johnson, Manchester's Black Boxing Hero and Communist*, (Dropped Aitches Press, 1992)

Hicks, Stephen 'Johnny', *Sparring For Luck*, (Thap, 1982)

Hooker, Denise, *Nina Hamnett: Queen of Bohemia*, (Constable, 1986)

Jarrett, John, *Byker to Broadway: The Fighting Life and Times of Seaman Tommy Watson*, (Bewick Press, 1997)

Kircher, Rudolf, *Fair Play*, (Collins, 1928)

Leslie, Anita, *The Gilt and the Gingerbread: An Autobiography*, (Hutchinson, 1981)

Lister, Dudley S., *How To Box*, (Eyre & Spottiswoode, 1952)

Madden, Brian, *Yesterday's Glovemen: The Golden Days of Ulster Boxing*, (The Brehon Press, 2006)

Mayhew, Henry, *London Labour and the London Poor*, (Griffin, Bohn, 1861)

McInnes, Peter, *Clouting For Cash: Great Fights and Great Fighters 1939-1959*, (p.r.m., 1962)

Morton, H.V., *H.V. Morton's London*, (Methuen, 1945)

Newton, Andrew, Jnr., *Guide For Beginners: Learn How to Box*, (1945)

Odd, Gilbert, *Encyclopedia of Boxing*, (Hamlyn, 1983)

Odd, Gilbert, *Great Moments in Sport: Boxing Cruisers to Mighty Atoms*, (Pelham Books, 1974)

Odd, Gilbert, *Ring Battles of the Century*, (Nicholson & Watson, 1948)

Pearce, Elizabeth A. S., *the road to Cricklewood: a history of Edgware Road in London...*, (University of London, 1978)

Potts, Archie, *The Wearside Champions*, (Bewick Press, 1993)

Toulmin, Vanessa, *A Fair Fight*, (World's Fair, 1999)

Tschiffely, Aimé, *Bohemia Junction*, (The Long Riders' Guild Press, 2001)

Walker, Mickey with Joe Reichler, *Mickey Walker: The Toy Bulldog and His Times*, (Random House, 1961)

Walter, Gerard, *White Ties and Fisticuffs: The Story of Patsy Hagate*, (Hutchinson, 1951)

Wolveridge, Jim, *'Ain't it Grand' (or 'This Was Stepney')*, (Stepney Books, 1976)

Index

Index